LAW FOR THE RETAILER AND DISTRIBUTOR

J R LEWIS

THIRD EDITION

Jordans

ISBN 0 85308 052 6
Published by Jordan & Sons Limited.
Printed in Great Britain.

Contents

Preface

Much, inevitably, has happened since the second edition of this book was published. The law never stands still; new decisions are handed down by the courts, and new legislation is passed by Parliament. A considerable amount of this affects the retailer and distributor, making a new edition of this book necessary.

The major events have been the passing of the Consumer Credit Act 1974 and the Health and Safety at Work Act 1974, but these pieces of legislation tend to emphasise the peculiar problems faced by the writer of a law book. Although they are on the statute book, neither has completely come into effect: the Consumer Credit Act will be brought into effect in stages, repealing other legislation affecting the consumer, and the Health and Safety at Work Act will eventually replace the Offices,Shops and Railway Premises Act—but not yet.

Thus, while the Moneylending Acts 1900 and 1927, the Hire Purchase Acts 1965 and 1968, the Advertisements (Hire Purchase) Act 1967 and the Trading Stamps Act 1964 are doomed, they are not yet actually, and totally, repealed. So, this book must take account of these Acts as well as the repealing legislation. On the other hand some provisions have already taken effect: the licensing register for regulated agreements, the sending of circulars to minors, the supply of unsolicited credit cards, the liability of the creditor for breaches of contract by the supplier, the prohibition of canvassing, exempt agreements and the service of notice of variation of agreements, all these are now effective. But it must still be emphasised—some of the older legislation is still operative.

Reference is also made in this book to other Acts passed since the last edition: the Race Relations Act 1976, the Employment Protection Act 1975 and the Sex Discrimination Act 1975, but otherwise the original aims of the book have not changed—to allow the reader to deal with an outline of the legal system and the rules of law that touch us in our daily business lives—and to do this by avoiding legal terminology as far as possible, relying on a simple, readable form.

One further point should be mentioned. For students, a major upheaval has been instigated by the phasing out of the previous courses in distribution, for their replacement by option modules and core modules leading towards the awards of the Business Education Council. Full regard is paid in these pages to the needs of students preparing for BEC courses, and in particular for the option modules in Law Relating to Distribution, and in Business Law.

The scope of the book is such that it should afford retailers, distributors and students some insight into the legal basis upon which commercial practice is founded.

CHAPTER 1

Law and the Community

In most countries the birth of children is an occasion for joy and congratulations, but in some primitive societies it was regarded as a token of favour with the gods. Accordingly, great care was always taken that the gods should not be offended, and the child protected. This gave rise to certain practices among primitive tribes which would seem in later ages to have little point or reason. In southern India the husband, on being informed of his wife's labour pains, would immediately take to his bed. Among the Caribs the father would fast and lie in his hammock and above all would completely abstain from eating the flesh of the sea cow. The following of such customs by tribesmen who no longer knew why they followed them is a characteristic of early society; in these cases the tribe would have forgotten that the husband went to bed to make the spirit causing the pain think that it was he, the husband, who was really bearing the child. This gallant action would thus relieve his wife of suffering. The Caribs would have forgotten their old superstition that the father who ate sea cow would be penalising his future child by endowing it with little round eyes just like the sea cow.

Though they had forgotten the origins of these customs they followed the practices blindly—the argument is the same as that which the man who uses a cut-throat razor advances: "Well, it was good enough for my father, so it is good enough for me."

This is not a logical argument, of course, for it denies the fact of progress in society, but custom is entrenched as a system in us all. And so it is with the law. In early society the individual makes no rules himself, but every community needs rules to regulate the behaviour of the individual. The rules he obeys are derived from the society into which he is born. The penalty that is visited upon the community for breach of these rules is at first a religious one based on the tribe's superstitions. But these customs are the earliest source of law.

But what is law? It may be defined as a rule of conduct for men living in society. Custom is shaped by the co-operative act of the whole community, and is backed by religion. Later, however, this hardens into "law" imposed not only by religion but by the dictates of an individual, or of a group within that society. Little regard is initially paid to the moral state of the criminal: whatever the origins of the crime, punishment follows. The questions of intent and morality are later developments.

The whole development of an ordered legal system is based upon the conception and growth of the ordered society and the relationship to be settled between the individual and the society in which he lives. It finally matures into the principle that every man, whatever his rank or station, has the right to be protected by the machinery of the law. But this principle in itself is not enough. It is too easy and too dangerous to speak only of the rights which the individual possesses in society. Dangerous, because the man who demands his rights may well transgress upon the rights of his neighbour by doing so.

It must be seen from this that it is necessary to speak also of obligations imposed by the law. The example of freedom of speech will serve to illustrate this point: it is one of the proud assertions of the individual in the democratic state that he has the right to speak his mind, the right to hold opinions and express them, the right to do these things without being penalised by the state itself. But does this mean that he is entitled to call his neighbour a thief and a liar, to say that his Member of Parliament accepts bribes, to publicly put it about that his grocer habitually overcharges and underweighs? Obviously it does not. But why is this? The reason is that while the individual may express his opinions freely he is not entitled to express such opinions as may infringe the rights of other members of society—namely those rights which entitle a man to the protection of the law whenever his character is called into question. His protection lies in the Law of Defamation whereby libels and slanders uttered against him can be sued upon and damages for the loss or injury he has received can be obtained by him from the person who uttered the defamatory statements.

The same principle applies throughout the law and throughout society generally. To each man his rights, but to each man his obligations also. But there is no reason why he should follow the laws laid down in the blind way that his forefathers followed the customs ordained by their social conditions. For he can see clearly the necessity for prohibitive laws once he realises this simple truth, that in the regulation of society it is necessary to protect interests other than his own, if anarchy is to be avoided. This can only be achieved by the acceptance of the obligations placed upon the individual by the law as well as the insistence upon the rights endowed by that same legal system.

It must be recognised even though it would seem that morality and law do not go entirely hand in hand. For they cannot do this where moral principles are tempered by the doctrine of convenience. Commercial honesty, even today, is dependent not so much upon moral values as upon the force of public opinion reflected in the laws made by Parliament. To many the word "law" has an unpleasant sound, denoting restriction of freedom. But morals are personal to the individual even though they are generally conditioned by the society in which he lives, and cannot form the basis for society's conduct. Thus, general principles of convenience must be brought in and the instincts of the individual must be to a certain extent submerged and restricted in order to obtain the maximum benefit for society as a whole. This is the function of law, but not its whole function, for its very machinery is largely directed towards the upholding of the rights of the individual against the state. In this way a certain balance can be achieved: the law restricts the rights of the individual, but the machinery of the law—the courts, the judges, the rules of evidence—protect him against the utmost rigours of the law where "right" is on his side.

TYPES OF LAW

We have seen that the origins of law lie in the customs followed in primitive society. But what form has the hardening of custom taken as it has been turned into law in the English system? To discuss this it is perhaps useful to deal first with the use to which the word "law" is put. First there is *imperative law* which is a rule imposed in the form of a command, then there is *scientific law*, which is simply the general principle expressing the operation of the universe, such as the law of gravity or the law of tides. There is *moral law* which is concerned with the principles of right or justice and there is *customary law* which is any rule actually observed by men voluntarily. Finally, there is *international law* which consists of rules governing states and their relation to one another, and what might be called *civil law* or *state law*, the law of the state or of the land, the law applied by the law courts and practised by the lawyers.

English law has its origins in customary law; it has the additive of moral law borrowed in part from ecclesiastical (church) law. It has the imperative nature bestowed upon it by the authority of Parliament and the courts. But it is not really necessary to delve into its nature too deeply, for this is a problem which has extended the imaginations of many great writers in legal theory. Rather it is necessary to speak of the types of law which we see in the English legal system, and these

3

are, basically, two, with the addition of a third system which is not strictly legal in origin but has been brought into the legal system. The three types of law are therefore Common Law, Statute Law and Equity.

Common Law

When William the Conqueror became King of England he instituted the Domesday survey, with which most people are familiar. In principle a census, it was kept up to date by commissioners who rode out regularly around the country, but it also formed the structural basis upon which was built the Common Law, for Anglo-Saxon England was administered by customary law which varied from district to district. This was changed in the course of time by the King's commissioners who rode out on circuits established by Henry II. Faced with so many customary rules it is no wonder that when they returned to Westminster they talked among themselves, comparing the better of the customs and criticising the worse. They naturally came to apply the better of these customs throughout the country, so that in the course of time the "laws" ceased to be local in nature and came to be based on the better of the customs discovered by the King's commissioners, or Itinerant Justices as they were called.

These customs then came to be applied throughout the country; they were the customs or laws which were common to the whole country; they were the common law. The circuit system established under Henry II was the origin of our own circuit system today, and the Itinerant Justices were the forerunners of our own Assize Judges. Indeed the Assize system, which used in effect the same commissions that were used by the Itinerant Justices, was a system which ran in an unbroken sequence from the twelfth century.

The Common Law, the law built up through the decisions of the courts of justice (for in time the law made in the shires by the Itinerant Justices was also used in Royal Courts established at Westminster), forms a large part of English law, a part which is still being developed today but which does not have its former pre-eminence within the system. It is also sometimes called "unwritten" law since it is not formulated in documentary form but consists of judgments given by judges on the particular facts of the cases before them. These judgments then form "precedents" so that later cases based on similar facts to the earlier decisions will be decided in the light of the earlier decisions. In this way modern judges are guided by the decisions given by their predecessors on the bench and the Common Law is given form and certainty.

4

Statute Law

The development of early English law was almost wholly brought about through the case law of the Common Law, but even in the twelfth century we find examples of legislation, or Statute Law. Legislation is the formal statement of law in documentary manner and with the growth in the power and importance of Parliament the influence of legislation upon the general body of English law was bound to increase.

In its early development the Common Law was of primary importance, since it was through this medium that the rule of law was established. As Parliament became stronger and more vociferous the early importance of the Common Law was eventually subordinated to the Statutes passed by Parliament, until the present position was reached whereby the judges maintain that they simply "declare" law and do not make it, and the Common Law principles can be overruled by Act of Parliament. In the fifteenth and sixteenth centuries the position and relationship between the two types of law was not so clearly formulated, so that Lord Chief Justice Coke held the Common Law to be above all other. The fluidity of the situation is shown by the fact that when he was dismissed from the bench by James I he became a Member of Parliament and then was loud in his claim that the Common Law must defer to the superiority of the Act of Parliament!

Nowadays it is commonplace for a judge to comment on the unsatisfactory state of the law he is called upon to apply and then to declare that he is powerless to change the law, this being the function of Parliament alone. It cannot be doubted therefore that in its power to overrule and change Common Law principles, Statute Law—that is the law made by formal act of the House of Commons and the House of Lords and the Queen acting together—is the superior form, having taken away the former primacy of the Common Law.

Equity

This system was the child of the defective state of the Common Law. The rules developed by the Common Law Courts at Westminster and by the judges on circuit were handicapped by the fact that they were limited in scope, immature, unable to cover all contingencies and therefore gave rise to injustice on many occasions. To obtain justice the individual would petition the King, who was the fountain of justice.

It became the practice to call upon the Lord Chancellor to deal with these petitions. An ecclesiastic, he was the "Keeper of the King's

5

Conscience", and the natural development from this was that petitions came to be referred directly to the Lord Chancellor. He heard these petitions in Chancery, which in the course of time became a court—but not a court of law, since the official did not use Common Law rules. These had already proved insufficient to meet the petitioner's needs, so the Lord Chancellor would follow his own ideas of justice to give a remedy to the petitioner.

Such "ideas" would obviously vary with individual Lord Chancellors, which would be difficult for lawyers called upon to advise clients, and it should also be noted that such tampering with the decisions of the law was not favoured by the Common Law judges themselves. By the seventeenth and eighteenth centuries the system of justice and fairness devised in the Court of Chancery had hardened into definite rules which were more easy to define from the point of view of the legal profession—but they were not rules of law, they were rules of Equity. Equity may therefore be defined as that extraordinary system of justice developed in and administered by the Court of Chancery alongside the development of the Common Law.

Though Equity grew up in the Court of Chancery as opposed to the Common Law Courts it is now administered in all the Common Law Courts also. This was the effect of the Judicature Acts 1873–5, which created a single system of central courts to administer both Common Law and Equity. Moreover, where the rules of Equity and the rules of law came into conflict it was laid down by the Acts that the rules of Equity were to prevail. This was of course necessary, although the ancient rivalry between the Common Law Courts and Chancery had died a natural death by the seventeenth century; the necessity for this step can still be seen in some instances such as the case where the legal rule demands written evidence in a particular form for a contract to be upheld, whereas Equity will uphold the contract in spite of the lack of form if there has been part performance by one party. This particular point is discussed later in Chapter 4.

The contribution of Equity to the legal system as a whole has been great; the trust, and the remedies of specific performance of contracts and injunctions to restrain the actions of another, are examples which might be noted.

Sources of Law

The most important sources of English law are of course Legislation, Case Law and Equity, with Custom, once a very important source, being only minor in nature nowadays. There are other sources however—an important example is the Law Merchant. In the Middle

Ages a body of international customs existed to regulate transactions between shipmasters and cargo owners, between merchant and merchant. Maritime customs existed in various ports, mercantile custom was applied in courts of fairs and markets. By the eighteenth century the local courts of this nature had virtually disappeared, but mercantile law and a large part of maritime law also had been incorporated into the common law. Important parts of our law such as the law relating to bills of exchange and the law of marine insurance thus originated in the "lex mercatoria".

A more modern source of law is to be seen in the practice of delegating to other bodies the power to legislate, which in theory is vested in Parliament alone. Modern government is a complex activity bedevilled with technical problems with which the Houses themselves are equipped to deal in part only. This, allied to the fact that Parliament has neither the time nor the inclination to deal with all the items and details of necessary legislation (such as, for instance, the time at which Okehampton's public park should close for the night) means that the power to deal with such minor legislation must be given to others.

In practice Parliament delegates to the Queen (acting through her Ministers) the power to legislate by Order in Council; it delegates to Ministers and heads of Government Departments, local authorities and public corporations, and sometimes to superior courts, powers to legislate within a particular field.

The delegation of this power is not absolute, for Parliament reserves the right to withdraw or curtail the delegated powers, and any acts by, for instance, a local authority, may be declared void if the act lies outside the scope of the powers granted to it by Parliament. This is known as the doctrine of "ultra vires". As an example of delegated authority the by-law of the local authority is useful; most people have at one time or another come across the restrictions imposed by the local authority—or at least noted the formidable posters with black headings and small, near-unreadable print displayed in prominent positions around the town.

CIVIL AND CRIMINAL LAW

There are few of us who have not been tempted by the apples in another's garden; there are few of us who have not succumbed to the temptation. Nor have we been deterred by the fearsome sign "Trespassers will be prosecuted". Nor in fact need we be. For the trespasser cannot be prosecuted (though he can be sued!) and the owner of the sign displays a woeful ignorance of legal principles. He

7

shows that he does not know the difference between civil and criminal actions, between civil and criminal law.

Nor did our ancestors applying their primitive law draw a very clear distinction between offences which were "criminal" and those which were "civil". Both were wrongs done by persons in society, against the customs of that community. Now, although the Wolfenden Report in 1957 stated that there is no definition of what amounts or ought to amount to a crime, the distinction between civil and criminal law is an accepted feature of the legal system.

The criminal law is concerned with those offences which affect the society as a whole by their gravity, rather than the individual alone (although some offences affecting only the individual may be called criminal). Thus, trespass is a civil offence as in nuisance and breach of contract; murder and theft are criminal offences. The distinction is shown in the proceedings which follow the perpetration of the offence: the civil offence results in a "suit" where a "plaintiff" sues a "defendant"; the criminal offence results in a "prosecution" of the "accused". It is the individual injured who sues, but it is the State which prosecutes. Again, the purpose of a civil action is the compensation of the person who has been injured, but the purpose of a prosecution is the punishment of the guilty person. The distinction is then carried through to the trial itself, where the rules of procedure also differ.

Common Market Law

The foregoing is concerned specifically with English law, but since January 1, 1973, English law has received an "injection" from outside, in the form of Common Market law. Commercial law is the law of the market place and the stated object of the Treaty of Rome is to make one market of western Europe for the sale and exchange of goods and services. The treaty envisages that each member state of the Community will by and large keep its own peculiar commercial law but the EEC Commission will from time to time issue Directives with a view to encouraging member states to bring their commercial laws into line. Uniform laws on bankruptcy and trade-marks for instance will be formulated in future and within the Treaty itself there are rules governing competition in trade between the member states of the European Economic Community. Some of these rules are mentioned later; the point to be noted is that since the accession of the United Kingdom to the EEC such rules become part of English law.

CHAPTER 2

Machinery of the Law

Believe it or not there are some people who actually enjoy going to law; there are some who continually run to the law courts to commence actions to the extent they become a nuisance, and eventually are regarded as "vexatious litigants" because they are really abusing their right to go to law. In the main, however, going to court is the last thing a businessman will want to do. It may be that his reputation could suffer as a result or the goodwill he has built up could disappear overnight; it is quite likely to be an expensive exercise in terms of time, money and health.

Even so, there are many occasions when there is nothing else a businessman can do other than commence an action. For instance, it may be that all his efforts to persuade another trader to pay for the goods ordered have been unsuccessful. Or again, a trader may find that when the lease of his business premises runs out the landlord wants him to leave and is insistent about it. And there is always the matter of nuisance or negligence or defamation or theft ... The reasons for going to court are numerous, but the problem for the businessman is: what court will the matter come before?

The court system was considerably overhauled by the provisions of the Courts Act 1971. The restructuring had become necessary for a number of reasons—the assize courts sat infrequently and were poorly located with regard to the distribution of population; assize timetables tended to be overloaded with criminal work; the assize judges spent a great deal of time travelling, and dependence upon part-time judges at quarter sessions was inconvenient. The system proved somewhat inflexible for the modern world and so the Act made a number of changes, abolishing the courts of assize and quarter sessions and setting up the new Crown Court, to deal exclusively with criminal cases, staffed by High Court judges, Circuit judges and Recorders sometimes sitting with justices of the peace. The Crown Court can sit wherever and whenever the Lord Chancellor determines.

For administrative purposes the country was divided into six circuits and the courts work on a three tier basis. In the first tier, civil and criminal cases are dealt with respectively at centres designated for High Court and Crown Court sittings. The second tier consists of centres designated for Crown Court sittings only, served as is the first tier by High Court judges, Circuit judges and Recorders. The third tier consists of Crown Court centres where the High Court judges do not serve.

THE CIVIL COURTS

County Courts

There are about four hundred towns in which a county court sits; they are served by Circuit judges and they deal with such matters as actions in contract and tort (excluding defamation) where the claim does not exceed £2,000; actions concerning land where the net annual rating value does not exceed £2,000; trusts, mortgages and partnership matters under £15,000. Some courts outside London also have an unlimited jurisdiction in bankruptcy matters and also in winding up companies with a paid up share capital not exceeding £10,000; some can also entertain proceedings brought under the Race Relations Act 1968.

There are some cases which *must* be brought in the county courts—certain claims under the Rent Restriction Acts and the Hire Purchase Act, for instance, but generally speaking the High Court has a concurrent jurisdiction—that is, a case can be brought either in the High Court or the county court.

The small retailer should be warned that it is more expensive to go to the High Court! For this reason, if the defendant is in agreement, it is possible to bring some actions in the county court even though they would normally fall outside the limits of the county court's jurisdiction. The great majority of civil claims are in fact brought in the county court.

Magistrates Courts

Most of the cases dealt with by magistrates are criminal in nature but the magistrates courts do have a certain civil jurisdiction. They deal with the enforcement of a restricted category of debts, for instance, and they exercise important functions in regard to the licensing laws. A committee of between five and fifteen local magistrates form a licensing committee and hold an annual meeting—sometimes known as a "brewster session"—and between four and eight transfer sessions

10

during the rest of the year. *Juvenile Courts* deal with applications for adoption and civil care proceedings relating to children and young persons; the *Crown Court*, though mainly a criminal court, does have some licensing jurisdiction and hears appeals from magistrates courts in affiliation proceedings and rating and licensing matters.

The superior courts in civil matters consist of the High Court, the Court of Appeal and the House of Lords.

The High Court

The civil jurisdiction of the High Court is wide and so has been split: there are three divisions of the High Court. Each division operates as an ordinary court (with one judge) or as a divisional court (with at least two judges). The three divisions are as follows.

Queens Bench Division. This is headed by the Lord Chief Justice of England who is assisted by about forty-two *puisne*, or ordinary, judges. It handles all those kinds of cases which are not expressly allocated to one of the other divisions, and it tries a large number of contract and tort cases. By section 2(1) of the Administration of Justice Act 1970 an Admiralty Court was created as part of the Queens Bench Division to deal with admiralty matters such as salvage and collisions between ships, and by section 3(1) of the Act a Commercial Court was constituted as part of the Queens Bench Division to deal with certain commercial cases.

Chancery Division. The Lord Chancellor is head of the Chancery Division but in practice he does not sit; the work is really done by the Vice-Chancellor, assisted by ten *puisne* judges. The court deals with those matters formerly dealt with by the old Court of Chancery, and this includes trusts, partnership actions, mortgages, bankruptcy and company law matters. It is to this court the trader might eventually come for specific performance of his contract or if he has a conveyancing problem. And if he has been having a long argument with his tax inspector about the calculation of his income tax liability or the revenue due upon goods he has shipped into the country, it is the Chancery Division which might give him the answer. There are separate courts in the Division, the Companies Court and the Bankruptcy Court, to deal with company matters and bankruptcy cases respectively.

Family Division. The grocer who finds his wife disputing ownership of the house and shop may find himself in this since it deals with, among other things, property disputes between husband and wife. The head of the Division is the President, and he is assisted by sixteen *puisne* judges.

11

The Court of Appeal

If an appeal is to be made, either on a question of fact or of law, from the High Court or from a county court, it will lie to the Court of Appeal. This is called a rehearing of the case but in fact the court relies on a transcript of the evidence presented in the lower court. The appeal may be allowed in whole or part, or dismissed. If it is allowed the court may substitute its own decision for that of the earlier court, or it may order a retrial. The work of the court is undertaken by the Master of the Rolls and the Lords Justices of Appeal, but the Lord Chancellor, ex-Lord Chancellors, the Lord Chief Justice, the President of the Family Division and the Lords of Appeal in Ordinary are also members. Sometimes a High Court judge is appointed by the Lord Chancellor to sit, in addition. The court normally works in divisions of three judges; in important cases five or more judges sometimes appear.

The House of Lords

This is the highest civil court of appeal for England, Wales, Scotland and Northern Ireland. The work is done by an Appellate Committee of the House of Lords, consisting of a maximum of eleven Lords of Appeal in Ordinary, the Lord Chancellor, ex-Lord Chancellors, the Master of the Rolls and peers who have held, or hold, high judicial office. The quorum for an appeal is three and the Committee normally sits in divisions of three or five. Individual judgments are given as printed opinions in most cases. Appeals normally lie from the Court of Appeal but appeal direct from the High Court is possible in some limited circumstances.

Two other courts may conveniently be mentioned here, each possessing a special jurisdiction.

The Restrictive Practices Court

The law and procedure of this court is now governed by the Restrictive Practices Court Act 1976. The court deals with agreements registered by the Director General of Fair Trading, and applications for exemption from the provisions of the Resale Prices Act 1976. Appeal from decisions of the court on points of law can be made to the Court of Appeal (Civil Division). The Restrictive Practices Court is staffed by three High Court judges, one judge from the Court of Session in Scotland, one from the Supreme Court of Northern Ireland

and up to ten other members who are qualified by their experience in commerce, industry or public affairs.

Employment Appeal Tribunal

This body was brought into being to hear appeals on questions of law from Industrial Tribunals and the Trade Union Certification Officer. Appeals are made on matters such as redundancy, equal pay, sex discrimination, trade union certification, and questions arising out of the Employment Protection Act 1975.

The Tribunal consists of judges of the Court of Appeal and the High Court nominated by the Lord Chancellor, one judge from the Court of Session and lay members appointed because of their knowledge or experience in industrial relations. It may sit on divisions anywhere in Great Britain—normally with a judge and two or four lay members giving equal representation to employers and workers.

THE CRIMINAL COURTS

Magistrates Courts

These, and the *Juvenile Courts* are the inferior criminal courts. Magistrates are laymen appointed by the Lord Chancellor on the recommendation of local advisory committees; no legal qualification is required. A lay magistrate receives no salary but can claim expenses. Stipendiary magistrates are solicitors or barristers of at least seven years' standing, appointed by the Crown on the recommendation of the Lord Chancellor and they are salaried. Each magistrates court has a clerk to the justices whose function it is to advise the magistrates on the law.

The magistrates courts have powers of summary trial over such offences as driving without due care and attention. As a general rule summary offences punishable with at least three months' imprisonment may be tried on indictment if the defendent so chooses. (An indictment is a written or printed accusation signed by an officer of the Crown Court and naming the defendant, the charges and the court of trial.) Magistrates also undertake committal proceedings—that is, they conduct a preliminary enquiry to decide whether the defendant has a case to answer.

Crown Court

The Crown Court can be classified as a superior court; it sits in various specified places and deals as a court of trial with serious offences such as murder, manslaughter, burglary and so on. The type of judge that sits is determined by the nature of the offence and all proceedings on indictment are tried by judge and jury. The Court also deals with committals for sentence, where a person is found guilty or has pleaded guilty, in a magistrates court and has been committed to the Crown Court for sentence. The Court also has a certain appellate jurisdiction.

Court of Appeal (*Criminal Division*)

This court was established by the Criminal Appeal Act 1966 which abolished the Court of Criminal Appeal. To hear appeals from the Crown Court the court must consist of an uneven number of judges—usually three. The Lord Chief Justice or a Lord Justice of Appeal normally presides.

The House of Lords

Either side can appeal to the House of Lords from the Court of Appeal (Criminal Division) with leave of the Court of Appeal or of the House of Lords. A point of law of general public importance must be involved.

INSTITUTIONS OF THE EEC

No account of the machinery of the law would now be complete without mention of the European Court of Justice. It is one of the main institutions of the Common Market system, the others being the Council of Ministers, the Commission, and the Assembly.

Judicial control in the Community is largely left to the separate states making up the Community—whether or not an action can be brought in the European Court of Justice is a matter of national judicial policy. The only exceptions to this are contracts involving officials of the Community, or contracts including an arbitration clause giving exclusive jurisdiction to the Community Court.

The Court of Justice comprises one judge from each member state and one other. It deals with two matters in the main: if it is decided by a municipal court that a question of interpretation of the Treaty arises it can be referred to the European Court (and it must be referred if there is no further appeal possible from the municipal court—for instance, the House of Lords); secondly, the Court deals with matters involving action brought by organs of the Community, member states, or individuals who allege that obligations of Community law have been broken. But if a State wishes to make a claim against another State it must first go to the Commission with its complaint; only if the matter is not resolved can it then go to the Court.

The Court of Justice is not bound by precedent, and it does not enforce its own judgments—each member state must provide machinery for enforcement within its own system.

COURT OF LAW OR ARBITRATION?

So much for the system of courts, but what actually *happens* when, say, a wholesaler claims he has not been paid for cases of washing-up liquid he has delivered to a small grocery chain? If repeated requests for payment have met with no response the wholesaler will probably consult his solicitor.

The solicitor will eventually have to file the particulars of the wholesaler's claim in the county court office; the registrar will then arrange for a pre-trial review and will inform the wholesaler and issue a summons to the grocer, along with the particulars of the claim.

The grocer then has alternative courses open to him. He can make a payment into court of the whole amount, or a lesser amount than that claimed. If the wholesaler accepts, then the action goes no further, though the wholesaler can make an application for costs if these haven't been covered by the payment in. Alternatively, the grocer can admit liability and offer to pay at a certain rate. If this is agreeable to the wholesaler, the court will so enter judgment. If not, the action will proceed. A third alternative is to contest the claim. In this case the grocer's solicitor will file a defence, and perhaps a counterclaim, such as the counterclaim that the goods were never delivered, or were accepted in payment of a larger debt owed to the grocer by the wholesaler—and now the grocer wants the outstanding payment made!

If the action goes on there is a pre-trial review where the registrar gives the parties directions for the best way of dealing with the action. These directions should then be followed, a day is fixed for trial and notice is given to the parties.

A complicated business even before the businessmen ever get to court! And thereafter there can be all kinds of legal argument between the parties, dragging on for a long time, to the enrichment of the lawyers and the impoverishment of the businessmen. This is why many agreements in the trade contain arbitration clauses. It is true that if a dispute involves difficult legal problems they are best dealt with in a court of law. But the view is generally held by businessmen

15

that if the dispute is really concerned mainly with issues of fact, it would be as well to have the matter dealt with by arbitration.

This is so because it is easier to fix a time and a place for a hearing in arbitration proceedings to suit the convenience of the parties. The proceedings are also less expensive than a court action and the result arrived at more speedily. One further point should not be overlooked. A judge is not a business expert. But in an arbitration the parties will often be able to ensure that the arbitrator appointed is a man who can bring to his consideration of the dispute a special expertise in the subject matter of the argument.

For these reasons it is common for businessmen to include in a commercial contract they draw up, an arbitration clause by which they agree that in the event of any dispute arising upon the contract the dispute shall be referred to a named person as arbitrator (or otherwise specifying the method by which an arbitrator shall be chosen). If one party then tries to sue the other before submitting to arbitration the other party can apply to the court for the action to be stopped.

Arbitration proceedings are held in private. The arbitrator must conduct the proceedings in a judicial manner but the rules that apply in a court of law regarding procedure do not of course apply in an arbitration. After studying the evidence the arbitrator will make an award to one party or the other. This award is usually final but sometimes it can be sent back to the arbitrator for correction of an error.

But what if the wholesaler has gone to arbitration, won his case, and the grocer still fails to pay up? In such a case the wholesaler can *then* go to court to ask for the arbitration award to be enforced as though it were an award of the court.

LEGAL AID

One further matter might be mentioned in connection with the machinery of the law. It has already been mentioned that many people will be deterred from going to the courts for assistance by the very fact of the expense involved. Under the Legal Aid Act 1974 legal aid can be provided in civil and criminal cases. A legal advice and assistance scheme for matters outside the courts was introduced by the Legal Advice and Assistance Act 1972. Legal aid can involve representation by a solicitor or barrister, or legal aid in matters not involving litigation—by a solicitor taking steps, for instance, to make a claim or present an argument against a claim being made. Local committees of solicitors and barristers have been established to receive applications for legal aid.

The committees investigate the financial resources of the applicant, and the details are sent to the Supplementary Benefits Commission who may, after deciding what the applicant's disposable income and capital amount to, state the applicant should make a contribution to the costs of the proceedings. The local committees also enquire into the merits of the applicant's case. And that, in a sense, brings us back full circle to the "vexatious litigant"—who is unlikely to obtain legal aid!

CHAPTER 3

Persons Under the Law

Statements of principles of law in this book proceed on the assumption that the persons concerned are not subject to any legal disability; that is to say, the persons concerned have full legal capacity.

Some persons have an exceptional legal position, however, in that they are protected by the law or suffer disabilities imposed by the law. The mental patient and the bankrupt are examples. Another is the minor (or infant).

A minor is a person who is under 18 years of age. His position as far as contracts is concerned is governed by the Infants Relief Act 1874 which renders certain contracts void. In general he is liable for torts (civil wrongs) that he commits, but where the commission of the tort depends upon a specific intention being proved it may be that the infant's youth will be relevant.

Even more striking than the case of the infant at law is the instance of the "juristic person". A person, as far as the law is concerned, is a being which is subject to the duties imposed by the law and can claim the benefits given by the law. But in the same way that a human being need not necessarily be a legal person (an outlaw or a slave was not a legal person) so it is not necessary that the legal person should necessarily be a human being. For the law recognises the existence of juristic persons—legal persons which are not human beings.

In English law the only juristic person recognised is the corporation and perhaps to a certain extent the trade union. The position of the corporation is of particular relevance to the retailer and will now be discussed in some detail.

CORPORATIONS

Incorporation is a most useful method for dealing with common interests which are vested in a number of individuals, particularly so since it makes very much easier the management and protection of those interests. From the retailer's point of view the most important form of incorporation is that which arises under the Companies Acts 1948–1967, but it should be noted that corporations can also come into being by Act of Parliament or by Royal Charter. However, the remainder of this chapter will be devoted to a discussion of the formation of a company under the Companies Acts 1948–1967. (Where the phrase "Companies Act" appears hereafter, this refers to the Companies Act 1948.)

The trader who runs his own business always faces the risk of his business collapsing. This might well lead to his bankruptcy. If he has stock worth £10,000 and debts totalling £20,000, it is not only against his stock that his creditors will act. If the trader is made bankrupt, all his assets, both inside and outside the business he has been carrying on, will be brought into the melting pot for the benefit of his creditors. He will be a ruined man, without a penny to his name, with his house, his car, his personal possessions sold to pay his debts.

On the other hand of course the small trader might be running a most profitable business but is unable to expand that business in the way he sees necessary because of his own limited capital. One way in which he could raise that capital would be to allow other people, members of the general public, to buy an interest in his business. The money contributed could then be used for expansion.

To both the trader who fears the risk of collapse and the trader who wishes to expand a flourishing business, incorporation offers distinct advantages. The limited liability company is the answer to their prayers and doubts. The fearful trader will form a private company; the expansionist trader will probably form a public company. The risk of personal liability outside the assets of the business itself is eliminated and in the second instance the public may now be persuaded to invest money in the enterprise.

The objects desired by these two traders will be achieved because the law recognises the device of corporate personality. The important thing to note is that the newly formed company exists as a legal person quite independently of the members who make up that company. This means that any debts incurred by the company will be the debts of the company and not of the members. The members, who will probably be known as shareholders, will hold shares in the company. These shares will represent the amount of money that each has contributed, in cash or in some other consideration, or is prepared to contribute to the company funds. In normal circumstances the shares held will then limit the financial liability of the member. In other words, if the business fails the member loses the money he has paid or owes on the shares. Beyond this amount he is not liable. His house, his car, his personal possessions cannot be touched. His liability is limited.

19

This will be the case even though the member is the person who started the company, manages it personally, and holds almost all the shares in the company. For the company exists as another person; he can lend money to it, he can make contracts with it. The company is in law a different person entirely from the members. The classic example arose in the 1890s when a Mr Salomon sold his boot business to a company which he formed with six members of his family holding one share each. He himself held 20,000 shares. He lent the company £10,000, receiving loan certificates (debentures) as security. When the company was wound up the creditors argued that as Salomon and Co. was really the same person as Salomon himself he could not owe money to himself, and *their* debts should be paid first. The court disagreed: once a company is incorporated it must be treated like any other independent person and the motives of the promoters are irrelevant.

It is quite obvious that the use of such a device might well be a heavensent opportunity for the rogue who wants nothing more than to defraud the public. Because of this transparent possibility the Companies Acts have laid down strict provisions to prevent the device being used for purposes of fraud. To protect the general public and those people who invest their money in companies, the Act lays down that when a company is formed under the Act certain documents must be registered with the Registrar at the Companies Registration Office. The file kept by the Registrar is then open to inspection by the general public on the payment of a small fee. Thus, anyone who wishes to invest money in a company or give that company credit in any transaction can, if he wishes, obtain from the file the details as to the powers possessed by the company and he will also be able to discover what the financial standing of the company is likely to be.

What is the procedure to be followed in the formation of a limited company? Firstly, if several individuals wish to form a limited company they have to decide a number of things. If they intend to buy a business already in existence exactly what assets are to be transferred? How are they to be paid for? They can be paid for in cash, or they can be paid for by the transfer of shares. Thus, the small trader who wishes to form a company will sell his business to the company and take in return shares in the company. The big trading company which buys up a small trader may offer him cash, or shares in the company. Again, how much capital will be necessary for the company to run smoothly? Where will this capital come from? Will it be raised by the issue of shares alone or will it be raised by the issue of shares and debentures (certificates given in return for a loan of money to the company)? If the company is to be a private company shares only will probably be issued.

Once these points are decided, the first step to be taken is the preparation of a Memorandum of Association. This document must be registered with the Registrar of Companies and it will contain the name of the company, which can be almost anything provided it ends with the word "limited". It will also state the country where the registered office is situated, the objects or powers of the company, the amount of capital of the company and how the liability of the members is limited. The importance of this document can be seen in the fact that upon it the company depends for its existence and powers. It tells the world what the financial status and the powers of the company are and it shows who the promoters of the company are, since they are called upon to sign the document giving their names, addresses and descriptions together with the number of shares taken by each subscriber.

Before it is printed, it is as well to discover from the Registrar of Companies that the name given to the company in the Memorandum of Association can in fact be used. If the company is to be a public company the memorandum must be signed by at least seven subscribers: in the case of the private company only two subscribers are necessary. But all must hold shares in the company, though one share is sufficient.

The first step, the preparation of the Memorandum of Association, having been taken, the promoters of the company must then make arrangements for the carrying on of the business. These arrangements are made in the form of Articles of Association. The Articles will go into detail in regard to matters such as the appointment of managers of the business or directors in the case of a larger company. It will detail the method of allotting shares to members and state the rights of shareholders. It will state that the shareholders will be entitled to share certificates as evidence of their holdings, which will also appear in a register of members that will be kept by the company. Meetings, voting procedures, resolutions will all appear in the Articles and all the matters placed in the Articles will be binding as a formal contract between the company and the members of the company.

Strictly speaking, the preparation of Articles of Association is not necessary; the Act says that they *may* be registered. If they are not, the provisions of Table A in the first schedule to the Companies Act, which in fact is a specimen set of Articles for a Company limited by shares, will apply. If the company to be formed will be a private company the modifications necessary for private companies stated in Part II of the Schedule must be adopted if Articles are not registered. In practice, all private companies register Articles.

Once these documents have been prepared it is possible for the promoters to go ahead with the registration of their new company. They will file with the Registrar of Companies the Memorandum of Association, the Articles of Association (if any), a list of the people who have agreed to become directors of the company, together with the written consent of these directors, and with these documents will be sent a statutory declaration that the requirements of the Companies Acts have been complied with. If the company is to be a private company the list of directors and written consents is not necessary.

The promoters should file at the same time the place from which the business will be carried on, i.e. the registered office, and particulars concerning the secretary and directors of the company. Deed stamps will be due on the Memorandum and Articles of Association together with a registration fee, stamp duty on the nominal capital, filing fees, and if any assets have been transferred to the company a conveyance duty on these assets (with certain exceptions).

Once the company has been registered in this way it comes into legal existence. If it is a private company it can commence business immediately but if it is a public company, only if the amount of shares up to the minimum subscription have been allotted, can it begin business.

On registration, the Registrar enters the name of the company in the register and hands over to the company a certificate of incorporation which is evidence that all the requirements have been complied with and the company has been duly formed. Under section 9 of the European Communities Act 1972 he must also publish in the *London Gazette* (*Edinburgh Gazette* for Scottish companies) the fact that he has received or issued certain documents, such as the certificate of incorporation and a notice of the situation of the registered office. He must thereafter comply with this rule of "official notification" in respect of changes of registered office, or of directors, or orders for dissolution, etc. Official notification is important because the company cannot rely upon the happening of an event against some other person unless that event has been "officially notified". An example of a specified event would be the making of a winding-up order or the appointment of a liquidator, as well as the changes mentioned above.

Once the company is in business it will want to use business stationery. The Companies Act 1948 provided that the company name must appear legibly on all business letters and other stationery and the European Communities Act 1972 added to this provision. It states that all business letters and order forms must include the following particulars:

(a) place of registration and number with which the company is registered;
(b) address of the registered office;
(c) in the case of a limited company exempt from the obligation to use the word "limited" in its name, the fact that it is a limited company.

Moreover, if a company refers on its stationery to its share capital the reference must be to its paid up share capital.

Two of the advantages apparent in the formation of a company have already been noted: the businessman avoids personal liability to a large extent in that is it limited, and he can also obtain subscriptions from the public. This is not to say that all is wine and roses once the company is formed. The promoters of the company may have wished to obtain the advantages and benefits of incorporation, which include in addition to those mentioned above the benefit of a possible tax relief, but they must also accept the disadvantages inherent in incorporation.

It may be for instance that at some time they will be called upon to submit to an inspection of their affairs by investigating inspectors appointed by the Department of Trade. They will find that as directors they are not permitted to obtain any secret benefits from their directorships: their positions are fiduciary ones and if they obtain personal benefits they can be sued by the company for the return of those benefits. They will have to disclose to the company any interests they have in contracts the company is entering into. They will be bound by the offences created by the Companies Act in connection with fraudulent trading. In other words, the trader who wishes to form his business into a limited company will find that he has to submit also to a certain amount of control imposed by the Companies Act for the benefit of the public.

It is quite apparent, however, that the advantages of incorporation far outweigh the disadvantages. An extremely large part of trade and industry in Great Britain is carried on by limited companies, public and private. Three hundred thousand companies incorporated in this country can hardly be wrong!

Private Companies

Since many small businesses are incorporated as private companies it would perhaps be useful at this point to emphasise the main distinctions between the private and public companies, some of which have already been mentioned. A private company is defined by the Com-

23

panies Act specially, and in effect the following provisions apply to private companies:

(i) the right to transfer shares must be restricted (often to members of the family);
(ii) it may consist of two members only but must not exceed fifty in all;
(iii) it must not invite the public to subscribe for shares;
(iv) it may commence business immediately it is incorporated;
(v) the directors need not retire at 70.

These special provisions are not exhaustive; further details can be obtained in works on Company Law.

Partnerships and Unincorporated Associations

Two or more people can, of course, set up in business together without forming a limited company. Normally, provided they do not amount to more than twenty people all together they can form a partnership, which is defined as the relation which exists between persons carrying on business in common with a view to profit. The limit of 20 does not apply to practising solicitors, accountants, members of a stock exchange and others exempted by Board of Trade regulations.

The partnership is formed by contract, either express or implied, but even where there is no written contract a person can be liable as a partner if he holds himself out or allows himself to be regarded as a partner. For instance, if the manager of a shop acts as though he were owner he could be regarded liable as a partner of the owners to someone who has been misled by his actions.

Persons who intend forming a company and are working toward that end are not regarded as partners: in a 1970 case, *Spicer Ltd v Mansell*, M and B agreed to form a limited company for the restaurant business and B ordered some goods from Spicer, for the business. B went bankrupt and Spicer sued M, arguing he was B's partner but the court disagreed: the two had simply been carrying out work preparatory to forming a company and were not partners.

From the claim made by Spicer however it is clear that in law one partner is regarded as the agent of every other partner and of the firm itself—this is why they sued M for debts created by B. In a trading firm a partner always has implied authority to sell and buy goods for the firm, employ people and receive payment for firm debts, handle cheques in the firm's name, borrow money and pledge goods in the name of the firm. He cannot bind the firm by deed, however, unless he has been so authorised expressly, by deed.

24

An instructive case arose in 1968. D, T and L were in partnership as produce dealers but only D was an active partner. D asked M to join with him in the purchase of a potatoes consignment, as a joint venture. D failed to pay to M any profits from the venture and M sued the firm. T and L were held not liable because although D could bind his partners in any dealing connected with the firm, he could not bind them in any venture *outside* the business. So though D was personally liable to M, T and L were not.

It is possible, of course, that people who form a partnership later disagree and want to end the relationship. In such cases what happens to partnership property? It might amount to goods, or money, or even land if premises have been purchased for the business. The answer is the ex-partners will hold the property as joint tenants—it belongs to them jointly. It is possible, of course, that the partnership agreement may vary the *amount* of the shares held by individual partners; one may hold one-third, for instance, and the other two-thirds is shared between three or four other partners.

Where the partnership is ended the assets must be sold, the proceeds used to pay off partnership debts and then the partners share what is left. In contrast to *Salomon's case*, mentioned above, a partner advancing money to a partnership is really advancing part of the money to himself and so cannot obtain preference over other creditors. One particular asset that sometimes gives rise to difficulty is goodwill—this is a partnership asset and when one partner retires he is entitled to be paid by the other partners for his share of the goodwill. If it is not sold when a partnership is dissolved, each partner is entitled to carry on business under the old firm name and thus keep the goodwill. The difficulties this could give rise to are obvious—five traders in the High Street using the same firm name, for instance!

It should be noted that the concept of juristic personality does not extend to partnerships and unincorporated associations. The importance of this fact can be seen by a comparison of the position in these two instances with that of the limited company. Thus:

(a) The limited company exists as a distinct person.

The partnership does not.

Shares in the limited company are freely transferable (unless it is a private company).

The partner cannot transfer his share without his partners' consent.

Shareholders are not agents of the company.

Partners are agents of the partnership.

Shareholder's liability is limited.

The partner's liability is unlimited.

The winding up of an

A bankrupt partnership

insolvent company does not bankrupt its members.	means the bankruptcy of the partners.

(b) Unincorporated associations may exist for purposes other than trade; common examples are football clubs. Such associations do not exist as legal persons and so they possess none of the advantages of the incorporated body. It is simply a group of persons bound together by the rules of the association, its affairs usually being managed by a committee. If the association is formed for business purposes it can include not more than twenty members (ten, if the business is banking). If it has more than twenty members (or ten) it must be incorporated either by statute or letters patent or by registration under the Companies Act. These restrictions were lifted to some extent by the Companies Act 1967 in the case of certain partnerships, as we have seen. If the firm deals under a name which does not consist of the true surnames of the partners, the firm must be registered under the Registration of Business Names Act of 1916. The registration must disclose the name, nature and principal place of business, nationality, Christian names and surnames of the partners, and any other business occupations of the partners.

After registration a certificate is issued and must be prominently displayed at the principal place of business. The Act also states that all the firm's trade documents using the firm's name must show the names of the partners, and their nationality if not British.

Many people engaged in the distributive trades will be involved in Europe. As in England, so in Europe: companies are used for enterprises ranging from the "one man" business to large public companies. There are many differences in detail however but progress towards unification is under way. Two methods are being sought: the attempted harmonisation of the separate legal systems, and attempts to establish the European Company (the *Societas Europaea*). In relation to the first method, changes required by the EEC Directive of 1968 were incorporated into the European Communities Act 1972. The idea of the European Company is still an idea, in EEC draft form.

CHAPTER 4

Law of Contract

FORMATION OF CONTRACT

Many everyday transactions are carried out in a straightforward manner, whereby goods are sold over the counter and paid for immediately. Each transaction is a contract. The straightforward contract is not always possible, however, particularly where the goods to be sold are warehoused elsewhere, or are in bulk too great to be delivered at once, or alternatively, where the customer does not have with him the payment required. It has been well said therefore that "wealth in a commercial age is made up largely of promises" and it is the promise which forms the basis of the Law of Contract.

Where two parties are in agreement concerning a transaction, or their conduct would make a reasonable person assume that such agreement has been reached, the courts of law will enforce the agreement made between them. This broad statement of the function of the Law of Contract is subject to certain limitations, discussion of which takes up the greater part of this chapter; nevertheless, it is true to say that the law attempts to enforce agreements based on arrangements consented to by the parties to the contract.

It should here be pointed out that a contract does not need to be in writing to be binding upon the parties; a verbal contract is just as effective as one made in writing—though it might be more difficult to prove. With the exceptions, therefore, of certain contracts which *must* be made in writing or by deed (which will be discussed later) the verbal contract can be considered as effective as the written one.

A distinction must be drawn between contracts which are binding upon the parties, and arrangements which the law does not regard as legally binding. "All contracts are agreements, but not all agreements are contracts." Purely social or domestic arrangements, where the parties do not really intend to establish a legal relationship between themselves, have no legal effect. An example occurs in the case of the invitation to dinner; failure to turn up could hardly be regarded as a breach of contract. Of course, even those arrangements which are truly contractual in nature may yet be rendered legally ineffective if the parties stipulate in the contract that no legal obligations are to arise under the contract. In the face of such a stipulation the courts will refuse to interfere as they refused to interfere in *Rose and Frank Co v Crompton and Bros. Ltd* (1925). R agreed to buy carbon paper from C. The contract stated: "This arrangement is not entered into . . . as a formal or legal agreement and shall not be subject to legal jurisdiction in the Law courts . . ." R sued for breach of contract and non-delivery of the goods but the action failed—legal relations had been expressly excluded.

These are preliminary matters: it was pointed out above that all agreements will be enforced, subject to certain limitations. What are these limitations? Briefly, they might be summarised thus:

(1) The parties to the contract must be legally capable of making a contract.

(2) There must be an offer by one party which is accepted by the other.

(3) The agreement between the parties must be a genuine one.

(4) The agreement must be supported by consideration.

(5) The purpose of the contract must not be against the law.

(6) In some cases, the contract must be made in writing or by deed.

The effect of the lack of one or more of these requirements will vary: it would perhaps be simplest to discuss each of the circumstances in turn.

LEGAL CAPACITY

Persons under disabilities recognised by the law may lack legal capacity to make a contract—examples are mental patients and drunkards, and to a certain extent aliens. A more common instance arises in the case of the minor—that is, the person who has not yet reached eighteen years of age. The retailer who deals with a minor is dealing with a person who enjoys the protection of the law, a protection which is extended, in many cases to the detriment of the retailer, even to the "infant rogue". It is quite obvious that the shopkeeper who supplies goods on credit to a minor will not want to receive the goods back. He is more interested in getting the price for them. But if he wants to succeed in his claim he will have to show that the goods taken by the minor can be classified as "necessaries". In *Nash v Inman* (1908) the minor ordered eleven fancy waistcoats from a Savile Row tailor. When the tailor sued for the price of the waistcoats the minor's father stated his undergraduate son was already adequately supplied with such items of adornment. The court held the goods ordered were not necessaries so the tailor failed in his claim.

Necessaries are any goods which the minor requires for his maintenance and comfort; they must be goods with which he is not adequately supplied at the time and they must be suitable to his station in life. Goods which might be regarded as "luxuries" by one person may be necessaries to another—it largely depends on the minor's position. Generally speaking, however, luxury goods do not classify as necessaries. Food, clothing, and accommodation are obvious examples of necessaries, but the term can also include education or advice.

The reason why the retailer must show that the goods are "necessary" to the minor is that the law ordains, in protection of the minor, that otherwise an agreement to supply goods to a minor is absolutely void. This means that as far as the law is concerned the agreement has never come into existence. Furthermore, this will be the case even where the minor has falsely misrepresented his age to the shopkeeper. If, on the other hand, the retailer can show that the goods were necessary to the minor the contract is binding and the minor can be sued for the price. The importance of the classification to the retailer is obvious.

The Sale of Goods Act 1893, section 2, also provides that where necessaries are sold and delivered to the minor he must pay a reasonable price for those goods.

The agreements declared void by the law when entered into by a minor are those to supply non-necessary goods, to lend money and an agreement to repay a debt that someone had incurred as a minor in the past. But it should be noted that although all such agreements are declared void, the infant or minor can sue upon such promises, if it is the other party who fails to perform his obligation. So much is the minor protected from the "wicked" adult!

Certain other contracts, when entered into by a minor, are binding; we have seen one example in the contract for necessaries. Another example is the contract beneficial to the minor, provided it contains an element of apprenticeship or service.

All other agreements made by the minor are voidable; that is to say he can refuse to regard them as binding upon him provided he exercises such power to deny the contract before he becomes 18 or soon after. In fact, he is given a certain grace beyond that time; the extent of this grace will depend on the circumstances.

Offer and Acceptance

An offer is essential to the making of a contract but it need not be made expressly, in words; it can be implied from the conduct of the parties. But it is essential that the person making the offer should "mean business". The shopkeeper who announces in the local press that he will sell goods at a particular price at a particular time is not necessarily making an "offer" which can be accepted by any party who takes the trouble to attend the sale. In *Harris v Nickerson* (1873) H went to a sale advertised by N, an auctioneer, but all the furniture in which H was interested was withdrawn. H sued N for damages for the loss of his time and expenses in attending the sale. The court held the advertising of a sale was a declaration of intention and not an offer which could be accepted by attending. It is not essential that the offer should be made to a particular person, on the other hand—an offer which is made to the world at large is a perfectly good offer capable of acceptance by any person who complies with the terms of the offer. In *Carlill v Carbolic Smoke Ball Co* (1893) the company advertised their "smoke ball" as a remedy against influenza and offered to pay £100 to anyone who used it as prescribed and yet contracted influenza. "To show their sincerity" the company deposited £1,000 at the bank. C bought and used the smoke ball but contracted influenza so she sued for £100. The company denied the existence of a binding agreement. The court held (i) an offer can be made to the world at large and can be accepted by anyone who bought the article and used it as prescribed; (ii) C need not communicate her acceptance of the offer since by implication acceptance would be made when the conditions laid down in the advertisement were complied with; (iii) the advertisement was a genuine offer since it was backed by the £1,000 deposit. Legal relations with users of the "smoke ball" were intended.

The requirement as to the offer or "meaning business" serves to distinguish the genuine offer from the "invitation to make an offer". The retailer who displays goods in his window with price ticket attached is not making an offer; he is inviting the public to come into his premises and make him an offer for the goods displayed, and the price tag is only a guide as to what price will be acceptable to the shopkeeper. Were this not to be so, the difficulties would be obvious: a £5,000 fur coat accidentally marked at £500 in the shop window, with three customers simultaneously approaching an assistant and "accepting" the offer, will serve as an example. In fact, of course, the three customers cannot accept the offer because there has been no offer. *They* have been invited to *make* an offer, and it is then up to the assistant to accept or reject the offers that they have made.

The same reasoning can be applied to the case of the self-service store. It would be ridiculous if the customer who picked up a packet of washing powder, then changed her mind and replaced it on the shelf, should find herself being sued for breach of contract by the retailer. The display of goods does not amount to an offer; it is an invitation to the customer to take the goods and offer to buy them at the cash desk. This offer can then be accepted or rejected by the assistant. The classic example is seen in *Pharmaceutical Society v Boots Cash Chemists (Southern) Ltd* (1953) where goods were sold in B's shop under a self-service system. Customers selected the purchases from the shelves and took them to the cash desk where the price was paid. The court decided that the contract was completed when the cashier accepted the offer to buy and received the price.

The offeror may attach any conditions to the contract that he desires, but if they are to be effective they must be communicated to the other person before or at the time the contract is made. He obviously cannot add conditions later. If a customer pays for a second-hand car only to be told that the dealer has decided not to give it to him until Christmas, this being a condition that he has just added to the contract, the customer would have every right to be loud in his complaints!

Many firms attempt to get over the difficulty of communicating conditions to customers by incorporating the conditions in a document and asking the customer to sign the document, thereby certifying that he has read and understood its terms and conditions. Subject to what is noted later in relation to exemption clauses, once the customer signs such a document it makes no difference whether he has read and understood the terms or not, for he is bound by his signature and the conditions are regarded as having been communicated. But the document must be a contractual document—a mere receipt does not classify as a contractual document. Thus where Mr Thornton took a ticket from the machine at the car park entrance, drove in, parked his car and later suffered an accident in the car park, the conditions stated on the ticket were not binding on him. The decision in *Thornton v Shoe Lane Parking Ltd* (1971) was that the ticket was only a receipt and there had been insufficient notice of limitation of liability given to Thornton.

But what of the retailer who misrepresents to the customer the terms of the contract contained in the written document? The answer is found in *Curtis v Chemical Cleaning and Dyeing Co* (1951). C took a dress to the company for cleaning and was asked to sign a document which stated that the company was not liable for any damage to the article. She did not read this, having been told that the document simply excluded liability for damage to beads and sequins. The dress was stained through the negligence of the company. The court held the company was liable as the misrepresentation of the assistant, though

31

innocent, had excluded the effect of the clause.

It is possible that the retailer has promised to keep the offer open to a particular customer for some days; he is not legally bound to keep to this promise unless he has been paid to do so. He should, nevertheless, tell the customer of his intention to withdraw the offer, for if the offer is accepted before notice of the withdrawal is received there will be a binding contract.

As with the offer, so the acceptance may be made by words or implied from the conduct of the parties. The mere intention to accept an offer will not be enough to found a contract. In *Felthouse v Bindley* (1862) B, an auctioneer, was instructed to sell J's horses. J's uncle, F, wrote to J about a particular horse, offering £30.15s for the animal and stating: "If I hear no more about him, I consider the horse mine." J made no reply but told B not to sell the animal; by mistake it was in fact sold. F sued B in conversion. It was held that J's silence could not amount to an acceptance so F could not succeed. The rule is that silence does not amount to consent. Nor can an acceptance be made by accident: if a customer orders a grand piano, making the offer to buy by a letter which crosses in the post a letter from the seller offering to sell the same piano for the same price, there will be no contract. There have been two offers, but there has been no acceptance.

Where the negotiations are made through the post the situation is slightly complicated by the time lag between the posting of a letter and the receipt of the letter. An offer can be accepted at any time before that offer is withdrawn. Once it is withdrawn any attempted "acceptance" is ineffective. But imagine the following situation: the customer offers to buy a garden roller by a letter received by the seller on the 5th March; the seller posts a letter of acceptance on the 7th March only to find that the customer has posted a letter of withdrawal of the offer on the 6th March, a letter which is not received by the seller until the 8th March. Who is going to suffer in this situation? The seller, because the letter of withdrawal was posted before the acceptance was posted? The customer, because the acceptance was posted before the withdrawal was received? *Byrne v Van Tienhoven* (1880) is a case in point. VT wrote from Cardiff to B in New York offering tinplate at a fixed price. The day the offer was received B telegraphed an acceptance, but three days earlier VT had sent a letter of withdrawal which did not arrive until B had confirmed his acceptance by post. B sued for breach of contract, when VT denied the existence of the contract. It was held that B should succeed since there was a binding contract from the time that the offer was accepted, and the withdrawal was ineffective since it had arrived after acceptance was made. In fact, in such matters as the use of the post, the courts apply the following

32

rules:

An offer becomes effective when it is received.

An acceptance becomes effective when it is *posted*.

A withdrawal of an offer becomes effective when it is received by the other party.

Thus, the effect of the application of these rules is that if the revocation (withdrawal) is never received it can never become effective—to be effective it must be received before acceptance is made. The receipt of an acceptance on the other hand is never necessary—proof of its posting is all that is necessary.

These rules might well be regarded as being rather arbitrary, but it must be remembered that whatever solution is used, someone must be hurt. Other countries use other systems but the difficulties cannot be surmounted and in England the position is as outlined above.

As far as the topic of offer and acceptance is concerned, it remains only to point out that the acceptance must be made in a definite manner with no terms added: the addition of new terms to the "acceptance" make the reply nothing more than a counter offer. The customer who offers to pay £20 for a new jacket does not have his offer accepted when the tailor says: "I agree to make you a jacket but the price will be £25 not £20." All that has happened is that the seller has made a counter offer, which is then open for the customer to accept or reject. In *Hyde v Wrench* (1840) W offered his farm to H for £1,000. H made a counter offer of £950 but when this was refused he agreed to pay £1,000. W refused to sell to him and H sued for specific performance of the agreement. The court decided H could not succeed since the counter offer had destroyed the original offer. If the statement added to the "acceptance" is merely a request for information and not a variation of the terms—such as, for instance, "I agree to make the jacket, but will you pay in advance?" it will not be a counter offer but a perfectly good acceptance of the original offer.

Finally, where the words "subject to contract" or like phrases are added to the acceptance the agreement does not become legally binding until such a contract has been prepared. No obligation arises until the document containing the terms of the agreement has been completed.

THE GENUINE AGREEMENT

The words "subject to contract" imply that final agreement has not been reached; in fact if any part of the contract is left for future negotiation between the parties the agreement will not be binding. Any vagueness or indefinite wording will give rise to this result, so phrases

33

such as "on the usual terms" or "to be supplied as and when required" should be avoided. In *Scammell v Ouston* (1941) O agreed to buy a motor van from S, the balance of the purchase price to be payable "on hire purchase terms". The court held the contract was not in being since it was too vague; hire-purchase agreements varied greatly and no precise meaning could be attached to this phrase. There were no trade customs or previous dealings between the parties to which the court could refer and so the agreement was not enforceable. The court will admit such agreements and enforce them if it can discover what the "usual terms" are from previous dealings between the parties, or from the customs of that particular trade, but where neither of these can be referred to the agreement will be void for incompletion. The agreement *was* held binding in *F. & G. Sykes (Wessex) Ltd v Fine Fare Ltd* (1966). S agreed to supply F with broiler chickens for five years. The contract specified 30–80,000 chickens per week during the first year but mentioned no figures thereafter. On the other hand it stated that differences between the parties could be referred to an arbitrator. This in fact made the contract binding because the number of chickens could be ascertained by arbitration.

Nevertheless, the advice for retailer, wholesaler, or any person entering a contract is obvious enough: make sure that the terms of the agreement are set out in a definite and straightforward manner.

Exemption clauses

Some reference has already been made to the use of exemption clauses in contracts. The courts do not favour such clauses but they commonly appear in written agreements in the distributive trades and if the parties have agreed to the contractual terms they will normally be binding (but see page 69).

The use of exemption or exclusion clauses in contracts has drawn the attention of Parliament, and by the Unfair Contract Terms Act 1977 no one acting in the course of a business can exclude his liability in contract or tort for death or bodily injury arising from negligence. This is so whether he attempts to do so by a term in the contract or by giving or displaying a notice. He *can* exclude liability for other loss arising from his negligence—but then only if he can show that the exemption was reasonable in the circumstances.

By section 3 of the Act where a business makes a contract on its own written terms of a standard kind it cannot exclude or vary liability for breach of contract unless it can show the exemption to be reasonable. These provisions, as well as the ones noted above, apply to all contracts except those relating to land, patents, shares, contracts

34

affecting the formation or the internal management of companies, and insurance.

The Act also deals with exclusion clauses in contracts for the sale of goods, but further discussion of these provisions may be left until the general contractual rules relating to the sale of goods are dealt with in Chapter 5. But what of the situation where the exemption clause relied upon by the retailer is a valid one? The rule is that if it is communicated to the customer it is binding on him.

This does not mean that the retailer relying on an exemption clause has to prove that the customer actually *read* the exemption clause. It is enough to show reasonable steps were taken to communicate the terms to him. But even if such steps have been taken the clause can be overruled by an *oral* agreement. This is what happened in a 1970 case between *Mendelsohn* and *Normand Ltd.* When he left his car at N's garage M was told not to lock his car, but the attendant promised to lock it after he had moved it. The attendant then gave a ticket to M; it excluded the company from responsibility for loss of the contents of the car. When a suitcase was stolen from the vehicle it was held that the oral promise, given by someone with ostensible authority to give it, overrode the exemption clause in the contract.

Of recent years it has been emphasised that an exemption clause cannot be used to escape liability if the dealer has committed a "fundamental" breach of contract—for instance, if a car dealer sells a car for use on the road and it turns out to be unroadworthy he has committed a fundamental breach. But even in such cases, *if the language of the clause is clear and definite enough* it can apply in spite of a fundamental breach. As one judge put it: "it cannot be said . . . that the resources of the English language are so limited that it is impossible to devise an exclusion clause which will apply to at least some cases of fundamental breach."

Nevertheless, the general principle is that seen in *Farnworth Finance Facilities Ltd v Attryde* (1970) where the buyer obtained a new motor cycle from a hire purchase company. The contract stated the cycle was supplied "subject to no conditions whatsoever express or implied" and that it was not subject "to any condition that the same is fit for any particular purpose". The cycle was in fact unroadworthy. This was held to amount to a fundamental breach, the buyer could repudiate the contract and the finance company could not rely on the exemption clauses. (This case arose before the 1973 Act—see page 69).

Apart from the question of vagueness and exemption clauses there are other grounds on which a contract can be rendered invalid, or worthless—where in fact there is no genuine agreement.

Mistake

Not all types of mistake will invalidate a contract. The customer who buys a tin of coffee from a shopkeeper cannot claim the return of her money simply because she thought that the tin contained tea—assuming, of course, that the seller was innocent of any misrepresentation and did not know that the buyer was mistaken. A mistake *will* operate to avoid the contract where it is a mistake as to the identity or existence of the subject matter of the contract. A lady sees two basket chairs in a shop window, marked £30 and £20 respectively. She offers to buy the "chair in the window" meaning the £20 chair. The assistant agrees to sell it to her, meaning by "it" the chair marked £30. If both parties are mistaken as to the other's intentions they are mistaken as to the identity of the chair being sold: there is no contract because they are talking about different things. In *Couturier v Hastie* (1852) C shipped Indian corn from Salonica and H, the agent, negotiated a sale on their behalf in London. Before the voyage was over the corn had heated and fermented and was sold elsewhere. The buyer repudiated the contract and C attempted to recover the price of the cargo from H. The court held the contract was based on the existence of the corn, but as it had been sold at the time the contract was made the corn was not capable of transfer and so the agreement was avoided. Similarly, if the chair the lady desires to buy has already been sold to someone else it cannot be sold to her by the assistant because that particular chair no longer exists as the subject matter of a contract between the two parties. This is what happened in *Raffles v Wichelhaus* (1864) when W agreed to buy cotton "to arrive ex Peerless from Bombay ..." from R but W meant the *Peerless* sailing in October while R meant another and different ship also called the *Peerless* sailing in December. It was decided that there was no binding contract between the parties because they were talking about different ships.

A second type of mistake which invalidates a contract arises where there is a mistake as to the identity of the other party to the contract. The jeweller who thinks that he is dealing with Lord Blank of Blankshire may succeed in avoiding liability on the contract if he can show that he was in fact dealing with Sam Shiftless, late of Dartmoor, Devon, a rogue who trades upon his likeness to his lordship. But the jeweller will have to show that his mistake as to his customer's identity was material and important to the formation of the contract.

If the jeweller is selling valuable rings and refuses to accept a cheque until proof of identity is offered, then he has made the identity of the person in his shop material and he can avoid the contract. But if he deals with the person in the shop without caring whom he is dealing with, the mistake will not operate to avoid the contract.

The question is of some importance, for in cases such as these the one party is usually fraudulent; he intends getting the goods on credit, or by passing a bad cheque, in order to sell the goods to someone else and make a pleasant profit. Where this occurs, the true owner of the goods can get them back from the innocent party who has paid the rogue good money for them, but only if the owner can show an operative mistake as to the identity of the rogue in the first place. For in this circumstance, the jeweller did not intend passing the goods to Sam Shiftless, but to Lord Blank. This means that Sam cannot get ownership of the goods, and so cannot pass good title (ownership) to the innocent third party. Thus, the owner can get them back.

Everyone will agree that this is a little hard on the only completely innocent person in the transaction (for at the very least the owner has been guilty of negligence in not ascertaining the true identity of the rogue). In *Cundy v Lindsay* (1878) for instance, Blenkarn wrote to L ordering some goods, using the address similar to Blenkiron & Co. and signing in such a way that the letter seemed to be from that company. L knew of the company's reputation and sent the goods as directed. Blenkarn did not pay for the goods but sold them to C. L sued C for conversion of the goods. The court decided there had been no intention to deal with Blenkarn so there was no contract with him. C was liable, therefore, to L. If the mistake as to identity is not fundamental and material to the contract, ownership *can* be passed to the third party by Sam Shiftless and the defrauded seller cannot get the goods back. The true test as to whether the mistake is operative or not is to decide whether the seller intended to deal with a *particular* person or not. If he did, there is no contract between him and the rogue. If he did not, then the question of identity is immaterial, and there is no way of getting the goods back from the third party. There is always the rogue to be sued, by either party, of course. The difficulty is that he has probably disappeared!

"This is another case where one of two innocent persons has to suffer for the fraud of a third," the judge said in *Lewis v Averay* (1971). This case underlines the difficulty in "face to face" situations and makes it appear that to establish an operative mistake in such circumstances will not be easy. Lewis advertised his car for sale; the rogue said he was Richard Greene (of "Robin Hood" fame) and offered to pay by cheque. As proof of identity he produced a special admission pass for Pinewood Studios with his photograph and name on it. Lewis handed over car, log book and test certificate and accepted the cheque. It bounced. Meanwhile, the rogue had sold the car to Averay. Had there been a contract between Lewis and the rogue, so that title would pass to Averay? The Court of Appeal said there had.

Two of the judges involved emphasised that in face to face contracts there must be a presumption that the contract does exist, though a contract voidable for fraud. The test in all cases is a factual one. The question to be asked is:

"To whom was the offer made?"

If the answer is "To the person standing there, whoever he might be," then there will be a valid contract when the offer is accepted.

If the answer is "To the person whom the rogue makes himself out to be," then the offer is not made to the rogue standing there, and so cannot be accepted by him so as to form a valid contract.

The frequency with which such cases arise only serves to illustrate how thorny a problem the one of identification really can be.

A third type of mistake which operates to avoid a contract is where the mistake is as to the nature of the document signed. The housewife who guarantees payment of the young salesman's bank overdraft by signing the document put before her will not be liable if she can show:

(a) there was a radical difference between what she signed and what she thought she was signing;
(b) she had not been careless in making the mistake; and
(c) she would not have signed the document if she had known its true nature.

The defence she would raise to the salesman's claim in such circumstances would be *non est factum*; it was "not her deed" because consent to the document was totally lacking.

The principles here stated were laid down in *Saunders v Anglia Building Society* (1970). G owned a house. L placed a document in front of him for signing, telling G that the document was a deed of gift to P, G's nephew. In fact this was untrue; the document was a transfer on sale from G to L, for £3,000. G relied upon *non est factum* and asked for a declaration from the court that the transfer was void.

The House of Lords held in this case that the transfer was not void for G could not show that by her conduct she had satisfied the conditions laid down. In the first instance the document she had signed was not *radically* different from that which she had thought she was signing. Secondly, there was no doubt that her mistake had been due to her own carelessness. Thirdly, she had failed to show to the satisfaction of the court that she would not have signed the document had she been aware of its true nature.

All this merely emphasises that when a party signs a contractual document a contract will normally be formed on the terms of that document even if the person signing it has not read it. It is possible that the contract can be set aside on the grounds of fraud or misrepresentation but if the person signing simply says later that he was mistaken as to the nature of the document his *non est factum* plea is subject to strict limitations.

One judge has put it this way: "a person who signs a document, and parts with it so that it may come into other hands, has a responsibility, that of the normal man of prudence, to take care what he signs, which, if neglected, prevents him from denying his liability under the document according to its tenor."

So the answer is clear—read the document, don't sign until you understand what it's all about. You *may* be able to get out of it if you can show you were mistaken as to what it was all about, but you won't if you were careless in signing in the first place!

Misrepresentation

A statement can amount to misrepresentation even though the maker of the statement does not know of its falsity: it is enough if he has been careless in making that statement, or has made it without bothering to discover whether it be false or true. The misrepresentation need not be a statement in words; conduct will suffice. If the person in the shop is dressed like a bishop with the intent to defraud the shopkeeper into giving him credit, then this will amount to a misrepresentation in the same way as a verbal statement that he is the Vicar of Dymchurch would do.

To amount to misrepresentation the statement must be a statement of fact, as opposed to one of law, or intention, or opinion (though a statement of opinion will be treated as one of fact in those circumstances where no reasonable person would possibly have held such an opinion). In *Smith v Land and House Corporation* (1884) the Corporation advertised their property, stating that it was at the present held by one "Fred Fleck" who was described as "a very desirable tenant". S agreed to buy the property but discovered that Fred Fleck had not paid his rent for some time and was about to file his petition for liquidation. Specific performance of the contract was refused and the contract rescinded, since the description of Fred Fleck was not an expression of opinion but a misrepresentation.

The misrepresentation must actually mislead the innocent party: this means that he must know of the statement and must have thought it true. If he does not act on the statement, or relies upon his own judgment, he cannot claim on the grounds of misrepresentation.

It has been said that mere silence cannot amount to misrepresentation and as a general rule this holds good. The seller of a car need not disclose to the buyer the fact that the car is burning as much oil as petrol; the seller of a packet of crisps need not disclose that the crisps have lost their crispness. The law says "Caveat Emptor" which, roughly translated, means that the buyer should look out for himself (though the Sale of Goods Act 1893 has something to say on this).

Nevertheless, there are exceptions to the general rule that silence does not amount to misrepresentation. The first arises where the seller makes a statement which though true initially becomes untrue later. If, when the contract is made, he does not inform the buyer of the change in circumstances his silence will be conduct amounting to misrepresentation. Similarly, the general rule does not apply to contracts of "utmost good faith" (*uberrimae fidei*) where all facts material to the formation of the contract must be disclosed. Examples of contracts *uberrimae fidei* are contracts of insurance, contracts for the allotment of shares in a company, and contracts preliminary to family settlements.

Misrepresentation may be innocent, or fraudulent, but the Misrepresentation Act 1967 also states that innocent misrepresentation is either negligent or non-negligent.

If the misrepresentaion is made honestly and without negligence the other party can terminate the contract, or refuse to perform it or, if he wishes the contract to continue, he can affirm it. If the misrepresentation is made innocently, but with negligence the other party can claim damages and the judge or arbitrator can also declare the contract good and award damages instead of rescinding (or terminating) it.

If the misrepresentation is made fraudulently the other party can claim damages and/or rescind the contract, refuse to carry it out, or if he wishes, affirm the contract.

It should be added that if the misled person wants to avoid the contract he must do so promptly but it is necessary to go to court—all he needs to do is give notice to the other party. But what if the other party, being a fraud, has disappeared? This is what happened in *Car and Universal Finance Co Ltd v Caldwell* (1965). The rogue, called Norris, bought a car by fraud and when his cheque "bounced" he disappeared. The car owner informed the police and the Automobile Association and asked them to trace the car. The court held that he had done all that was reasonably to be expected of him in the circumstances and by his actions he had successfully avoided the contract. As he had done this before the rogue purported to resell the car, the original owner's title to it prevailed.

The Misrepresentation Act 1967 also deals with exclusion clauses

—that is, clauses which exclude or restrict either

    (a) liability incurred by a party who makes a misrepresentation before the contract was made, or

    (b) the right of the party affected by such misrepresentation to avail himself of any remedy open to him.

Section 3 of the Act states that any such clause shall be of no effect unless, in the proceedings arising out of the contract, the court or arbitrator allows it to be relied upon as being fair and reasonable in the circumstances.

Duress and Undue Influence

Another ground for avoiding a contract is Duress. A case was reported in 1957. A woman was alone in her flat when there was a knock at the door. She opened the door; the defendants entered the flat and refused to leave. They forced her to sign a receipt for a jewel case and its contents which they then took away. When they had gone she found they had left a cheque for £90. The court agreed that there was no valid contract for the sale of the jewel case and its contents in spite of the signed receipt. The "sale" had been obtained by duress.

There are few instances, other than this reported case, in modern times. Violence may be used to steal, or force one's opinions upon others, but only rarely is it used to make a person enter a contract. The common law doctrine of Duress applies only in circumstances such as those above where a person is forced to enter a contract under actual or threatened violence or imprisonment towards the contracting party or his near relative. Similarly, a contract can be avoided where Undue Influence has been exercised. The law recognises that undue influence may be exerted upon those people in a special relationship: the parent upon the child, the guardian upon the ward, the solicitor upon the client, the trustee upon the beneficiary. Where such a relationship occurs and undue influence is pleaded by the child, etc., the court presumes that undue influence has been used and it is up to the parent, etc., to show that no such influence was in fact exercised.

CONSIDERATION

The doctrine of consideration applies to all contracts other than those made under seal (see p. 48). The law refuses to enforce "mere agreements" unless they are supported by consideration.

What is consideration? It can be defined as the promise given for a promise; or it can be defined as the promise given for the act of

41

another party. It is possible to describe it in the language of purchase and sale. The customer who pays for goods to be delivered to his house can sue if they are not delivered—for he has furnished consideration, in this case the payment. The shopkeeper who promises to deliver goods on Wednesday can sue if the goods are refused at the door—for he has provided consideration, in this case the delivery of the goods. In the first instance the payment of money has "bought" the promise to deliver goods; in the second instance the delivery has "bought" the promise to accept and pay for the goods.

If the agreement lacks consideration it cannot be enforced (unless it is under seal). Thus, a person cannot sue on a contract unless he has provided consideration, and it must be he himself who must provide the consideration. Consideration supplied by another is useless—it must come from the person who sues.

The consideration need not be "adequate"—the wholesaler who has agreed to supply goods worth £500 to a retailer in consideration of an immediate payment of £100 cannot say that the contract is bad for lack of consideration, for although the sum is "inadequate" in relation to the value of the goods it is nevertheless the sum agreed to by the parties and so it is valuable consideration. Gross inadequacy may of course be evidence of fraud.

To amount to consideration the act or promise must involve some sacrifice. If it is a promise to do something that he is already bound to do anyway the promise may not be valuable consideration. If the lady owes the butcher £100 and the butcher agrees to accept £90 in full satisfaction of the debts he can still claim the other £10. If she points to his acceptance of £90 as a defence to his claim he can argue that there was no contract between them that the law will recognise. His promise not to sue for the outstanding £10 was bought with the payment of £90. But since the lady was already under an obligation to pay that money to him she has provided no consideration at all.

A word of warning should be sounded here, however. Even though the creditor has accepted a smaller sum in such circumstances, he can still sue for the larger amount if his acceptance was obtained in an inequitable or unfair way. *D. and C. Builders* had a claim for £482 against Mrs Rees. Mrs Rees knew the builders were in financial difficulties, so she offered them £300 in full settlement, saying if they wouldn't accept that they'd get nothing. Under such pressure the builders accepted. In the court case that resulted in 1966 the builders were held entitled to the outstanding £182, since they had in effect been "held to ransom" by Mrs Rees.

But we were speaking earlier of the lady and the butcher, to whom she owed £100. Were she to pay the £90 in a different way (by cheque, where the butcher was entitled to cash) or at a different time (in January where the debt was not due until March) or at a different place (in York where the payment is due in Plymouth) then if this is done at the request of the butcher she *has* provided consideration: she has done more than was strictly necessary and that "more" involves a sacrifice on her part which will be accepted as valuable consideration. It is important to note that the consideration must not be past. The second-hand dealer who sells a table to a buyer cannot be sued on a promise, given after the sale is complete, that the table is free from woodworm. There is no consideration for this promise. The paying of money for the table cannot be the consideration, for it is in the past, it is part of an earlier, completed transaction, it bought the table, not the promise! The only exception to this rule, if it is really an exception at all, is in the case of the negotiable instrument: a cheque is treated as having been given for valuable consideration even though that consideration has been given in the past.

ILLEGAL CONTRACTS

If the contract is made for an illegal purpose it will be void. Thus, an agreement to buy gramophone records that are banned in this country could not be sued upon since the courts would regard the contract as void for illegality.

A contract will be void not only where its purpose is illegal: if any part of the contract is tainted with illegality the taint will affect the rest of the contract and render it void. Thus, an agreement to provide a customer with a screwdriver would be illegal if the seller knew that the screwdriver was to be used to force the lock on a door for purposes of burglary. The purpose of the contract itself—the sale of a screwdriver—is not illegal; the sale is tainted, nevertheless, with the illegality of the use to which the screwdriver is to be put. Were the seller to be ignorant of the intentions of the buyer the position would be different, of course.

Some contracts are declared illegal by statute, others are declared illegal by the courts on the ground of public policy. Such contracts include contracts against religion, in absolute restraint of marriage, impeding the course of justice, trading with the enemy (here, residence in an enemy country makes the trader classify as an enemy), contracts tending to encourage bribery and corruption or to injure the safety of the country, and contracts in restraint of trade. This last type of contract will be of some importance to the retailer and merits some discussion.

43

Any contract which is made for an illegal or immoral purpose will be declared void by the courts. The Common Law declared that all contracts in restraint of trade were illegal also, but the modern attitude is not quite so sweeping as this and the courts regard some contracts in restraint of trade as enforceable. But the basic attitude remains the same: on the face of it, the contract is to be regarded as void. Only in certain circumstances will it be regarded as binding.

Agreements in restraint of trade are generally of three kinds: those where the employee agrees not to set up in competition with his employer within a certain area or a certain time; those where the seller of a business agrees not to open another business in competition with the person to whom he has sold out; those where a manufacturer places restrictions upon the sale of goods supplied by him.

Such agreements are *prima facie* (on the face of it) void but in fact the courts tend to regard the agreement as binding if it is reasonable both for the parties concerned and also in the interests of the public generally, provided that the restriction imposed is not too wide in nature and effect. If the agreement does not conform to these stipulations it will be void.

In the case of the employer/employee relationship the law accepts the fact that the employer might have trade secrets that the employee might become familiar with. The employee might impart these secrets to others for whom he works in the future. Similarly, the employee who obtains trade information about markets or becomes personally known to customers might well seriously affect his employer's business if he leaves and works for a rival firm in the area. Because of this, the courts will uphold a contract restraining the employee, but only if the restraint is reasonable—and what is reasonable is a matter of fact for the court to decide in the light of all the circumstances. A grocer's junior assistant is no more likely to obtain very much in the way of trade secrets than the boy on a newspaper round: neither of these is likely to damage his employer's business if he leaves to work for another. Restraints on such individuals would be unreasonable, whereas they might well be reasonable when applied to the managing director of a firm. This was pointed out in *Pearks Ltd v Cullen* (1912) where C was employed by P as a grocer's assistant and agreed not to work in a similar business within two miles of any shop belonging to the company at which he had been employed within the previous twelve months. He went to work for a nearby rival. P sued to enforce the agreement. It was held P must fail since the restrictive covenant was not necessary to protect their business, though it might have been otherwise had C been their manager and had access to trade secrets.

In all such cases the courts, while recognising that the employer might well have an interest to protect, yet lean heavily in the favour of the employee. Where the relationship between the parties is not of employer and employee but of vendor and purchaser of a business the situation is different. Much wider restrictions have been upheld in such cases—even world-wide restrictions against competition. This is justified by the fact that the vendor has been paid not only to transfer the assets of his business to the purchaser but also to refrain from future competition. In other words the payment takes into account the promise—but again, the question of reasonableness is important.

By way of contrast we might look at cases reported in 1970 and 1894—the one involving a "master–servant" relationship, the other a vendor–purchaser relationship.

In the 1970 case the employee had worked for five years as a milk roundsman. In his contract he agreed that for one year after leaving the job he would not sell milk or dairy produce to, or take orders from, people who had been customers of his employer during the last six months and who had been served by him. When he changed his job he went to work for a rival dairyman, serving on the same round. At the first hearing the court regarded the limitation as being too wide because it went further than was necessary to protect the employer's goodwill (it could have prevented the employee from working in a grocer's shop where he might be selling cheese or butter) but the Court of Appeal held that as the employer carried on only a dairy business the clauses, read in context, were clearly meant to restrict the employee's activities only when working as a milk roundsman.

The periods of restraint mentioned in the contract, namely twelve months and six months, were regarded as reasonable and so an injunction was granted, preventing the employee from continuing his job.

It is noteworthy here that the courts were concerned to look closely at the scope of the restraints—in time, in the matter of the customers, in the question of damage to the employer's goodwill. Where the case is one of vendor-purchaser of a business the same matters will be looked at but the whole scope of the enquiry broadens and the limitations that may be regarded as reasonable are likely to be much wider than those acceptable in employer–employee examples such as *Home Counties Dairies Ltd v Skilton*, above.

In the case reported in 1894 N sold his business to the company and promised that he would not engage in the manufacture of guns, explosives and ammunition, etc., or in any competing business for 25 years. He was made a managing director of the company with a salary of £2,000 p.a. with commission on net profits. When he entered into an agreement with competing firms, the company sought to enforce his promise of non-competition. It was held that the company could succeed. The covenant taken was not injurious to the public interest nor was it wider than necessary in view of the nature of the business and the limited number of customers, who were, mainly, Governments.

If a wholesale company were, for instance, to impose restrictions upon its employees, and some of these were valid, others void, a court will sometimes order the valid clauses to be severed from the void ones; the former will then be enforceable, the latter not. This will be done only where the severance will not affect the contract as a whole.

The third type of trade restriction, that practised by the manufacturer who places conditions of resale of his goods in the agreement whereby he sells the goods to the retailer, is covered by the Resale Prices Act 1976. The Act makes it unlawful for any supplier of goods to:

(1) include in an agreement for sale of goods a provision for minimum prices on resale in the United Kingdom, or

(2) require the inclusion of such a provision, or

(3) publish or notify to dealers minimum resale prices.

This does not mean they can't *recommend* resale prices for their goods. Agreements caught by the Act are void.

What if a supplier withholds supplies from a dealer, saying he has in the past sold at less than a certain resale price, or will do so in future? The Act in fact makes his action in holding back unlawful. An exception arises if during the last twelve months the dealer has been selling the same or similar goods as loss leaders—that is, to attract custom for other goods rather than to make a profit. In such a case the supplier *can* legally withhold the goods. But, on the other hand, what if the dealer had disposed of the goods in a genuine seasonal or clearance sale? In that case we are back to the general prohibition: the supplier must not withhold the supplies.

The Act also makes provision for some kinds of goods to be exempted by order of the Restrictive Practices Court from the general provisions against resale price maintenance—where for instance it would lead to a reduction in the quality or variety of the goods, or the number of shops would be cut down. Few exemptions have been made.

The Treaty of Rome

Since we have been discussing restraint of trade above it might be

46

convenient to point out here that by the terms of the Treaty of Rome certain rules are laid down concerning the free movement of workers and competition in trade.

The rules concerning competition prohibit all agreements, actions or arrangements which affect, or attempt to affect, the restrictions of free competition, either by preventing the lowering of prices or by promoting artificial price increases. It is a good answer to the charge to show that the consumer in fact is given a fair share of the benefits arising from the restrictive practice.

An example can be seen in the sole-distribution agreement. If the real purpose of the agreement is to allow the manufacturers or the distributor to extract from the public an inflated price it is barred. But if they do not prohibit exports to other countries in the Community and there is a substantial volume of competing goods available for other distributors to handle, the agreement is acceptable.

Effect of Illegality

The effect of illegality on a contract generally is that the contract is void and neither party can sue on the agreement. To this rule there are two exceptions. Where one party is innocent of any knowledge of the illegality, and was induced to enter the contract by the other, he can claim any money that he has paid over under the contract on the ground that he is not *"in pari delicto"* (equally to blame). The second exception arises where one party repents of the purpose of the illegal contract before such purpose is carried out; he also can recover money paid, but only if the purpose is still capable of performance. If it is now impossible to carry out the contract he has repented too late and cannot recover.

There are two Acts which may also be noted here, in passing, though they will be dealt with again later. The Race Relations Act 1976 makes it unlawful to discriminate against a person on grounds of colour, race or ethnic or national origins, in specified situations. The criminal law is also brought into action under the Trade Descriptions Act 1968.

FORMALITIES OF A CONTRACT

Some agreements are covered by particular Acts of Parliament and have to comply with rules laid down by them. An example is an agreement to dispose of certain consumer durable goods on credit with payment by instalments. Such an agreement must comply with any Hire-Purchase and Credit Sale Agreements (Control) Order in force. But

47

apart from such exceptions, generally, a contract may be made in any form, verbal or written, or it may be implied from conduct. The distinction usually drawn is between specialty contracts and simple contracts. A specialty contract is a contract made by deed, which is a written document "signed, sealed and delivered". A simple contract is a contract made in any other form—in writing, by word of mouth, or implied from conduct.

No consideration is necessary for a specialty contract, but a simple contract fails unless it is supported by consideration. Actions on simple contracts are barred after six years have gone by since breach, but in the case of the specialty contract the period is twelve years. If a deed covers the same ground as an earlier simple contract the simple contract is extinguished. Deeds are normally used where formality in the making of the contract is essential, such as in the sale or lease of property.

Some contracts have to be made in writing, though they need not necessarily be made by deed. Examples are contracts of marine insurance, contracts made under the Hire Purchase Act 1965, and contracts for the transfer of shares in a limited company.

In certain other contracts the writing must be in a specific form—it must conform to the requirements of section 40 of the Law of Property Act 1925. This states that the writing must contain the names and description of the parties, the essential terms of the contract, and must be signed by or on behalf of the person against whom it is to be used as evidence. Any writing conforming to these requirements can be used as a "note of memorandum" to support such a contract. Such written evidence is needed in two types of contract: the contract for the sale or other disposition of land or an interest in land, and the contract of guarantee (where the requirement is laid down by the Statute of Frauds 1677).

A guarantee should be distinguished from an indemnity, for the indemnity is not covered by the provisions as to written evidence and can therefore be sued on even though it is not supported by written evidence. A guarantor promises to pay if the debtor does not; an indemnity arises where the promise is to pay in any event. So the customer who says, "Let him have the goods and I will see you paid", or "I will see to the bill", can be sued on this verbal promise. He has given an indemnity and this does not need to be supported by a "note or memorandum in writing". But the customer who says, "Let him take the goods, and I'll pay if he does not", or "I'll guarantee payment if he fails to pay" cannot be sued by the shopkeeper unless this promise has been made in writing. Sometimes, the dividing line between a guarantee or indemnity is hard to draw, but basically it

48

depends upon this simple fact: is primary liability placed upon the person who promises to pay or is his liability only secondary? If his liability is only secondary—that is, he must pay only if the debtor fails to pay—it is a guarantee and must be supported by written evidence. If the liability to pay is primary it is an indemnity and a verbal promise is good enough.

In some circumstances, such as in the lease of land, even though the written evidence is not forthcoming Equity will assist the plaintiff by applying the doctrine of Part Performance. The court will order the defendant to keep to his promise where the plaintiff has partly performed his side of the bargain, and the person relying on the lack of written evidence is acting fraudulently.

DISCHARGE OF CONTRACT

Once the contractual relationship has been formulated the parties to the contract are under mutual obligations, the obligations placed upon them by the terms of the contract. These obligations do not last for ever, of course, and they can in fact be discharged by agreement between the parties, or by the performance of the contract. The obligations may also be discharged where one party has broken the contract terms, or where the contract has become impossible to perform.

DISCHARGE BY AGREEMENT

This needs little discussion. The parties agree to be bound by the contract no longer. The old contract may be substituted by a new one or there may be a term in the old contract which automatically brings the contract to an end on the occurrence of some event. If one party has performed his side of the obligation, however, the other must give consideration to him in order to obtain a full discharge from *his* obligations. This is known as the doctrine of accord (agreement) and satisfaction.

DISCHARGE BY PERFORMANCE

This merits fuller treatment. It is necessary first of all to emphasise that performance must be exact to discharge the party performing from his obligations under the contract. If the trader agrees to supply five hundred tins of peaches packed in boxes of ten he has not performed his obligation when he delivers five hundred tins packed in boxes of twenty. The buyer will be justified in refusing to accept them

49

and the trader cannot claim that he has done what he promised. His performance has not been exact. This is what happened in a 1921 case where A agreed to buy from B 3,000 tins of Australian canned fruit packed in cases containing 30 tins each. The right number of tins was delivered but some of the cases contained only 24 tins. It was held that the buyer was entitled to reject the whole consignment since the goods did not correspond with their description.

In some circumstances the performance will be so substantial that it will suffice: a tradesman who agrees to supply five sliced loaves and delivers four sliced loaves together with one he has sliced himself with a carving knife, and not too well at that, could probably claim that his performance of the contract was close enough to be sufficient. But "substantial performance" as a principle is indefinable: it all depends upon the construction made by the court in the particular circumstances.

If the goods are tendered according to the contract and the buyer refuses to accept them, the party tendering the goods is discharged from his obligations. The tender must, however, be made at a reasonable time and place, and if it involves the tender of money in repayment of a debt the tender alone does not amount to a good discharge. In *Startup v MacDonald* (1843) S agreed to supply linseed oil to M "within the last fourteen days of March". The oil was delivered on March 31st at 8.30 p.m. M refused to accept the goods because of the lateness of the hour. The tender was held to be reasonable and S was entitled to damages for M's refusal to accept the oil. But in cases where the tender does *not* amount to a good discharge the money must then be paid into court and if the creditor who has refused to take the money (probably on the grounds that he is owed a larger sum) does not succeed in showing the court that the tender was insufficient he will have to pay the costs of the court action. Where money is tendered it is the exact amount, without a request for change, that must be tendered, otherwise the tender can be refused. Equally, offering a cheque or some other negotiable instrument is not good enough—unless the creditor is prepared to accept the cheque, of course, and is objecting only to the amount of money stated on the cheque.

If there is a time stipulation in the contract it can be of importance in relation to the discharge of the contract. The lady who insists that the dress she has ordered must be delivered by Wednesday at the latest is justified in refusing to accept it on Thursday. She has made the time element material to the contract. If she telephones the shop on Thursday morning, asking if it has arrived, or telling them to send it to her as soon as it does arrive, she has then waived her insistence as to the time element and she cannot refuse it as having been delivered too late. It is still open to her thereafter to reintroduce a time limit—where she might say, "If it's not delivered by Saturday I don't want it at all!" Then, she has made the time element material again and tender after Saturday could be rejected. An example arose in 1950. O ordered a Rolls-Royce chassis from R. It was not delivered at the time specified in the contract so O waived the time condition. Some months later, when the work was not completed, O said that if the car chassis was not ready within four weeks he would refuse to accept it. The chassis was not delivered within the four weeks. The judge said O could refuse delivery later since he had made time of the essence of the contract after his initial waiver and four weeks' notice was reasonable.

If time is not made material, then the the goods must be tendered within a reasonable time: the court will decide whether the time is reasonable or not. We have seen that actions on contracts are barred after six years (or twelve, if the contract is a specialty contract). This means that failure to deliver, or to accept delivery, gives rise to a right to sue the party in default. The action must be brought within the six- (or twelve-) year period running after that date, except that if the plaintiff is under a disability such as infancy or being a mental patient the limitation period will not begin to run until the disability ceases. Once it starts to run, it cannot stop for subsequent disability. Again, where the cause of action is concealed by fraud or mistake the period will run only from the time that the cause of action could or should have been discovered.

DISCHARGE BY BREACH

If one party breaks his obligation under the contract the other can sue him for damages but, if the breach is sufficiently serious, where for instance the commercial purpose of the contract has been frustrated by the breach, he can not only sue for damages but he can also repudiate his own obligations under the contract. To claim discharge the innocent party must show that the other has committed a total breach of contract affecting a vital part of the contract; a partial breach will not be enough. Thus, the retailer who orders from the wholesaler Christmas cards which are not in fact delivered until December 24th, a month late, can repudiate the cards on the ground that the breach of contract has meant the destruction of the commercial purpose of the contract.

If the breach of contract is a minor one—where for instance there has been a short delay in paying for goods ordered from the wholesaler—the contract is not discharged. But as one judge put it in

1971 "... the case would be quite different if the defendants' breaches had been such as reasonably to shatter the plaintiffs' confidence in the defendants' ability to pay for the goods".

But what if one party simply repudiates an agreement? Does this discharge the contract? Clearly the answer must be no. Generally, the contract will end when the repudiation is *accepted* by the other party.

DISCHARGE BY FRUSTRATION

This arises where the claim is made that the performance of the contract is rendered impossible by subsequent events—the purpose of the contract is said to be frustrated. An example occurs where there has been a change in the law. If a pet-shop owner orders 500 budgerigars from a wholesaler, and Parliament then prohibits the sale of budgerigars through fear of the spread of psittacosis, the petshop dealer need not take delivery of the birds any more than the wholesaler need deliver the birds: the change in law has frustrated the contract. It is impossible to perform. Similarly, if the subject matter of the contract is destroyed the contract will be discharged by frustration. If the retailer decides to hire a van to deliver his fish and chips he is under no obligation to the owner of the van if the vehicle is destroyed by fire before the hire commences. It should be noted that if he takes the lease of business premises, however, the agreement will still be binding upon him if the premises are burnt down, for a lease passes an interest in the land as well as the use of the property. So even if the shop is a smoking ruin he will still be liable to pay the rent due under the lease.

Another example of discharge by frustration arises in the case of personal illness. If the contract is one involving personal service—for instance, the casual help who promises to come in at the weekend to help with the stocktaking—illness will be a good discharge from his obligations. It can also give his employer a reason to discharge the contract though not to claim damages, because there has been no "breach". An example arose in *Condor v Barron Knights* (1966). C was 16 years old, a drummer in the Barron Knights band. His duty under his contract with them was to play seven nights a week. When he fell ill a doctor said he was fit to play only four nights a week. Could the band terminate his contract? The court said they could: in the business sense C's illness had made continuation of the contract impossible.

Finally, if the contract depends upon the occurrence of a future event which does not materialise, the contractual obligations will be discharged. The bakery shop that agrees to supply £200 worth of

52

cakes and ale to a wedding reception which is called off because the bashful bridegroom has run off to sea might well find that the contract is discharged by frustration. Formerly, this would have meant that the bakery might have to bear the loss completely, unless the cakes and ale had been paid for in advance in which case the bride's father would bear the loss. This principle—"the loss must lie where it falls"—no longer holds good. Now, anything paid in pursuance of the contract discharged by frustration may be recovered, and sums due are not payable. But, at the discretion of the court, part or all of the expenses necessarily incurred under the contract can be recovered. In other words, if the bakery has received nothing by way of payment they cannot claim payment but, according to the circumstances, they might claim something by way of expenses provided the contract provided for payment in advance. Alternatively, if the bride's father has paid in advance he can recover his money, subject again to a claim for expenses incurred. It goes without saying, perhaps, that the bakery must attempt to sell the cakes and ale elsewhere if possible before making claims against the bride's father. In other words the bakery must attempt to minimise its loss.

It should be added that the contract will not be regarded as frustrated if the party has given an absolute undertaking as in a 1957 case, where Finnish exporters sold a quantity of ant eggs to English buyers "delivery: prompt, as soon as export licence granted". The sellers could not get an export licence so did not ship the ant eggs. Were they liable for breach of contract or was the contract discharged by frustration? The court pointed out that the sellers had undertaken absolutely that they *would* obtain an export licence so they were bound by the contract.

REMEDIES FOR BREACH OF CONTRACT

The final topic for discussion in this outline of the Law of Contract concerns remedies. It has already been noted that in some cases the plaintiff can ask for damages. Other remedies available to him are Specific Performance, Injunction, and he may in some circumstances sue on a Quantum Meruit.

DAMAGES

If the contract specifically states that a sum of money is to be payable in the event of a breach of contract that sum is called liquidated damages. It can be obtained quite irrespective of the actual loss suffered by the innocent party, provided that the intention at the time of the making of the contract was to genuinely assess the loss likely to occur in the event of a breach. If the purpose of stipulating the award was simply to force the performance of the contract, and was not a genuine attempt to pre-estimate the loss, the sum will be disregarded as a "penalty" and the court will order payment only of the actual loss if any suffered as damages.

An example arose in *Lamdon Trust v Hurrell* (1955). The hire-purchase price of the car was £558 and H paid a deposit and four instalments—total £302—but failed to pay the fifth instalment. L took the car back and sold it for £270, then claimed £122 under a clause in the hire-purchase agreement. The court said the clause was not a genuine attempt to pre-estimate damage but a penalty.

Where there is no sum stated in the contract as payable in the event of breach, the innocent party can claim as damages the actual loss that he has suffered—the sum awarded is called unliquidated damages.

The basic rule is one of compensation—the plaintiff can claim for loss suffered as a result of the breach. This loss can be financial, or damage to property; it can be personal injury or even distress: an example arose in *Jarvis v Swan Tours Ltd* (1973) where personal distress was caused when a holiday firm defaulted on its obligations.

Where no loss has been suffered the court can award nominal damages, just to acknowledge that a breach of contract has occurred.

Damages are related to actual loss, but the defendant will not be liable for *all* loss suffered. Suppose the retailer is liable to the customer for failure to supply new tyres for the customer's car. That gentleman may claim as damages the loss incurred through his inability to use the car for his business appointments—provided the retailer knew, or should have known, that the car was used for these purposes. But he will not be liable for extraordinary losses which he cannot be expected to anticipate—the price of the customer's mother-in-law's ticket by rail from Birmingham (the customer would have fetched her by car if the tyres had arrived in time!).

In *Pilkington v Wood* (1953) P employed W, a solicitor, to act for him when he bought a house in Hampshire. When P decided to sell the house he discovered his title to the property was defective. W admitted negligence. P claimed as damages the difference in value between the house with good title and its value with bad title, plus hotel, travelling and telephone expenses which would not have been incurred had he been able to sell the house and move to Lancashire as he intended, and interest on a bank overdraft he had found necessary to take. The court said the additional damages could not be claimed since they could not be reasonably supposed to have been in the contemplation of the parties when P bought the house or likely to result from breach of P's contract with W.

Where a claim for damages is made the plaintiff must show that he has attempted to minimise his loss. In *Darbishire v Warran* (1963) D's Lea-Francis shooting brake was badly damaged in a collision due to W's negligence. Although told that the repair of the car would not be an economic proposition D ordered the work to be done and then sued W for the difference between the cost of repairs and the sum received from the insurance company's assessment of the car's value. The court said that in having the car repaired D had not mitigated his loss. He should have bought a similar car to the Lea-Francis with the sum given by the insurance company. On the other hand a person is entitled to take reasonable steps to retain his position in such cases. This was emphasised in *Daily Office Cleaning Contractors Ltd v Shefford* (1977), when D, having had his Rambler Ambassador damaged by S's negligence, hired a Jaguar XJ6. It took 25 weeks to repair the Rambler and S compained that D should have "shopped around" and got a smaller car as replacement. The judge disagreed, saying D "was entitled to hire a Jaguar XJ6 as being a car of comparable status to that of their damaged vehicle." From this it follows that if a shipper has a cargo of bananas on his hands because the defendant has refused to take delivery of them he cannot expect to obtain the contract price as damages simply by leaving the bananas in the hold to rot. He must attempt to sell them elsewhere at the best price that he can get. His damages will be the difference between contract price and the price he actually received for the cargo. If the contract price was £1,000 and he sold the bananas for £500 the amount of damages claimed will be obvious. What is less obvious is the situation where the price of the goods is fixed—as in the case of a motor car for instance. In this new situation the dealer will be able to recover a sum equal to the profit which would have been made. In *Thompson Ltd v Robinson* (1955) R agreed to buy a car from T but refused to take delivery. T returned the car to the manufacturers and claimed from R the amount he would have received by way of profit on the transaction. At that time, the supply of cars exceeded the demand in that area. The court held that T was entitled to his claim as to profit.

Specific Performance

Instead of claiming damages, the plaintiff might ask the court to order the defendant to do what he had promised to do under the terms of the contract. In other words, the plaintiff asks for a decree of Specific Performance. The court will make such an order only where the award of damages would not sufficiently recompense the plaintiff

55

and protect his interests. The decree will not be issued where the contract is one that would require the continual supervision of the court as was the case where M agreed to provide a porter at the residential flats occupied by R. The porter spent much of his time elsewhere, and boys and charwomen carried out his duties as porter. The court would not grant an injunction to restrain the breach nor order specific performance of the contract. Nor will Specific Performance be ordered where the contract does not impose mutual obligations upon the parties—as will be the case where one of the parties is an infant and the contract is voidable at his option. The order is never made to enforce contracts involving personal service.

INJUNCTION

This is an order directing the defendant to cease committing an act in breach of contract. It is not granted where the award of damages would be sufficient protection of the plaintiff's interests or where the court could not enforce the decree. It is enforced by proceedings for contempt of court.

Although Specific Performance does not lie in a contract for personal services, the same result can be obtained by the use of the Injunction. If the managing director of the firm breaks his five-year contract and goes to work for a rival firm he cannot be forced to return by an order of Specific Performance: the order does not lie where the contract is for personal services. He can, however, be served with an Injunction which will forbid him from working for the rival firm in breach of his contract. The likely effect of this will be that he will have to return to his old employers and complete his contract—although it is still open to him to take another post, provided that it involves work different from that done for his old employers and covered by the contract and the injunction. He could, for instance, always work as a delivery boy. This was the dilemma facing Bette Davis, the film star, in 1936. She could obtain work other than as an actress, but she was bound by her agreement, under her real name, Nelson, with Warner Brothers, to work only for them as an actress. She broke this promise by entering into an agreement with another party and the film company sought an injunction to restrain her. The court held the injunction would be granted for the continuance of the contract or for three years whichever was the shorter. A *temporary* restraint against dismissal *can* be ordered; in *Hill v CA Parsons & Co Ltd* (1972) H was dismissed with inadequate notice as a result of trade union pressure to maintain a closed shop. The court granted an injunction restraining the employers from dismissing H until adequate notice had been given. This is not the same as specific performance, of course, because the employer can always suspend the employee on full pay if his presence proves embarrassing!

Like Specific Performance, injunction is an equitable remedy and is granted only if in all the circumstances it is just and equitable to do so.

Injunctions are also sometimes granted to enforce *lawful* restraints of trade, and in exceptional circumstances can be granted to order the seller of goods not to withhold delivery, as in *Sky Petroleum Ltd v VIP Petroleum Ltd* (1974).

Quantum Meruit

This remedy may be applied where the contract has been substantially performed, or where performance has been frustrated by the act of the defendant. The plaintiff will sue on a *Quantum Meruit* ("as much as he has earned") for the work that he has done under the contract. For instance, the shopkeeper who orders extensions to be made to his premises, a lump sum to be payable to the builder on completion of the work, cannot rely on the fact that the work is shoddily done to withhold the sum payable. He can be sued, on a *Quantum Meruit* and will have to pay the sum named in the contract, subject to a deduction he can make, equal to the amount required to put the shoddy work right in accordance with the terms of the contract. An example is *Hoenig v Isaacs* (1952). X agreed to decorate Y's flat and fit a wardrobe and bookcase. On completion he was to be paid £750. When the work was done Y complained of faulty workmanship. The court said X could recover from Y £750 less £294 (the cost of remedying the faulty workmanship).

Similarly, if a retailer agrees to supply goods over a monthly period for £100 payable at the end of the month, the customer's refusal to accept any more goods after £50 worth have been delivered means that the retailer can sue for £50 at least.

If it is the retailer who refuses to supply the goods the position might well be different. Then, the frustration of the contract is self-induced—it is the retailer who has brought about the circumstances which frustrate the performance of the contract—and he cannot sue. This is what happened in a 1935 case. M chartered a steam trawler from O to be used only for fishing. M applied for otter trawl licences for five ships but was granted three; none of these was used for the chartered ship. M argued that the charter was frustrated, for no licence was available for the ship. The court said the charterparty had not been frustrated since the failure to allocate a licence to the particular ship was due to M's own choice.

57

CHAPTER 5

Sale of Goods

Several of the examples given in the previous chapter have been contracts where the basis of the agreements has been the transfer of goods from one person to another. This is inevitable where one of the parties to the contract is a retailer since he is, after all, selling goods as a means of livelihood. Nevertheless, it should be noted that the agreement for the sale of goods is given a special significance by the law: although it is largely governed by the general law of contract, it has received the special attention of Parliament as a transaction and the rights and duties of the parties to the contract and, to a certain extent, the terms of the contract themselves are covered by the Sale of Goods Act 1893, as amended by the Supply of Goods (Implied Terms) Act 1973 and the Unfair Contracts Act 1977.

In the course of this chapter the special considerations to be given to contracts for the sale of goods will be outlined. Though these requirements are placed in statutory form it should nevertheless be noted that they are based upon the practice of merchants themselves. Only where commercial practice had failed to cover situations likely to arise in a mercantile transaction did the Sale of Goods legislation step in to cover the point. And it must also be remembered that a great part of the law developed by commercial practice was accepted and merged into the Common Law in the sixteenth and seventeenth centuries. This, the Sale of Goods Act expressly does not touch or affect, for the Act itself states that its provisions are not to be taken to have replaced the general law of contract. It states that the rules of agency and the effect of fraud, misrepresentation, duress, undue influence, mistake, etc., which have been dealt with in the preceding chapter, do apply to the sale of goods and only where the provisions of the Act actually conflict with common law principles is the Act to be regarded as overruling the Common Law.

The sale of goods is then to be regarded as a special contract which is largely covered by the Common Law but which also enjoys the privilege of special legislative provisions. Before these provisions are discussed it is necessary to define what is meant by a contract for the sale of goods. The Act itself defines a contract for the sale of goods as one whereby the seller agrees to transfer goods for a price, but this tells us little that we do not already know from our own observations. Such a definition is necessary nevertheless, because of the fact that there are certain other transactions commonly met with in the commercial world which are very similar to the contract for the sale of goods. Since these other transactions are not in fact covered by the Sale of Goods Act it is necessary to distinguish them, for it would be wrong to include them when the various special provisions of the Act are discussed or applied.

In the first place the contract for the sale of goods should be distinguished from the contract of exchange. The definition of a contract for the sale of goods in the Act speaks of "money consideration, called the price". So the customer who pays for his weekend joint by giving the butcher a sack of potatoes or a trip around the bay in his yacht is not indulging in a contract for the sale of goods. This is a contract of exchange, potatoes for meat, and is not covered by the Sale of Goods Act. The position is slightly more difficult where payment is made partly in money and partly by handing in goods, but in the past the attitude of the court has been to treat such a contract as one of sale of goods.

A contract for the sale of goods must also be distinguished from the contract of hire purchase. The hire-purchase agreement will be dealt with in greater detail in the next chapter along with the general law relating to consumer credit transactions, but it will be useful at this point to describe how it differs from the contract of sale under the Act. The first thing to note is that the resemblance between the two types of transaction is close, the more so because the basic idea behind the hire-purchase agreement is to transfer ownership in the washing machine or whatever else is the subject of the agreement to the buyer. In this it cannot differ from the contract of sale. But the difference between the two agreements is that when the retailer sells the refrigerator to the customer the destination of the goods is determined: the refrigerator is going to pass into the ownership of the buyer as soon as the contract is completed; whereas in the hire-purchase agreement the destination is not so determined. The refrigerator is then handed over to the customer who obtains *Possession*, not ownership; he hires the goods with an option to purchase them finally. Not until that option is taken up at the end of the hiring period, or before—under the terms of the agreement—will ownership pass to the customer.

The retailer is very much the middleman in these transactions, of

59

course, since the financial arrangements are almost always made by a firm which specialises in hire-purchase facilities. Nevertheless, both the retailer and the customer should realise the essential nature of the hire-purchase agreement and the distinction between this and the contract of sale. For the customer does not "buy" the goods, he hires them; he does not get ownership, he gets possession only. The finance company becomes the owner of the goods and may be able to retake them if the hire-purchase instalments are not paid. But more of this later. Before the contract of hire-purchase is dealt with in detail the provisions of the Sale of Goods Act 1893 relating to conditions and warranties in contracts of sale, delivery of goods, and the rights of the seller will be dealt with.

CONDITIONS AND WARRANTIES

In most contracts of sale it is possible to discover terms which the parties are intended to carry out. The retailer might order the latest line in men's shoes or raincoats, "delivery to be made by the 15th August". The wholesaler might agree to deliver ladies' dresses in bulk "provided the theatre production lasts beyond the month". These terms are not basically necessary to the contract, for the contract is one whereby the seller sells and the buyer buys, but such terms are included in order that the parties should be protected in the event of non-delivery at a convenient time or closing of the production before the next orders are dealt with.

Such terms expressly inserted in contracts for the sale of goods are described as conditions either precedent or subsequent: if delivery is not made by the 15th August the condition precedent to the formation of the contract has not been fulfilled; if the theatre production closes down within the month the condition subsequent to the formation of the contract has not been carried out. The 1893 Act states that where there is a condition in a contract for the sale of goods, if that condition is broken the contract can be repudiated: in the first case mentioned above the retailer could refuse to accept the goods when they are delivered after the 15th August. He rejects the goods, he repudiates the contract.

Not all stipulations in contracts are conditions, however; some are called warranties. The warranty can be regarded as different from the condition in that if a condition is broken the innocent party can either repudiate the contract and he can sue for damages for breach of the condition. But if a warranty is broken the only right that the innocent party has is to sue for damages; he cannot have the choice of rejecting the goods and repudiating the contract.

60

The condition and the warranty can be distinguished because of their effect in the event of a breach, but this is not a very satisfactory way of drawing a distinction between them. Unfortunately, this is the only way it can really be done, for this is the method used by the 1893 Act. It does not specifically define a condition any more than it defines a warranty. It speaks of both simply as "stipulations".

Is it possible then to define them more precisely? It is, but again the definition is hardly satisfactory. It is possible to define the term condition as being a stipulation that is more important than a warranty, and a warranty as being a stipulation less important than a condition—the importance of the distinction being reflected in the effect that follows from a breach of either. With this unsatisfactory situation we must be satisfied.

Whether it be a condition or a warranty, however, it will be of little effect unless it actually forms part of the contract.

In *Hopkins v Tanqueray* (1884) T, at an auction, assured H that a certain horse was "perfectly sound in every respect". Next day H bought the horse, but it turned out to be unsound. Could H sue successfully? The answer was he could not, for the statement was a mere representation not a warranty in the contract. So if the statement is made *before* the contract is formed or *after* it is completed it is nothing more than a "mere representation" in the first instance and a promise unenforceable for lack of consideration in the second. (See the rule as to past consideration in the previous chapter.)

Even though there are no conditions or warranties expressly stated in the contract, if it is a contract for the sale of goods certain conditions and warranties will be implied; that is to say the court reads into an agreement for the sale of goods stipulations that are not in fact there, stipulations that might not even have been intended by the parties. This is one of the peculiarities of the contract for the sale of goods. Even though the parties make the contract for themselves the Sale of Goods Act says that certain conditions and warranties are always to be taken as being present where the contract concerns the sale of goods. These conditions and warranties are of importance, both to the retailer and to the customer, since upon them largely depend the liabilities of the respective parties. The implied conditions will be dealt with first, then the warranties to be implied in contracts of sale will be dealt with.

Implied Conditons

Strangely enough, the one condition that might be thought to be implied—that is, the condition that the goods actually exist—is not im-

61

plied at all! The 1893 Act deals quite definitely with this point and states that if the goods which are the subject of the contract have perished at the time the contract is made no liability is to be placed on the parties. In other words, the seller can make an agreement to sell non-existent goods to a buyer and he will not be liable to the buyer on that contract. If, for instance, a shopkeeper agreed to sell a tin full of bags of potato crisps to a customer, he would not be liable for breach of contract if the buyer found, on getting home, that the tin was half empty, someone having stolen the bags, unknown to the shopkeeper. No condition as to the existence of the bags had been made in the contract, and no condition as to their existence is implied by the Act.

One condition that *is* implied in a contract for the sale of goods, however, that is almost as basic as the one mentioned above, is that the seller is taken to have given an implied condition that he has a right to sell the goods. This will normally mean that by selling the goods to the buyer he is in effect telling the buyer that he has the right to sell the goods, telling him that he owns the goods and can pass ownership, or telling him that though he does not own them he is acting on behalf of the owner and can pass ownership to the buyer. That such a condition is basic and necessary is obvious: we have already seen the position where a thief steals goods and sells them. The person who buys from the thief can no more obtain ownership of those goods than can the person who buys goods from a rogue who has obtained them by fraud.

What will be the result in this type of situation where the seller does not possess the right to sell? The first and obvious remedy available to the buyer when the real owner of the goods comes along and takes them back is to sue the rogue who "sold" them to him for damages. If the buyer has discovered the seller's inability to pass ownership before the contract is completed he can of course repudiate the contract. If he does repudiate the contract he is not allowed to retain any benefits he has received under the contract, but in some instances it is possible for him to make a real financial gain.

For instance, the housewife who "buys" a washing machine from a retailer will naturally be considerably annoyed when, six months later, her neighbour demands from her that particular machine on the ground that it is in fact hers. But she need not be annoyed, for she is in a very strong position. If the machine does in fact belong to her neighbour, the housewife can sue the retailer for breach of the implied condition that he had a right to sell the machine. She will be able to recover from him the full price that she paid for the machine. Nor can he ask for a sum to be deducted for the use she has had out of the machine. In other words she gets her money back, and the free use of

62

a washing machine for six months, with no hiring charge. In *Rowland v Divall* (1923) R bought a car from D and used it for four months before discovering D had had no right to sell the car for it really belonged to X. The court decided that R was entitled to recover the whole purchase price and need pay nothing for the use of the car during the four months he had possession of it. The housewives who are likely to find themselves in this position are very few and far between, admittedly, but this type of situation is far from impossible. It does happen! Indeed, it has even been suggested that if a thief sells a stolen crate of liquor to a wine merchant, who then sells it to a customer who drinks the liquor before the theft is discovered, the wine merchant would have to pay the full price back to the customer, for he had no right to sell the liquor in the first place. He would also have to pay the value of the liquor to the real owner. The customer on the other hand would have had a free crate of whisky! The moral of this tale is: deal only with reputable suppliers.

This is underlined by a 1954 case where A took a car under hire purchase terms and thinking she could sell it she transferred it to B who sold it to C who sold it to K who sold it to B, for £1,275. After using the car for eleven months B received a notice from the hire-purchase dealers who were still legal owners of the car, claiming the vehicle. A paid off the balance of the price within the week. B sued K nevertheless, claiming £1,275 (although the car was now worth only £800). The court decided that K was in breach of section 12(1) of the 1893 Act and "though the plaintiff's position was somewhat lacking in merit" B was yet entitled to the £1,275 and need pay nothing for the use of the car.

The implied condition applies also in the case of an agreement to sell; there the seller in effect promises he will have a right to sell the goods at the time when the property in the goods is to pass.

There are certain other conditions implied in a contract for the sale of goods that are concerned in the main with the quality of the goods supplied.

The first of these arises where the goods are sold by description (and the Supply of Goods (Implied Terms) Act 1973 adds that a sale of goods will not be prevented from being a sale by description merely because they are exposed for sale or hire and are *selected* by the buyer). In all such contracts the condition implied is that the goods must correspond to that description. If the shopkeeper advertises or offers for sale six-inch nails he is in breach of the implied condition if the nails are five and a half inches long. If the fish-fryer advertises he is selling hake the buyer can sue for breach of the implied condition if he is sold cod (quite apart from criminal liability under the Trades

Descriptions Act 1968). And the customer who buys a pint of the publican's "best bitter" only to find his palate denying the term will be justified in rejecting the pint of inferior brew that he is given.

The addition of extraneous matter to the goods sold can take those goods out of the description but the addition must be substantial. In *Ashington Piggeries Ltd v Christopher Hill Ltd* (1971) CH agreed to make up a food for mink according to an agreed formula; this was sold to AP. The formula included herring meal; the meal contained a chemical; reaction between chemical and herring meal resulted in death of the mink. Was CH liable to AP for breach of the condition that the food should correspond to its description? The House of Lords said not; there had been no "addition" to the herring meal sufficient to take the commodity out of the description "herring meal". The chemical affected the *quality* of the goods but did not affect the *identity*. (AP succeeded against CH under another section of the Act relating to quality: CH had provided food not suitable for the purpose it was to be used for—see below.)

A sale by description can occur even in the case of the sale of goods in a self-service store. No words are needed from the assistant: if the goods are clearly marked with a label or other description such as "EEMO WASHING POWDER—the wonder whitener" it will be a sale by description and will give rise to the implied condition that the goods will correspond to the description.

It should be noted that sometimes goods acquire a trade name and in these circumstances they need not correspond to the description. It has been well said that, "If anybody ordered Bombay ducks and somebody supplied him with ducks from Bombay the contract to supply Bombay ducks would not be fulfilled."

Where the sale is by sample and description the goods must correspond not only to the sample provided but also to the description given. In a 1948 case W sold some balloons to C by sample as "sample taken away . . . with all faults and imperfections". The court held this provision did not protect W since the bulk did not correspond with the sample. Thus, if the wholesaler's representative shows to the retailer a piece of Grade 2 cloth and says, "We can supply this Grade 1 cloth immediately", the fact that the retailer nods his head wisely and accepts the offer does not mean that when the cloth arrives, in accordance with the sample he is bound to accept it. He is not, for although the cloth is the same as the sample shown to him it does not correspond with the description: it is not Grade 1 cloth but Grade 2 cloth.

The 1973 Act made new provision to replace section 14 of the 1893 Act which dealt with implied conditions and warranties as to the quality or fitness of goods for any particular purpose under a contract of

64

sale. It states that where the seller sells goods in the course of business there is an implied condition that the goods supplied under the contract are of merchantable quality. But what is meant by merchantable quality? The Act states this categorically: they are of merchantable quality if they are as fit for the purpose(s) for which goods of that kind are commonly bought, as it is reasonable to expect. In deciding upon this question of "reasonableness" regard must be paid to the description applied to them, the price if it is relevant, and all the other relevant circumstances.

This places a clear obligation upon the seller, as did the 1893 Act. The seller is in business; he is taken to know what is merchantable; he must use his knowledge and skill and not sell goods that are not of merchantable quality.

This does not mean he cannot avoid liability entirely. It may be, for instance, that the goods sold suffer from obvious defects. If the buyer examines the goods before the contract is made and the defects should have been seen by him in that examination there is no implied condition of merchantability. Equally, if the retailer, aware of certain defects in the goods, draws the attention of the buyer to those defects before the contract is made, he cannot afterwards be held liable if the goods are found not to be of merchantable quality on account of the defects. They were pointed out to the buyer; he bought the goods knowing of the defects; he cannot complain thereafter.

Clearly, some defects would not be obvious—the suspicious beer drinker who holds his pint up to the light will never be able to discover that it contains arsenic so the implied condition would then apply even though he has "examined" the goods before buying them!

The condition as to merchantability under the 1973 Act depends upon relevant circumstances, as has already been mentioned. The price paid for the goods will often be an important factor. The toy bought for 50p can hardly be expected to last a lifetime; the overcoat bought for £80 can reasonably be expected to keep the rain out for more than a week. Merchantability is a quality that must remain with the goods for a reasonable time, of course; the retailer who sends frozen fish to the housewife is not discharged from his liability merely because the fish were frozen when they left him—they should still be frozen when they arrive.

In a case heard in 1970 Brown bought rayon cloth from Craiks Ltd, cloth manufacturers. Brown wanted the cloth for making dresses but Craiks understood it was to be used for industrial purposes. The price agreed was too low for dress cloth but higher than normal for cloth for industrial use. Should the goods be regarded as of merchantable quality? In that case the court said the buyer should have made it clear why he wanted the cloth—and the goods were to be regarded as of merchantable quality because he had not done so.

This brings us to section 14(3) of the 1893 Act as amended by the 1973 legislation. It covers the question of the circumstances where the buyer does in fact make known to the seller the purposes for which he requires the goods (which Mr Brown in the case above did not!). The section states that where a seller in the course of business learns from the buyer, either expressly or by implication, *any* particular purpose for which the goods are being bought, there is an implied condition that the goods supplied under the contract are reasonably fit for that purpose.

It makes no difference that the purpose mentioned by the buyer is a purpose for which the goods are not commonly supplied. As long as the buyer makes known the purpose the seller is under an obligation—the condition as to fitness is implied.

There is an exception to this. If the circumstances surrounding the sale are such as to show that the buyer is not relying on the seller's skill and judgment in such matters, or if the circumstances are such as to show it would be unreasonable for the buyer to rely on the seller's skill and judgment, the implied condition would not apply.

To take an example: if the buyer tells the car dealer he wants a car for racing and, seeing a model T Ford, he says he wants that one, and will not be dissuaded by the dealer's protests that it is hardly to be regarded as suitable for racing purposes, there would be no implied condition of fitness for the purpose the buyer has stipulated. He is not relying upon the car dealer's skill and judgment—indeed, he is going directly against it.

On the other hand, if the customer asks the shopkeeper for some effective pest destroyer there will be an implied condition as to fitness—and if the "pest destroyer" actually causes the flies the customer mentioned to breed in proliferation, the seller would be liable!

It should be emphasised that the sale must be in the course of business. The condition would not therefore arise where the sale is made between private persons—where a car owner sells his car to a friend, for instance. Manufacturers, wholesalers, dealers, retailers will be liable on sales only where completed in the course of business.

Prior to the 1973 amendments there had been a number of cases which stressed that the condition as to fitness applied not only to the goods themselves but also the containers in which they were carried. The obvious example is the bottle which bursts. The seller is liable—even though it might be difficult if not impossible for him to discover that the bottle was defective. An interesting case arose in

66

1954. W ordered a consignment of Coalite from R. Unknown to the parties, the Coalite contained an explosive material which blew up in the fireplace when W lit the fire. W sued for damages. Was the Coalite fit for the purpose intended? The defence argued the Coalite was not defective—it was the substance mixed with it that caused the damage! The court would have none of that argument. The goods were not merchantable. Furthermore, it was stated as long ago as 1905 that if the goods are defective—as in the case of adulterated milk—the seller would be liable even though the defect occurred through the act of another person.

What will be the situation where the sale is made by a person who is acting as agent for someone else? In such a case the implied conditions as to merchantability and fitness for the purpose they are to be used for will be implied just as they would be if the sale were made by the "principal" in the business. But the sale must be made in the course of business—if the agent is selling to a friend who knows he is not acting in the course of business it will not apply—and if the friend does not know of the situation immediately, as long as reasonable steps are taken to draw his attention to the fact that this is not a "business sale" before the contract is made, the conditions will not apply.

Apart from the foregoing it may be added that implied conditions and warranties as to fitness for a particular purpose can be annexed to the contract of sale by trade usage. Also, the condition as to "reasonable fitness" noted above applies wherever the sale is one where the price is payable by instalments—and "seller" in such cases can mean the person who conducts the negotiations before the contract is made. (See also page 87.)

It is as well to emphasise that such implied conditions arise in the sale of goods; that is to say, there must be a contract between the parties. Suppose mother sends father to buy some ice-cream. He buys four cones, keeps one himself, gives one to mother, one to son and one to the son's girl friend. After eating half of her ice-cream cone the girl friend discovers a mouse's tail in her mouth. When she recovers from her swoon she will doubtless be annoyed to discover that she has no remedy against the retailer on the basis of the implied conditions under the Sale of Goods Act. She can sue him, of course, but in negligence only, and then she will have to show that he has been negligent. If she were able to sue under the Sale of Goods Act all she would have to prove is the presence of the mouse's tail. But she cannot sue under the Act unless she is a party to the contract with the retailer, and in this instance she is not. Father could sue if the mouse's tail had appeared in his mouth, for it was he who bought the goods from the retailer. But the girl friend's remedy lies only in negligence, not in contract. The classic case is *Donoghue v Stevenson* (1932). A bought a bottle of ginger beer for her friend from a retailer. The friend consumed half of the liquid, then pouring out the remainder from the bottle, she discovered the remains of a decomposed snail. She suffered injury from nervous shock. She could not sue the retailer, for no contract existed between her and the retailer. She sued the manufacturers on the grounds of their negligence in supplying goods unfit for human consumption in an opaque bottle. The court said the manufacturers were negligent and liable to the consumer.

Implied Warranties

The 1973 amendment to the Sale of Goods Act states that in every contract of sale (other than those noted below) there is an implied warranty that the goods are free and will remain free until the time when the property will pass, from any charge or encumbrance not disclosed or known to the buyer before the contract is made. It adds that there is also an implied warranty that the buyer will enjoy quiet possession of the goods except so far as it may be disturbed by the owner or other person entitled to the benefit of the charge or encumbrance in question.

It will be remembered that the warranty is a term of the contract which is not so serious as the condition and a breach of warranty gives rise to a suit for damages only—the contract cannot be repudiated. The amendment noted above specifically recognises the position of the person who has some rights in the goods, not disclosed at the time of the sale—the buyer is entitled to quiet possession but cannot prevent the owner of the "benefit of charge or encumbrance" enjoying it.

The exception to these warranties arises in the situation where it appears from the contract of sale, or it can be inferred from the circumstances of that contract, an intention that the seller shall transfer to the buyer *only such title as he or a third person might have*. In such a case there is an implied warranty that all charges or encumbrances known to the seller and not known to the buyer have been disclosed to the buyer before the contract is made. In other words, where the title to the goods to be sold is known by both parties to be a limited one, the seller must inform the buyer of all charges and encumbrances he is aware of—otherwise he is in breach of warranty.

In addition, there is an implied warranty that neither the seller nor the third person (where the agreed intention is that the seller transfers only such title as that third person has) nor anyone claiming through or under them will disturb the buyer's quiet possession of the goods.

Naturally, anyone who has a charge or encumbrance on the goods which has been notified to the buyer before the contract is made *can* disturb his possession, but provided such charges or encumbrances are not known the implied warranty will apply.

Exclusion of Implied Terms

Is it possible for the retailer, or manufacturer, or wholesaler, or distributor to avoid the effect of terms implied in the sale of goods? The 1893 Act allowed this, stating quite clearly that the implied conditions could be varied or prevented from coming into effect by express agreement between the parties. There was such an agreement in *L'Estrange v Graucob* (1934) where the contract for sale of an automatic vending machine contained the clause: "any express or implied condition, statement or warranty, statutory or otherwise, is hereby excluded". The court decided that the seller had successfully excluded his obligations under the Sale of Goods Act.

The courts were always reluctant to allow dealers and manufacturers and such business organisations to remove this protection given to the buyer and the tendency was to allow terms to be excluded only where the agreement was quite specific on the point. This led to a kind of running battle, with company lawyers drafting carefully worded exclusion clauses in attempts to overcome the problem and the judges raising further hurdles in subsequent cases for the lawyers employed in business to overcome.

The situation is now governed by the Unfair Contract Terms Act 1977, which replaces section 55 of the Sale of Goods Act 1893 as amended by the Supply of Goods (Implied Terms) Act 1973. The Act draws a distinction between those contracts where a person is *dealing as a consumer* and those where he is not.

Section 6 of the 1977 Act states that the implied terms with regard to title in contracts of sale (section 12 of the 1893 Act and section 8 of the 1973 Act) cannot in any contract be excluded or restricted. But, in a contract where a person deals as a consumer, liability for sections 13, 14 and 15 of the 1893 Act and breach of sections 9, 10 and 11 of the 1973 Act (these relate to hire-purchase agreements) can *never* be excluded or restricted by a contract term.

And if the person is dealing otherwise than as a consumer? In such cases, liability can be excluded or restricted by a term of the contract "in so far as the term satisfies the requirement of reasonableness."

The 1977 Act introduced one more important change. The 1973 Act provided that an exclusion clause would be unenforceable to the extent that it was shown to be "not fair or reasonable to allow reliance on the term" and placed the burden of proof on the party attempting to avoid the exclusion clause. The 1977 Act reverses this: the party seeking protection of the clause must establish it as fair and reasonable.

What does all this mean in practice?

Let us take the example of the wholesaler and the retailer. The wholesaler agrees to supply goods to the retailer. The retailer is not "dealing as a consumer". The parties can include a clause in their agreement which excludes or limits liability for the implied conditions as to correspondence with description, or merchantable quality, or fitness for purpose and correspondence with sample—but any such clause will be effective only in so far as, taking all the circumstances mentioned in the Act into account, the clause is deemed "reasonable". The same situation arises where the clause attempts to restrict liability arising under sections 9, 10 and 11 of the 1973 Act, dealing with similar liabilities in hire-purchase agreements: liability can be excluded or restricted only "in so far as the term satisfies the requirement of reasonableness."

Now we come to the case of the retailer who deals with the customer: this will be a case where the customer is dealing *as a consumer*. Here, the conditions implied under sections 13, 14 and 15 of the 1893 Act cannot be excluded at all, or restricted, and any attempt to do so would be void and of no effect. The attempt would be foredoomed—and no reference can be made to the idea of fairness and reasonableness!

Section 7 of the 1977 Act deals with exclusion clauses arising under such contracts as those for hire, barter and for work and materials. As against a person dealing as a consumer, liability in respect of implied conditions as to correspondence with description or sample, quality or fitness for purpose cannot be excluded by a contract term. And the concept of reasonableness applies once again where the contract is one other than with a person dealing as a consumer.

It should be emphasised once more, however, that where the implied condition relates to title—section 12 of the 1893 Act and section 8 of the 1973 Act—the exclusion clause can be of no effect in *any* contract, whatever its nature.

These provisions of the 1977 Act are really an attempt to take account of the relative positions of the parties concerned. It is possible to allow businessmen in their dealings with each other a certain amount of latitude, in that they are freer to make their own bargains. In the case of the businessman and his customer the law considers that true freedom of contract is less likely to arise since the customer is to be regarded as a party in a less advantageous position, if only because he

70

lacks the knowledge, and expertise, and experience of the businessman who makes a living from such contractual arrangements.

But when the wholesaler wishes to exclude the operation of sections 13, 14 and 15 of the Sale of Goods Act regard is paid to what is, in the circumstances, "fair and reasonable". How is this matter to be resolved—one man's idea of fairness might not be another's—particularly where there is the possibility of legal action involved? The legislation makes specific reference to this. It states that, in deciding whether or not reliance on an exclusion clause negativing liability under one of these sections would be fair or reasonable, regard must be had to all the circumstances of the agreement between the parties.

In particular, the court would look at the following matters:

(a) The strength of the bargaining positions of the seller and buyer in relation to each other. This would take into account, among other things, to what extent the buyer could obtain the goods from some other source, and the extent to which there are suitable alternative goods available.

(b) The fact that the buyer might have received some inducement to agree to the exclusion clause. It will also be relevant to discover whether in accepting the clause the buyer had the chance to buy the goods, or suitable alternatives to them, *without* the exclusion clause, from any source of supply.

(c) The knowledge of the buyer in the sense that he knew or ought reasonably to have known of the existence of the clause, and its extent—from the custom of the trade for instance, or from some previous course of dealing between him and the seller.

(d) The conditions that might be laid down prior to operation of the clause. For instance, the parties might have agreed that sections 13, 14 or 15 might be excluded if some condition is not complied with by the buyer. The court would then ask itself whether it was reasonable, when the contract was made, to expect that compliance with the condition was practicable.

(e) Whether the goods were manufactured, processed, or adapted to the special order of the buyer.

It is always open for the court to decide that a term which purports to exclude or restrict any of the provisions of sections 13, 14 or 15 is not in fact a term of the contract, of course.

DELIVERY OF GOODS

The Sale of Goods Act states specific rules relating to the act of delivery.

By delivery is meant "the voluntary transfer of possession". This may be carried out by actually handing over the goods themselves or by handing over control of the goods—the transfer of keys to unlock the warehouse where the goods are kept, for instance. If the goods are held by a third person there will be no transfer until that third person gives an acknowledgment that he is holding the goods on behalf of the buyer. It is possible of course to pass delivery by a transfer of documents also. An example is delivery by transferring a bill of lading.

In the matter of delivery the question of time is not of importance unless it is made so by the agreement of the parties, though in fact commercial practice is such that time of delivery is always a factor of importance in the contract. If there is no time of delivery mentioned in the contract the goods must be delivered within a reasonable time, and again the court will decide what is a reasonable time. The element of reasonableness is applied also to the method of delivery: it must be at a reasonable hour and at the place of business, normally. Failure on the part of the seller to keep to the delivery date means that a condition of the contract is broken and the buyer can then reject the goods. He may, of course, decide not to enforce the time stipulation—in legal language he "waives the delivery time". It is always open to him to re-impose the time limit again, as we have already seen in the discussion as to the general law of contract. An example is seen in *Rickards v Oppenheim* (1950), the Rolls-Royce case already mentioned on page 51.

Not only must the seller deliver the goods at the right time (or a reasonable time) and place but he must also deliver the goods in the right quantity. If he delivers less than he has promised the buyer can reject them. If he accepts the goods he must pay the rate he would have paid under the original contract.

But the courts insist on adopting a reasonable attitude towards such failure to stick to the strict letter of the contract. In one case, the sellers agreed to sell 4,500 tons of wheat or 10% more or less. They actually delivered 4,950 tons and 55 lb. (without claiming payment for the 55 lb.). Could the buyers reject the goods? Common sense prevailed over mathematical logic and the court said the buyers were not entitled to reject the goods. The difference in the agreement and what was actually delivered was too small to be important.

Delivery of "part now, the rest later" will not discharge the seller from his obligation to deliver the right quantity, and again the buyer can reject such an arrangement and repudiate the contract.

In the same way, if the seller delivers more than he has promised, the buyer can reject them all, or reject the extra amount. If he accepts the goods he must, of course, pay for them at the contract rate.

EFFECTS OF THE CONTRACT

Transfer of Property

By "property" is meant ownership. While the property remains with the seller he is liable to take the risk of loss; the risk passes to the buyer with the "property". When does the property in the goods pass? It depends upon whether the goods are "specific" or "ascertained".

Specific goods are goods identified at the time the contract is made. The property here passes when the parties intend that it should pass. If the intention cannot be discovered the following rules apply:

(1) If the goods are in a deliverable state the property passes when the contract is made.

(2) If the goods are not in a deliverable state the property does not pass until they are put in a deliverable state and the buyer is given notice of it.

An example of what is meant by "deliverable state" arose in 1969. S bought carpet from PH but when it was delivered to the showrooms where it was to be laid it was sent away for stitching. It was returned next day in heavy bales—but was stolen. Who had to bear the loss—S, or PH? The court said the carpet was not in a deliverable state while it was in bales so property in the carpet had not passed to S. It was still the property of PH when it was stolen so PH had to bear the loss and S was not liable to pay the price to PH.

(3) If the price of the goods is to be reckoned by weighing, measuring or testing, etc., the property will not pass until this is done.

(4) If the goods are delivered "on approval" or "on sale or return" the property will pass when the buyer shows his approval or acceptance or retains the goods beyond the time specified, or if none, for more than a reasonable time.

The property in goods can still pass under (1), above, even though time of delivery, or of payment, is postponed. But in fact the basis of commercial practice, as is often the case, is somewhat different from the law! This is so in cases involving sales in a supermarket, or in a cash and carry shop. In these sales the buyer and seller usually intend that the property shall pass *when the price is paid*. An interesting case on this point arose in 1969—illustrating also the interaction of civil and criminal law. The cash and carry shop, C, had a till in which, when the price recorded reached £100, the numbers returned to zero. L selected the goods, placed them in a wire basket, took them to a cash desk and the manager operated the till. Unfortunately, he failed

73

to take into account the way the till worked—the register showed £85 and this is what he asked for. L paid up quite cheerfully, for *he* knew it should have been £185! The question was: did L commit the crime of theft? Had he stolen goods worth £100? The court said he had not. The parties intended property to pass when the price was paid; the manager handed the goods unpaid for to L (and was a duly authorised person with power to do so) so L could not be held guilty of *stealing* the goods—they had been given to him. It should be added that this doesn't mean cash and carry managers should henceforth refuse to operate tills: the case was brought under the Larceny Act 1916, and under the new Act, the Theft Act 1968, L would in fact have been found guilty!

Unascertained goods are goods not yet specifically identified, e.g. part of a quantity. In this case no property passes until the goods are ascertained, i.e.

(1) goods of the contract description and in a deliverable state are "unconditionally appropriated" to the contract, e.g. where the seller sets aside the goods ordered for delivery, or

(2) the seller delivers the goods to the buyer, or to a carrier to be taken to the buyer.

Transfer of Title

The seller of the goods cannot give a greater right in the goods than he himself possesses. Thus, only an owner, or his agent, can pass good "title to the goods".

There are certain recognised exceptions to this general principle, however.

One is the mercantile agent, who has possession of the goods and acts in the course of business. A second exception occurs where the goods are sold in market overt, according to the usage of the market, as long as the buyer bought in good faith without knowing the seller had no right to sell. But what is meant by "market overt"? It means in the City of London every shop in which goods usually sold in that shop are exposed for sale. The sale must be *by* the shopkeeper and it must be a place to which the general public is admitted. *Outside* the City of London, it means a market held on days stated by charter, custom or statute as market days, in the place stated as the marketplace.

A further exception often arises where A obtains goods by fraud from B. A's title is said to be "voidable". B can terminate the agreement because of the fraud but if A sells to C *before* B rescinds the contract, C gets good title to the goods provided he bought them in good faith and not knowing of the fraud. By way of illustration we can refer back to the case earlier mentioned on p. 40, *Car and Universal Finance v Caldwell* (1965). Norris, the rogue, sold the car but it was not until January 15 that a buyer in good faith acquired it. Caldwell on the other hand had informed the police and the A.A. on January 13—*before* the purchaser in good faith bought it. It could be shown therefore that no good title had passed. Caldwell had terminated the agreement before title had passed.

The above deals with cases of fraud, but what of stolen goods? If the thief is convicted of an offence connected with the theft the court can at the same time order the goods concerned to be returned to the owner by whoever has possession or control over them.

One further exception may be noted. Suppose a shopkeeper sells hi-fi equipment to a buyer and promises to deliver it, but then sells it to a different person. That person gets good title to it; the seller had retained possession and can pass title—though he leaves himself open to a claim for damages from the first buyer, naturally!

Rights of the Seller

So far, the emphasis has been upon the liabilities of the seller in the contract for the sale of goods, and the conditions protecting the buyer have been emphasised. This is not to say that the seller is without rights, however. In fact his rights are of two kinds: against the goods, and against the buyer under the contract. The rights he has in respect of the goods are called *real* in nature (concerned with the *res*, or thing, itself) while those against the buyer are called *personal* in nature.

Real Remedies

It is very necessary that the seller should have rights "against" (i.e. in respect of) the goods, for it may well be that when the buyer fails to pay for the goods the reason is that he *cannot* pay for them. There would be little point in the seller suing him in such circumstances.

What the seller can do instead of suing the buyer is to sell the goods to someone else, but he cannot do this if the goods have been delivered to the buyer. He has relinquished his rights in the goods in that case.

In effect, three real remedies are given to the seller who has not been paid; these remedies are provided by the Sale of Goods Act.

The first remedy is the use of the *unpaid seller's lien*. This is a right to retain the goods until the whole of the price payable has been paid or tendered. Usually, the lien will be exercised only as a preliminary step before the goods are resold to another person.

The seller will have no right to exercise such a lien if there is more than one contract concerned—that is, where there are separate goods to be paid for separately—nor will the lien be allowed where the goods have been sold on credit (unless the term of credit has ended or the buyer has become insolvent). Furthermore, it is essential that the unpaid seller is still in possession of the goods, for the lien is really the right of the "unpaid seller of goods who is in possession of them . . . to retain possession of them".

The lien of the unpaid seller will be lost to him if the price is paid or tendered, or if he delivers the goods to a carrier to take them to the buyer. It will similarly be lost if the buyer or his agent lawfully obtains possession of the goods or if the unpaid seller waives his right to enforce the lien.

The second real remedy available to the seller is the right of *stoppage in transitu*. Where the buyer of the goods has become insolvent the unpaid seller who has allowed the goods to leave his possession may resume possession as long as the goods are still in transit by stopping them *in transitu* (in the course of transit). He may then retain possession of the goods until payment of the price has been made or tendered to him.

Goods are deemed to be in transit when they have passed out of the possession of the seller and have been placed in the possession of a carrier by land or water but have not yet reached the buyer. Normally, the transit will be ended by delivery to the buyer, but if the buyer rejects the goods the transit is not ended, for the carrier continues to have possession of them.

If notice of stoppage is given to the carrier and the carrier nevertheless delivers the goods to the buyer the seller can sue the carrier for conversion.

It should be noted that the use of the right of stoppage *in transitu* does not bring the contract automatically to an end. It merely allows the seller to retain the goods until payment is made or tendered.

The third real remedy provided by the Act is the seller's *right of resale*. Once the lien or stoppage *in transitu* has been used as a remedy, a sale by the seller to a third party will give that third party ownership of the goods. But this is not a right of resale—and in these circumstances the first buyer could sue the seller. The right of resale arises only where the goods are perishable in nature, or where, after giving notice of the intention to resell, the seller within a reasonable time receives no payment or tender of payment from the first buyer. If a right of resale is expressly reserved in the contract, of course, this can be exercised immediately the buyer is in default.

Quite apart from his real rights, the seller has personal rights he may exercise. Thus, he may *sue for the price* stipulated in the contract; this will be available when the property in the goods has passed to the buyer. If the property in the goods has not passed, the seller may sue for *damages for non-acceptance* of the goods. In such circumstances the measure of damages will be the difference between the price payable under the contract and the price actually obtained on resale to a third party—this will normally be done in an attempt to mitigate the loss caused by the non-acceptance (a principle already discussed on page 55). An important point to note here is that the state of the market for the goods in question must be taken into account. But if the non-acceptance is of little importance to the seller, where for instance he can dispose of the goods with ease because demand far exceeds supply, he may obtain nominal damages only and will not be able to claim the full amount of profit that he would have received. An example arose in 1957, in *Charter v Sullivan*. S ordered a car from C and then refused to take delivery when it arrived. C claimed as damages the loss of profit that he would have received on the sale. The court held the demand for cars of this type exceeded the supply available and C could sell all the cars that he obtained. He was entitled to nominal damages only.

If the seller is ready and willing to deliver the goods and requests the buyer to take delivery of them, failure to take delivery within a reasonable time will mean that the seller can sue for any loss occasioned, and also for a reasonable charge for the care and custody of the goods.

AUCTION SALES

Special rules apply to auction sales.

Each lot is *prima facie* deemed to be the subject of a separate contract of sale and the sale is complete at the fall of the hammer. Until then, a bidder may retract his bid. The seller, or any of his employees acting for him, cannot bid nor can the auctioneer knowingly take such a bid unless notice is given that the sale is subject to the owner's right to bid. A reserve price can be placed on the goods; each bid is then accepted only conditionally until the reserve is reached.

The auctioneer selling goods makes certain implied undertakings:
He warrants he has a right to sell.
He warrants he knows of no defect in the principal's title.

He undertakes to give possession when he receives the price.

He undertakes possession will not be disturbed by the principal or himself.

The usual situation is that the conditions of sale are contained in a printed document—the sale catalogue. These may well include limiting clauses but they can be overruled by express oral warranties at the time of the sale.

"Knock Out" agreements where dealers agree, for payment, not to bid against each other for certain articles are outlawed by the Auctions (Bidding Agreements) Acts 1927 and 1969.

Mock Auctions

The situations that the Mock Auctions Act 1961 is designed to prevent are those where goods are sold to a bidder either at a price lower than the amount of the highest bid, or part of the price at which it is sold to him is repaid or credited to him (or stated to be so). The Act also strikes at cases where the right to bid for any lot is restricted or stated to be restricted to persons who have bought or agreed to buy one or more articles, or where articles are given away or offered as gifts.

The Act applies to any lot which consists of or includes plate, plated articles, linen, china, glass, books, pictures, prints, furniture, jewellery, articles of household or personal use or ornament or any musical or scientific apparatus or instrument.

The Act makes it an offence to promote or conduct or assist in the conduct of a mock auction at which lots to which the Act applies are offered for sale.

Offences under the Act may be punished by a fine not exceeding £100 where the conviction was a summary one. Alternatively, imprisonment for not more than three months may be imposed, or both imprisonment and fine. If the conviction is one on indictment a fine not exceeding £1,000 may be imposed, or imprisonment for not more than two years, or both.

EXPORT SALES

Export sales involve a foreign element and will not necessarily be governed by English law so the English exporter who wishes English law to apply will insert a stipulation in the contract to that effect. Where the situation is governed by English law a number of different types of contract can be carried out, the terms of which have in many cases become standardised. Special rules sometimes apply as to the passing of the property in the goods but a detailed discussion lies beyond the scope of this book.

INTERNATIONAL SALES

The foregoing has been concerned with "domestic" sales of goods, but there also exists a Uniform Law on the International Sales of Goods (ULIS). This has been given statutory effect by the Uniform Laws on International Sales Act 1967 and this Act is part of English law. A considerable number of firms in this country now specify ULIS as the proper law of their international contracts. In any case the following points should be made: ULIS applies to international sales only (though a State could make it part of domestic law); it does not cover hire-purchase contracts; questions of mistake, misrepresentation, fraud or duress are not dealt with; it contains no definition or interpretation of trade terms; and it does not deal with securities, negotiable instruments or shares. There are some important divergencies between ULIS and existing English law—for instance, under ULIS risk passes with delivery of the goods. In addition, ULIS does not cover the formation of the contract: this is dealt with in the Uniform Law on the Formation of Contracts for the International Sale of Goods (ULFIS).

Once again, though ULFIS applies only where the concluded contract would be governed by ULIS, it is interesting to note some of the more important divergencies between English law and ULFIS. Some of these can be compared with the contractual rules mentioned on page 33.

(1) The offer does not bind the offeror until communicated to the offeree and ceases if withdrawal is communicated to the offeree before or at the same time as the offer.

(2) After an offer is communicated to the offeree it can be revoked unless the revocation is not made in good faith or in conformity with fair dealing, or unless the offer states a time for acceptance or otherwise indicates it is firm or irrevocable.

(3) A qualified acceptance does not amount to a counter offer unless it materially changes the terms of the offer.

(4) An acceptance is not complete unless it is communicated to the offeror.

(5) An acceptance through the post becomes effective only when delivered at the address of the offeror.

As far as the application of these laws is concerned the questions to be asked, therefore, are:

(1) Is there a contract for the international sale of goods?

(2) Does ULIS apply?

(3) Does ULFIS make the contract valid?

If the answer to the first two questions is negative it is English law which will apply; neither ULIS or ULFIS has application.

CHAPTER 6

Consumer Credit

The Final Report of the Committee on Consumer Protection was issued in 1962 and led to the passing of the Hire-Purchase Acts and the Trade Descriptions Act 1968, as well as the Consumer Protection Act 1961 (which preceded the Report but actually implemented some of its recommendations). The 1961 and 1968 Acts will be dealt with in the next chapter, but it is necessary here to consider the impact of the Consumer Credit Act 1974, which was passed as a result of the Crowther Report on Consumer Credit.

CONSUMER CREDIT ACT 1974

The Act provided a framework, with detailed provisions regarding consumer credit to be provided by regulations and so the Act is not yet fully in force. The following account assumes its implementation.

Regulated Agreements

Certain agreements are regulated by the Act. They are of two kinds: consumer credit agreements and consumer hire agreements.

A *consumer credit agreement* is one where the creditor provides the debtor with credit not exceeding £5,000—but it does not cover cases where the debtor is a company. A *consumer hire agreement* is one by which goods are hired under an agreement which is capable of lasting for more than three months and does not require payments in excess of £5,000. If the hirer is a company the agreement is not covered by the Act.

But what if the retailer wants to get an overdraft from the bank, or use a credit card to obtain credit? Are these "regulated agreements"? The answer is yes: they are classified as *running-account credit*: credit where the amount is not fixed by the agreement (even though the agreement usually fixes a maximum limit). If the agreement is within the £5,000 limit it is classified as a regulated agreement (even where the agreement contains a clause allowing the limit to be exceeded temporarily).

Some credit agreements are exempt from the Act even where they are below the £5,000 limit. Thus, where credit is secured on land and granted by a local authority or building society, it is exempt from the Act, as are certain low-cost consumer credit agreements where the rate of interest is below a certain level, and where the number of payments under an agreement are four or less. Similarly, consumer hire agreements for the hire of telephones and gas and electricity meters are exempt.

Sub-categories of these definitions are included in the Act in sections 11 and 12. In particular, a distinction is drawn between debtor–creditor–supplier agreements, and debtor–creditor agreements. In the first of these cases there is a business agreement between creditor and supplier; this means there will often be responsibility for defective goods placed on the creditor as well as the supplier. Thus, where a customer obtains goods from the retailer and the credit is obtained from a finance company, the finance company can be held liable if the goods or services are defective. This will arise in debtor–creditor–supplier agreements; it can also arise where the creditor (the finance company) makes the contract directly with the customer.

It follows that if a customer presents himself to a retailer or distributor and buys some goods on credit, flourishing an Accesscard or Barclaycard, and then finds the goods obtained are defective he can certainly bring a claim against the supplier—but at the same time, or alternatively, he can bring his claim against the credit card company. Similarly, if the retailer has been guilty of misrepresentation or breach of contract the customer can make his claim against the credit card company as well as or instead of the supplier—for they are jointly and severally liable. The distributor who wishes to avoid this rule can do so, however—by pricing the goods at less than £50 or more than £10,000! UDT v Taylor.

30,000   *100*

Licensing

Under the Act consumer credit and consumer hire businesses must be licensed. This means that not only finance houses must be licensed, but also any retailer who enters into credit sale, conditional sale or hire-purchase agreements with a customer. But the Act also covers "ancillary businesses". These are any businesses which handle credit brokerage, debt-adjusting, debt-counselling, debt collecting or credit reference agencies. It follows that the retailer who does not actually enter into credit agreements with his customer himself, but arranges

82

finance for them with a finance house, will himself have to be licensed. The administration of the licensing system falls to the Director of Fair Trading.

Advertising and Canvassing

The Act supersedes the regulations introduced under 1967 legislation and enumerates various offences that may be committed in respect of advertising credit. They include:

(a) advertising the supply of goods or services on credit when they are not also offered for cash (section 45);
(b) issuing advertisements which are false or misleading in a material respect (section 46);
(c) sending a minor a document inviting him to seek information about credit or to obtain credit (section 50);
(d) issuing an unsolicited credit card (section 51);
(e) canvassing debtor–creditor agreements off trade premises (section 49).

Under section 44 of the Act regulations will be made to ensure that advertisements do not mislead and are true in substance. They are likely to require advertisements to give a clear indication of the cost of the credit by stating a true annual percentage rate or else to indicate that such information is available. Their objective will be to achieve truth in lending transactions.

Under section 52 of the Act it is an offence to infringe regulations as to the contents and form of a quotation of credit terms.

This brings us to the question as to what formalities are required by the Act as far as regulated agreements are concerned.

Formalities

By section 173 the parties to a regulated agreement are prevented from contracting out of the protection provided by the Act for the debtor and hirer. But what formalities are demanded by the Act?

A creditor or owner under a regulated agreement can enforce it only if it fulfils the requirements of sections 55 and 60–65. These lay down the following.

(1) The agreement must contain specified information; for instance, as to the true annual cost of the credit.

(2) All the terms (except implied terms) of the agreement must be stated in the written agreement, or in some other document referred to in the written agreement. They must include details of the debtor's

right, if any, of cancellation, and comply with regulations as to form and contents (such as names and addresses of the parties, amounts and due dates of payments, true cost of credit, in accordance with regulations to be made under section 60).

(3) The agreement must be signed by the customer in person and by or on behalf of the creditor or owner.

(4) The customer must be given one copy of the agreement when he is given or sent the agreement to sign. Often, the agreement is not actually made when he signs it; he must then be given a second copy later. This copy must be sent within seven days of the making of the agreement. (This stipulation is necessary because in many triangular arrangements of this kind the customer signs a proposal or offer in the first instance, and the agreement is only made when the finance house accepts the offer by posting an acceptance to the customer.)

(5) Where the regulated agreement is proposed to be secured by land the customer must receive his copy of the agreement at least seven clear days before he is sent by post the *actual* agreement to sign.

Cancellation

Some regulated agreements can be cancelled by the customer if he changes his mind after having signed the agreement. An agreement is cancellable if the agreement was signed elsewhere than at the trade premises—at home, for instance, or at the customer's own trade premises. But this is only so if the negotiations included oral representations made by the creditor or owner or dealer in the customer's presence. The object of this provision is, of course, to prevent salesmen pressurising customers into credit agreements, and to allow a cooling-off period for the customer when he can think over the concluded agreement.

The cooling-off period begins when the customer signs the agreement and lasts until the end of the fifth clear day after he receives his second copy of the agreement. He can cancel the agreement up to that time by giving or posting a written notice of cancellation to the creditor or owner—or in the case of a debtor–creditor–supplier agreement, the dealer.

If the cancellation arises in a *debtor–creditor–supplier* agreement for restricted use credit, or consumer hire agreement, the customer can recover payments already made. He must return the goods but need not actually take them back—he can wait for them to be collected. He can also retain them until he is paid back his deposit or instalments, but in all such cases must take reasonable care of the goods for 21 days after serving notice of cancellation. He need not

84

return perishable goods, or goods supplied to meet an emergency, or goods which were consumed before cancellation. In other words, if the customer buys plants in a garden, or spare parts for a car, in an emergency, he is under no duty to return them after cancellation of the agreement. He will of course be liable to pay for those goods after cancellation.

If the cancellation arises in a *debtor–creditor* agreement or in an unrestricted use credit agreement the customer must repay, usually with interest, any credit he has already received.

The retailer as agent of the creditor

Under section 56 of the Act the retailer or distributor who conducts negotiations with the customer is regarded in a debtor–creditor–supplier agreement as the agent of the creditor. This means that the creditor will be liable for any misrepresentations made by the retailer or distributor and any money paid to the negotiator will be regarded as having been paid to the creditor. The negotiator is also regarded as the creditor's agent for the purpose of receiving written notices —such as notices of an offer to enter an agreement, or of cancellation—from the customer.

Enforcement of agreements

If a creditor or owner wants to enforce a regulated agreement he must bring his action in the county court.

If he wishes merely to sue for payments he can simply commence proceedings. In certain other circumstances he must first serve a default notice. These circumstances are where he wishes to terminate the agreement, demand earlier payment of a sum, recover possession of goods, enforce a security, or treat any right given to the debtor or hirer by the agreement as ended, restricted or deferred. And if he wants to do any of these things for reasons other than a breach of the agreement by the debtor or hirer and if the agreement is of a specified duration (such as a hire-purchase agreement) he must serve notice of his intention.

The notice must give the debtor or hirer at least seven days warning and the default notice must make clear what the debtor or hirer can do to make right his breach of agreement. If he *does* make good his breach the breach is thereafter regarded as never having happened.

The court has power, additionally, to re-open agreements which are extortionate in their terms (e.g. if it grossly contravenes principles of fair dealing). Where the debtor or hirer dies, his relatives can continue the agreement if it is of specified time duration—the creditor or owner cannot terminate it merely because of the death of the original contracting party.

The above constitutes the general regulations laid down by the Consumer Credit Act, but since hire-purchase agreements are of particular importance to the retailer and distributor we may now look at the law relating to such agreements, falling as they do under the Consumer Credit Act.

HIRE PURCHASE AGREEMENTS

The nature of the hire-purchase contract

Under a hire-purchase contract goods are delivered to a person who agrees to make periodical payments by way of *hire*; after the stated hire instalments have been paid he has an option of *buying* the goods. It is therefore a granting of possession (bailment) to the hirer combined with an option to purchase—but the unfortunate thing is that the man in the street who takes goods on hire-purchase often fails to realise this and regards the goods as his own immediately he takes possession, to deal with as he wishes.

The member of the general public is also surprised on occasions to discover that when he signs the hire-purchase agreement in the shop he is usually signing a proposal form directed not to the retailer, but to a finance company. The questions that arise therefore are: What is the relationship between the hirer and the retailer? What will happen if there is something wrong with the goods—can the retailer be sued by the hirer?

The retailer and the finance company

The retailer, as owner of the goods, will often wish to use the resources of a finance company in order to carry out the hire-purchase transaction. This is particularly the case in the car trade or where electrical goods of considerable value are being sold. In such cases the finance company provides the money to buy the goods from the retailer and naturally makes a charge for this service upon the hire-purchaser. What the hire-purchaser often fails to realise is the nature of the triangular arrangement undertaken, and the position and powers of the hire-purchase company financing the contract.

First of all, when the customer agrees to buy the goods from the retailer on hire-purchase, using the services of a finance company, the retailer sells the goods to the finance company under an outright *con-*

tract of sale. The finance company thus becomes owner of the goods and pays the price to the retailer.

The finance company then enters into the hire-purchase agreement with the customer, who undertakes to pay the charges, including the finance charges, directly to the finance company. He will not obtain title to the goods until, after the last instalment is paid, he exercises his option to buy.

It follows from this that there is no contract as such between the retailer and the customer: no contract of sale, no contract of hire-purchase. Does this mean the retailer cannot be sued by the hire-purchaser? It may be he could take the same step as the ice-cream eating girl friend mentioned earlier and sue the retailer in negligence—if it could be shown that the goods put into circulation by the retailer were dangerous, on account of a defect the retailer should or could have known about. But could a claim be made in contract?

There is one circumstance where the retailer might be liable—where a special contract over and above the hire-purchase contract has been established between retailer and hire-purchaser. This would be the case where the retailer has given an express warranty to the customer as to the quality of the goods. An example arose in 1950. A car salesman showed a car to the buyer saying "it's in perfect condition and good for thousands of trouble-free miles". The buyer then agreed to buy the car through a finance company on hire-purchase terms. The car was in poor condition, however, and the buyer, Mr Brown, later sued Sheen and Richmond Car Sales Ltd., the car dealers, on the warranty the salesman had given him. The court held the car dealer had given an undertaking to Brown to induce him to enter the contract: in effect "if you enter the hire-purchase agreement I will promise the car is in good condition". The car dealer was liable on that promise.

How much is the dealer likely to have to pay where this warranty arises? More than he might imagine: he can be held liable for all the damage suffered by the hire-purchaser, which will include his liabilities under the hire-purchase contract. Nor is it limited to the difference in the value of the goods as warranted by the dealer and the true value of the goods. The dangers for the dealer in making such statements are obvious.

Recourse agreements. Sometimes a finance company will enter into a recourse agreement with the dealer—this extends the liabilities of the dealer in that he agrees to pay the finance company if the purchaser defaults on the agreement. How much will it cost the dealer? The answer is—the whole amount of damages suffered by the finance company—not just a sum equivalent to the instalments in arrear before the hire-purchase contract was terminated. In *Goulston Discount Co Ltd v Clark* (1967) the hire-purchase price of the Jaguar was £458. The finance company paid the dealer £300 and the dealer gave the customer a trade-in price for his old car of £100. The customer paid a few instalments, defaulted, the finance company retook the Jaguar, resold it for £155 and then claimed £157 from the dealer under a recourse agreement. He argued that only £74 (the instalments due prior to the retaking of the car) was due. The court told him to pay £157.

Refinancing arrangements. Under a refinancing arrangement the car dealer buys the car from the owner under a straight contract of sale and then *resells* it to a finance company which then gives the original owner hire-purchase terms. Such arrangements are not restricted to cars, of course, but it can really amount to the original owner getting a loan on the security of the goods actually retained in his possession. The courts have said that if the parties are aware of the true nature of the transaction, the hire-purchase transaction is a sham and void as an unregistered bill of sale. But if the transaction is intended as a *genuine* hire-purchase agreement (for instance, if the finance company was not aware of the irregularity of the arrangement) the transaction is valid and binding upon the original owner who, for instance, defaults on the repayments and wants to avoid liability on remaining instalments!

The dealer as agent of the finance company

The principles of agency will be dealt with in more detail in Chapter 10 but the question here to be answered is: when a dealer negotiates with a customer for a hire-purchase agreement, and perhaps takes a deposit from him, is he acting for himself, or as an agent for the finance company?

The general rule was stated by Lord Justice Pearson in 1965: "In a typical hire-purchase transaction the dealer is a party in his own right, selling his car to the finance company on his behalf and not as general agent for either of the two parties." But a 1969 case, *Branwhite v Worcester Works Finance Ltd* is instructive.

Branwhite agreed to trade in his car to get a Rapier from Raven car dealers on hire-purchase. Terms were agreed, Branwhite signed the finance company's proposal form and hire-purchase agreement without reading them and the Raven manager fraudulently inserted higher figures, on the basis of which the finance company paid him the inflated cash price. When Branwhite received a copy of the agreement he noticed the difference, particularly in the higher repayment terms demanded of him, but did nothing when reassured by Raven's manager. Later, the finance company took back the Rapier for Branwhite's failure to pay the instalments. It was held they could not recover the instalments from Branwhite because the Raven manager's fraud had made the hire-purchase agreement invalid; on the other hand Branwhite could recover the deposit from the finance company because they had paid Raven the sale price of the Rapier, *less* the amount of the deposit and therefore could be treated as having received the deposit.

The dealer certainly will be the agent for the finance company where he delivers the goods to the hire-purchaser after the hire-purchase agreement has been completed. Moreover, the dealer is regarded under the Consumer Credit Act 1974 as the agent of the finance company in respect of representations he makes regarding the goods during the negotiations that lead up to the making of the agreement. This includes any conditions or warranties made. The dealer is also an agent for the finance company as far as receiving notice of cancellation by the prospective buyer or hirer is concerned. These points will be dealt with again later.

It can be seen from the above that the finance companies have been acting from a position of strength over the years—sometimes demanding that the retailer agrees to act as guarantor for the hire-purchaser's debt—which means that if the customer fails to pay the instalments the retailer has to pay the balance owing. It is then up to the retailer to enforce the hire-purchase agreement against the hire-purchaser as best he may.

One method the retailer may take in protection of himself is not to act as guarantor personally, but to ask the hirer to provide his own guarantor—either as part of the original hire-purchase agreement or as a separate agreement entered into with the retailer. In this way the retailer protects himself in the same way as the finance company protects itself at the expense of the retailer.

Owners claiming damages

If the hire-purchase agreement is terminated by the hirer breaking the contract, or by the owner giving notice of termination when the hirer has broken the contract, how much can the owner claim by way of damages?

If there is a minimum payment clause, by which the purchaser has agreed to pay a calculable amount if a breach does occur, the owner can claim that sum—unless it is so exessive as to amount to a penalty (see page 54 *ante*).

89

Otherwise, the amount depends upon the circumstances. For instance, the breach may be a repudiation of the agreement. This would happen where the hirer fails to pay several instalments and makes it clear he has no intention of sticking to the agreement. In such a case the owner can claim all the loss he has suffered as a result of the hirer's failure to carry out the agreement.

On the other hand, instalments may be in arrears but the hirer does not intend to repudiate the agreement. If the owner terminates the contract in these circumstances as he may be entitled to do under a clause in the contract, he can claim only the amount of instalments unpaid up to the date of the termination. The importance of the distinction between these two sets of circumstances can be seen in the case where a Mr Baldock was sued by Financings Ltd in a case reported in 1963. The finance company claimed £538—the loss they had suffered for failure by Baldock to carry out the contract. They got £56—the unpaid instalments. The reason? Baldock had never intended repudiating the agreement. In fact, he had told the company he could raise the outstanding money within a few days but the company had repossessed the goods and terminated the agreement. So £56 it was. The moral for the owner who seeks to terminate is: tread delicately.

Credit Sale and Conditional Sale Agreements

The main legislation dealing with hire-purchase agreements was the Hire Purchase Act 1965. This legislation, it has already been noted, is to be replaced by the Consumer Credit Act 1974 which is in the process of implementation. The 1974 Act uses new terminology ('debtor' for 'hirer', and 'creditor' for 'owner') and applies not only to hire-purchase agreements but also to credit sale and conditional sale agreements. The conditional sale agreement is one whereby

(a) the instalments are not limited to five or more and
(b) unlike the credit sale agreement, the property in the goods remains with the seller until the instalments are paid, or other conditions specified are fulfilled.

Additionally, in the credit sale agreement property passes to the buyer in accordance with the law relating to the sale of goods.

How does the conditional sale agreement differ from a hire-purchase contract? In a conditional sale agreement the buyer has possession under a contract of sale; under a hire-purchase agreement he has possession of the goods under contract of bailment.

Hire-purchase agreements that fall under the 1974 Act are those agreements which classify as regulated consumer credit agreements under the Act. To be such, the hire-purchase agreement must fulfil two conditions:

    (1) the debtor (hirer) is not a company or body corporate;

    (2) the amount of credit must not exceed £5,000.

The credit consists of the capital borrowed, not the deposit nor the interest or finance charges. So if the total amount repayable is greater than £5,000 this doesn't matter—provided the capital sum borrowed is £5,000 or less it is caught by the 1974 Act.

The contents of hire-purchase agreements caught by the Act conform to the general principles laid down for regulated agreements in the Act. The protection afforded by the Act cannot be contracted out of.

Right of cancellation. Some regulated agreements can be cancelled as under the previous legislation, where a "cooling-off" period was introduced. These rights of cancellation last only for a few days, the idea being that if the agreement was signed at a place other than the trade premises the debtor can have second thoughts and still escape from the agreement at no cost to himself.

The retailer as an agent

It was earlier pointed out that if a dealer makes representations during the negotiations before the agreement is made the Act states that he is deemed to have made the representations as an agent for the owner or buyer. What is the effect of this situation?

In the first instance the finance company will be held liable for any such statements made by the dealer during the course of negotiations, but, more important, the dealer himself may be found liable to the hirer for breach of a "collateral warranty". This arises where it is shown the hirer would not have entered the contract had the representations not been made.

The representations mentioned include conditions and warranties. The Supply of Goods (Implied Terms) Act 1973 implies the following conditions in *all* hire-purchase agreements (including those where the hire-purchase price is £5,000, and even where a company is the hire-purchaser):

    (a) an implied condition that the owner has the right to sell the goods at the time when property is to pass (section 8);

    (b) where the goods are let by description an implied condition that they will correspond to that description (and to the sample if the letting is by sample and description) (section 9);

    (c) where the owner lets goods under a hire-purchase agreement in the course of business, an implied condition that the goods are of merchantable quality (except for defects drawn to the hirer's attention before the contract was made, and for defects the hirer should have discovered where he examined the goods before making the agreement);

(d) where in the course of business the owner is told by the hirer of the purpose for which the goods are required, an implied condition that the goods are reasonably fit for that purpose (except where the hirer shows he is not relying on the owner's skill or judgment) (section 10);

(e) under a letting by sample, an implied condition that the goods will correspond in bulk with the sample, that the hirer will have a reasonable opportunity to compare bulk with sample, and that the goods will be free from defects rendering them un-merchantable, which would not be apparent on reasonable examination of the sample (section 11).

The following warranties are also implied:

(i) an implied warranty as to title and quiet possession (section 8);

(ii) where the intention is to give a "limited" title, an implied warranty that all charges known to the owner have been disclosed to the hirer before the agreement was made and that the hirer's quiet possession will not be disturbed by owner or third person concerned (section 8(2));

and the Act adds that implied conditions and warranties as to quality or fitness for a particular purpose may be annexed to hire-purchase agreements by usage.

The question that then arises is whether or not the dealer or the finance company can exclude liability under these implied conditions and warranties by contracting out. It will be noted that the implied terms stated above are similar to those implied in contracts for the sale of goods, and the position regarding exclusion of the terms is also similar. These can be an exclusion by means of an express condition or warranty inconsistent with a term implied by the Act but in any case section 8 provisions cannot be excluded. Also, in the case of consumer agreements (where the owner acts in the course of business and supplies goods ordinarily supplied for private use or consumption and the hirer is a private person not engaged in hiring as a business transaction) no exemption from sections 9, 10 or 11 or any part of them is possible. In contracts other than consumer agreements exemptions from sections 9, 10 or 11 shall not be enforceable to the extent that it is shown it would not be fair or reasonable to allow reliance on the exclusion clause. The determination of what is fair or reasonable is based upon similar considerations to those already mentioned in the sale of goods (see page 69).

Where the agreement is a conditional sale agreement a breach of a condition, express or implied, that is to be fulfilled by the seller must be treated as a breach of warranty and not as a ground for rejecting the goods and treating the agreement as repudiated. This only applies, however, if it would have been so treated as a breach of warranty in a corresponding hire-purchase agreement with the owner to carry out the condition. (This removes the application of section 11(1)(c) of the 1893 Act from conditional sale agreement—see page 60).

Terminating the contract

The agreement itself may lay down grounds for termination for instance, where the hire-purchaser exercises the option usually included: the option to return the goods to the owner. But there can also be termination where the agreement is broken.

The contract will be broken where the hire-purchaser fails to keep up payments on his instalments—normally, the agreement states that in such a case the owner can terminate the agreement by giving notice to the hirer. If the transaction is covered as a regulated agreement by the Consumer Credit Act 1974, however, there are certain restrictions placed upon the creditor's right to terminate.

(1) If he wants to terminate for some reason other than a breach of contract by the debtor he must first serve a written notice, with seven days' warning, on the debtor.

(2) If there has been a breach of the agreement by the debtor, the creditor can terminate only after serving, with seven days' warning at least, a *default notice*, and he must allow the debtor in that seven days' period to put right his default, if he can.

So how can the debtor escape the consequences of termination? Suppose, for instance, a retailer has obtained some expensive refrigerating equipment on hire-purchase terms, and has failed to keep up his payments. What options are open to him?

There are three situations that may be discussed.

(1) First of all he can take the perhaps obvious step of paying off the arrears before the end of period on which the default notice expires.

(2) Alternatively, having received the default notice, he can make an application to the court for a time order. If he gets one, this will allow him extra time to raise the money to pay off the arrears.

(3) Thirdly, if the goods are "protected goods" he can point out to

the creditor that he must sue for the sum owed, or for return of the goods. And when he is sued, he can ask the court for a time order. If this request is successful it is open to the court to alter the instalment pattern on the equipment and extend the repayment period. But what is meant by the term "protected goods"? By section 90 of the 1974 Act goods let under a regulated hire-purchase agreement are protected if the debtor is in breach of the agreement but has paid or offered to pay at least one-third of the total hire-purchase price. The creditor can recover possession of the goods then only by a court order.

If the debtor does not avoid the consequences of termination, of course, the creditor can also usually claim a sum by way of damages, in addition to recovering possession of the goods.

But what is the situation if the creditor seizes the "protected goods" without going to court for an order? The debtor will then find that the agreement is terminated—and that means he is released from all further liability for the rest of the instalments. Indeed, he can even recover all instalments and other sums he has already paid! So it is an unwary creditor who tries to take back protected goods without a court order.

A rather different circumstance arose in 1970 in *Bentinck Ltd v Cromwell Engineering Co.* The hirer obtained the car on hire-purchase, paid the deposit and a few instalments, then fell into arrears. The amount paid was in excess of one-third of the purchase price so the goods were "protected goods". The car was damaged in an accident and was left at a garage; he left no instructions regarding repair and when the finance company finally traced him three months later he made no further payment before disappearing. Six months later the company took the car from the garage.

The policy behind the "snatch-back" provisions is clear enough, and allows the hirer time to pay, but it could hardly be said that this case really fell into the "snatch-back" category. The Court of Appeal held that on the facts the car had been abandoned—the hirer no longer had possession personally or through an agent so when the finance company retook possession it did not recover it "from the hirer" under the terms of the "snatch-back" provision (section 90) of the Act. It followed that the retaking was lawful.

The point of the action generally was that the defendant dealers had entered into a contract of indemnity regarding the hire-purchase agreement and this had therefore not been terminated by an "unlawful" retaking of the car. So the agreement still stood. The action on the indemnity therefore succeeded and the defendant was forced to pay the outstanding balance—the difference between the hire-purchase price under the agreement and that already obtained by the plaintiff by way of deposit paid by the hirer, instalments subsequently paid, and proceeds from the ultimate sale of the car.

The debtor's right to terminate. The debtor under a regulated agreement is given the right to terminate the contract at any time by giving notice to the creditor: section 99 of the 1974 Act. But, as well as returning the goods he must:

(a) pay all arrears of instalments due;
(b) pay damages for any loss caused by his failure to take reasonable care of the goods; and
(c) pay *either* the minimum payment stated in the agreement, *or* the amount necessary to bring his payments up to half the total hire-purchase price, *or* the loss sustained by the creditor as a result of the termination.

As far as (c) is concerned, he'll obviously pay whichever is the smallest sum, but as an alternative to all this he can, of course, merely pay off all the instalments, early, and thereby become owner of the goods immediately. This will also entitle him to some rebate of his interest charges.

Protection afforded car buyers

Most of the law relating to Hire Purchase is now stated in the 1974 Act, but the Hire Purchase Act 1964 is not entirely dead and finished with. Special protection afforded to buyers of motor vehicles is contained in the 1964 Act and this part of the Act is still in force. It is probable that the protection is even wider than that under the 1974 Act in that it applies to private purchasers who are companies, and there is no statutory limitation placed on the value of the goods, as there is in the 1974 Act.

It should be noted first of all that the protection does not apply to car dealers or car finance houses: the 1964 Act does not regard them as "private purchasers". What the Act states is that where a private purchaser obtains a car in good faith, and without realising that the car is the subject of a hire-purchase agreement or a conditional sale agreement (in which cases the seller may not have property in the car) he is not penalised. Though the seller may not have ownership of the car, since it is still vested in the finance company, the private purchaser obtains good title—he is thus protected against a claim by the original owner or seller.

An example should make this clear. If Brown enters a hire-purchase agreement with the finance company and then, before he has paid the price of the car, sells the car to White, ownership of the car passes to

95

White even though, strictly speaking, Brown did not have ownership to pass. The finance company can certainly proceed against Brown, but the car cannot be retaken from White. In other words, the private purchaser is protected, but the civil or criminal liability of the hirer or buyer who sells the car in contravention of his contract with the finance company is not affected. The important point to remember, however, is that the private purchaser *had no notice of the hire-purchase agreement and took the car in good faith.* If he knew of the agreement he is not protected.

CHAPTER 7

Consumer Protection

The law has traditionally protected consumers—through contractual remedies available to the buyer of goods against the person selling them under the Sale of Goods Act 1893, and through remedies in tort to persons who could prove negligence under the "neighbour" principle.

Reference has already been made to the contractual remedies available; in Chapter 8 there will be discussed the remedies available in tort. In this chapter we may concentrate on particular legislation that has been specifically passed to protect the consumer—notably, the Consumer Safety Act 1978, the Trades Descriptions Act 1968 and other legislation covering the sale of food and drugs.

CONSUMER SAFETY ACT 1978

The Consumer Protection Act 1961 gave the Minister power to impose safety regulations on a prescribed class of goods. The regulations related to the composition or contents, design, finish or packing of specified goods as well as to warnings or instructions required. The Act thus made it possible for *any* person affected by a breach of the regulations to bring an action, whether he was the immediate buyer or not.

A number of regulations were issued—relating to fireguards, nightdresses, carry-cots, toys, and the wiring colours for electrical appliances. A new Act was passed in 1978, however, repealing the 1961 Act and broadening the coverage previously given.

In the first instance, the Minister may make regulations applying to goods generally—not just to a prescribed range or class of goods. These regulations may also require that goods conform to certain standards, that testing or inspection of goods must be carried out, and may require that warnings or instructions should accompany the goods or be marked on them.

A further extension of the Minister's powers is seen in the provision whereby he may, by regulation, prohibit persons from supplying, offering or agreeing to supply, exposing for supply or even *possessing* for supply, goods or component parts of goods which he considers are not "safe" or do not satisfy the requirements of the regulations.

Criminal penalties support these powers—the retailer or distributor who commits an offence can find himself facing a maximum of three months imprisonment and a fine of up to £1,000—though it is a good defence to show he took "all reasonable steps and exercised all due diligence to avoid committing the offence".

It is not necessary that the Minister bring an action himself, however. By section 6(1) of the Act "Any obligation imposed on a person by safety regulations or a prohibition order or a prohibition notice is a duty owed by him to any other person who may be affected by a failure to perform the obligation and a breach of that duty is actionable . . ."

As we shall see in Chapter 8, the consumer who is injured may bring an action in negligence, but it may now be simpler for him to use the 1978 Act and argue breach of statutory duty.

TRADES DESCRIPTIONS ACTS 1968 AND 1972

The emergence of these Acts brought something new into the field of consumer protection in that the criminal law was brought into play—provision was made for the criminal prosecution of any person who misdescribed goods or services he had available. By "trade description" is meant any indication, direct or indirect and by whatever means given, of any of the following matters relating to goods or parts of goods:

(a) quantity, size or gauge;
(b) method of manufacture, production, processing or reconditioning;
(c) composition;
(d) fitness for purpose, strength, performance, behaviour or accuracy;
(e) any other physical characteristics;
(f) testing by any person and the results;
(g) approval by any person or conformity with a type approved by any person;
(h) place or date of manufacture, production processing or reconditioning;
(i) person by whom manufactured, produced, processed or reconditioned;

(j) other history including previous ownership or use.

It then states that a "false trade description" is one false to "a material degree", displayed so it is associated with the goods in the consumer's mind—and it need not be in writing but can be made orally.

And the offence itself? It is a criminal offence under section 1 of the Act to

(a) apply a false trade description to any goods, or
(b) supply or offer to supply any goods to which a false trade description is applied.

A businessman would "apply" a trade description by affixing it to the goods themselves or to anything in or on or with which the goods are supplied. Similarly, it would be an application where the description is made in an advertisement relating to the goods. An "offer to supply" could of course be inferred merely from the fact that the seller has possession of the goods, and it should be noted that where an offence has been committed it is no good the director, or manager, or secretary or other such officer arguing the offence was committed by the company—if it is shown that the officer in question consented or connived at the offence, or it arose because of his negligence, he too will be liable to prosecution. This is one example where the individual cannot hide behind the cloak of incorporation!

Are there any defences that can be raised to a prosecution under the Act? For instance, it may be that an offence has been committed but the *intention* to commit the offence had not been present. What is the situation then? The Act makes specific reference to defences. One such defence is *Mistake*. If the offence was committed purely by mistake the offender will not be penalised. But the courts have shown that they view this defence very carefully, and it would be no use, for instance, simply to say the offence was committed by an employee. A second defence arises where there is *Reliance on Information* supplied by another person. A third defence is *Default of Another*. If it can be shown that the offence was committed as the result of the act or default of some other person (an employee) no liability will follow. This is what happened in 1970, in *Becket v Kingston Bros* where K bought turkeys from Denmark, carrying labels stating "Norfolk King Turkeys" which they were not. The managers of all branches were told to stick new labels on the turkeys, correcting the misdescription but one did not. K was charged with an offence under the Act. The defence of default by the manager was successfully raised. Similarly, in *Tesco Supermarkets Ltd v Nattrass* (1972) faulty supervision by a shop manager led to goods being sold with a false indication as to price. The company succeeded in showing that it had exercised all due care and diligence and the shop manager, though an employee, was "another person" in the meaning of the Act. A further defence would be *Accident* or other cause beyond the control of the person charged but perhaps the most common will be the taking of all *Reasonable Precautions* and the exercise of all due diligence to avoid an offence by the person charged or anyone under his control.

Special consideration is given regarding an advertisement: where the offence is committed in an advertisement it is a defence for the publisher to prove he received the advertisement in the ordinary course of business and had no reason to believe the publication would amount to an offence. The publisher is thus protected—the writer of the advertisement who wants to sell the goods is not!

It should be emphasised that in all the defences mentioned above it is essential to show that all reasonable precautions and due diligence was shown. And though an offence may have been committed it has no effect upon the contract that might have been made. That will remain valid as a contract for the sale of goods—the aggrieved party will merely take action on grounds of misrepresentation. By section 1 of the Criminal Justice Act 1972 magistrates and the Crown Court have the additional power to order compensation to be paid to victims who have suffered loss.

But who otherwise will enforce the provisions of the Act? The task is given to weights and measures officers employed by local authorities. They have the power to enter premises, seize and examine goods, make test purchases and bring prosecutions in their own name with the approval of the Department of Trade. They must give notice of test and of intended prosecution. It is a separate offence to obstruct such an officer in the execution of his duty.

Trade Descriptions Act 1972

The 1968 Act was supplemented in 1972 by an Act which extended the requirements as to the marking of imported goods. It made it an offence to supply or to offer to supply in the course of trade goods made or produced abroad unless they carry a conspicuous indication of the country of origin. This applies to goods to which a United Kingdom name or mark is applied, or a name or mark likely to be taken as such (whether or not the UK name or mark actually exists). The offence is not committed if the United Kingdom mark or name is not visible and is not likely to become visible to a customer inspecting the goods.

It should be emphasised that the Act applies only to goods sold in the course of business, and it has no application to second-hand goods or to goods to be used as containers or labels for other goods.

This Act extends the provisions found in the 1968 Act which prohibit the importation of goods bearing a false indication of their place of origin, and restrict the importation of goods bearing trade marks which if used within the United Kingdom would infringe the exclusive rights of the proprietor.

Misstatements other than False Trade Descriptions

Apart from offences committed under the 1968 Act as being false trade descriptions there is a series of other offences that might be committed in relation to misstatements concerning goods. These might be grouped under three headings.

(1) *False indications as to price.* Price wars within the distributive trades, with consequent confusion in the minds of consumers, led to the necessity for some action to be taken on this front. In the event, the 1968 Act stated that it is an offence for anyone to give a false indication that the price stated is equal to or less than a recommended price for the goods. Equally, it would be an offence to state the price differs from the price at which they were previously offered by him (the false "sale" price, for instance), and it is also an offence to indicate that goods are being offered at a price less than the price they are actually being offered at.

An example arose in 1972, which also illustrates that the term "offer" under the Act does not necessarily mean the same thing as "offer" in the general law of contract. David Greig Ltd displayed a bottle of fruit juice in their self service store with the price marked on top and the bottle labelled "the deposit on this bottle is 4d refundable on return". At the cash desk was a notice: "In the interests of hygiene we do not accept the return of empty bottles. No deposit is charged by us at the time of purchase."

The court held that this amounted to a misleading indication as to the price of the goods, given when the bottle had been placed on display. The notice at the cash desk in no way enabled the firm to avoid criminal liability. And by section 6 of the Act "A person exposing goods for supply or having goods in his possession for supply shall be deemed to offer to supply them."

Under the general law of contract, however, it could be argued that the notice at the cash desk might well be regarded as a term in the contract whereby no deposit was charged and the price marked on the bottle was the price of the contract. It follows therefore, that while

101

"display" under the Act can amount to an offer, under the general law of contract it amounts only to an "invitation to treat"—so it would be possible to commit a criminal offence by displaying the goods and yet this would not amount to an offer in contract. For the general law is that the contract is formed at the cash desk in circumstances such as these (see page 31) and notices which come to the customer's attention before acceptance may form part of the terms of the contract.

S 12

(2) *Royal Patronage.* The Act prohibits false representations in the course of business or trade, concerning royal patronage or approval or royal awards. Also prohibited are false indications that goods or services supplied are of a kind supplied to any person.

S 14

(3) *Services, accommodation, facilities.* The retailer who knowingly or recklessly makes a false statement about services, accommodation or facilities provided in his trade or business commits an offence if the statement relates to the provision of these, or the time or manner of them, or the person who will provide them, or the examination, approval or evaluation of them by any particular person, or the location or amenities of any accommodation so provided.

A case arose in 1972. A builder named Ben Cohen agreed to build a garage for a customer named Bailey and stated orally that the work would be completed within ten days. In a written estimate he stated it would be like the garage erected by Bailey's neighbour. In fact, the garage was not like Bailey's neighbour's garage, and the work was not completed in ten days. He was charged with recklessly in the course of trade making (a) an oral statement false as to the time a service was provided and (b) making a written statement in an estimate which was false as to the manner in which a service would be provided.

The court held that no offence had in fact been committed. They said that a promise relating to what was to be done in the future could not be false at the time it was made because the promise did not refer to an existing fact. Therefore, it was not possible to say whether the statement was true or false. It was true that the promise amounted to a breach of warranty, but Parliament had never intended that the Act should be used in such circumstances. The offence under the Act was the making of a statement as to what had been done in provision of the service.

The duty of enforcing these provisions also falls on the weights and measures inspectors. But they have other work to do in addition.

WEIGHTS AND MEASURES ACT 1963

Over the years a large amount of legislation both public and local in character, dealing with weights and measures, had arisen for the

102

protection of the consumer. Many of these Acts have now been repealed, in whole or in part, and the Weights and Measures Act 1963 is the main piece of legislation now dealing with the matter.

The Act is set out in Parts. Part I is concerned with units and standards of measurement and Part II deals with weighing and measuring for trade. Equipment used in the distributive trades of types prescribed by the Department of Trade must be passed by an inspector of weights and measures. With some exceptions the equipment must bear a stamp to that effect. The Department can issue certificates of approval for patterns of equipment, and equipment may be marked to show it complies with that pattern.

It is Part IV of the Act, together with Schedules 4 to 8, that gets down to the detailed provisions protecting the consumer against short weight or measure. The general principle in these provisions is that the consumer must be properly informed as to the weight of the goods or the quantity of the goods that are on sale.

The general effect of the provisions is that the goods must be sold by net weight or if they are prepacked the container must not exceed a permitted weight. Moreover, it must be marked with the net weight of the contents. If not, the weight must be made known to the customer in some other way.

There are obvious difficulties in this as far as some goods are concerned. One example is paint, sold by capacity; another would be sand, sold by volume. Fruit and vegetables can hardly be sold under these regulations so these are exceptions, as are goods sold by length such as ribbons and elastic.

On the other hand, the Act lays down specified weights or quantities for some goods—these can be sold only under such rules. Milk must be sold in pints, half pints, quarts and so on (except where it is sold in automatic machines); on licensed premises gin, rum, vodka and whisky can be sold only in specified fractions of a gill as shown by notice on the premises. Other examples of goods to be sold only in specified made-up quantities are cereal breakfast foods, tea, coffee, jam, butter, margarine and dried fruits.

The requirements relating to these, and other goods sold by retail such as meat, fish, poultry, cheese, bread, lard, eggs, sand, solid fuel are to be found in the Schedules to the Act, which also deal with lubricating oil, liquid fuel, fertilisers, perfumes, toilet preparations, soap, ribbons and thread, seeds, nails, cleansing powders, detergents, paints, polishes, cigarettes and stationery.

The Department of Trade can stipulate the way in which prepacked goods are to be marked and what equipment must be made available to customers to weigh goods for themselves. It is an offence under the

Act to sell short weight or a lesser quantity of goods where they are sold by measurement or number.

But what of the retailer who has bought wholesale certain goods which are pre-packed and which he has no opportunity to examine or weigh or count? There is a safeguard open to him, in fact. What he should do is to buy only from a reputable supplier who is prepared to give him a written warranty with the goods. Alternatively, the only defences open to him against a prosecution brought under the Act are to prove that the offence was committed by mistake or accident, or was due to causes beyond his control.

Trading Stamps Act 1964

During the last ten years the practice of issuing trading stamps as a method of attracting custom has grown and become widespread. The proliferation of agencies wishing to set up as suppliers of such incentives made legislative control of the boom imperative and the result was the Act in 1964, which provided that no one should carry on business as the promoter of a trading stamp scheme unless he fell within the definition in the Act of a company or an industrial and provident society. In this way some attempt was made to control the promoters of such schemes.

The schemes themselves were also subjected to legal control. In the first instance the stamps themselves must be clearly marked on the face with a value expressed in coin of the realm. The name of the organisation issuing the stamp must also be so marked. The question of value arises in addition under the provision that promoters or operators of trading stamp schemes must not publish advertisements which are misleading or deceptive or which attempt to convey the value of the stamps by reference to what the holder has to pay in order to obtain them.

The Act also introduced the "cash demand" provision. If the holder of the stamps with an aggregate cash value of not less than 25 pence asks for them to be redeemed the promoter of the scheme must redeem them by paying that aggregate cash value.

More important, perhaps, for the retailer, is the provision of the Act which states that if a shop operates a trading stamp scheme it must keep posted in a place where it can conveniently be read by the customers a notice containing certain information. This information must include a statement of the cash value of the stamps, and the number of trading stamps a customer is entitled to when he makes a purchase or other transaction in the shop. At the same time the shop must keep a copy of a current catalogue where it can conveniently be read or consulted by customers.

The Supply of Goods (Implied Terms) Act 1973 substituted the warranties to be implied on redemption of trading stamps for goods, and the situation is now governed by section 16 of the 1973 Act. The substitution means that a new section 4 applies in the Trading Stamp Act. This section states that there are three implied warranties in every redemption of trading stamps for goods—warranties that cannot be excluded.

(i) An implied warranty on the part of the promoter of the scheme that he has a right to give the goods in exchange;

(ii) an implied warranty that the goods are free from any charge or encumbrance not known or disclosed to the person obtaining the goods before or at the time of redemption, and that he will enjoy quiet possession of the goods except so far as it may be disturbed by the owner or other person entitled to the benefit of any charge or encumbrance disclosed or known;

(iii) an implied warranty that the goods are of merchantable quality. This does not apply where the defects were drawn to the attention of the person obtaining them before redemption, or at the time of redemption, nor does it apply where he examined the goods and did not notice defects he ought to have noticed before or at the time of redemption.

Once again, these terms are similar to those that now apply to contracts for the sale of goods and contracts of hire-purchase.

What of the effect of VAT on trading stamp activities? The tax itself and its incidence is dealt with in more detail in Chapter 9 but it may be noted here that delivery of stamps to retailers and others is not to be regarded as a supply of goods for the purposes of VAT and so no tax is charged upon the stamps themselves when they are delivered to retailers, or given by retailers to their customers. Provision is made for VAT calculations in respect of goods given in exchange for stamps to customers, however.

FOOD AND DRUGS

The law has intervened with positive effect in the sale of food and drugs and drink to ensure that the consumer obtains goods of reasonable quality. Contractual liability can arise, as we have already seen, both under the general law of contract and the law relating to sale of goods. Liability can also arise in tort as may be instanced by the negligence case of *Donoghue v Stevenson*. There are also duties imposed by the criminal law however, and it is these with which we may concern ourselves here.

The Food and Drugs Act 1955 brought together all previous law and established a system where the consumer is protected against inferior food products. It also ensured that the preparation and service of food and its contents was made subject to ministerial control. It did not, of course, affect any contractual or tortious claims that suffering consumers might have against persons selling inferior goods to them.

Thus, under the Act, it is an offence to add a substance to food so as to render it injurious to health if it is done with the intention that the food shall be sold for human consumption in that state. Equally, it is a criminal offence for any person to sell, offer or expose for sale, or have in his possession for those purposes, any food intended for human consumption which is unfit for that consumption. A separate offence is committed with each item of food so offered, sold or exposed.

What is the situation if the food is sold in innocence of its state? In order to be convicted of the offence it is not necessary to show that the retailer knew of the defect in the food. So the butcher who sells meat without knowing its impurity was such as to make it unfit for human consumption cannot deny liability—his ignorance is no excuse. Nor would he escape liability by showing it was all the fault of an employee who allowed the meat to get into the impure state. As long as the employee was acting within the scope of his employment the butcher will be liable—and as we shall see, it will not be enough for him to argue he had expressly forbidden the employee to do the act complained of.

How then can he defend himself? One defence is to show that the purchaser of the meat was given adequate notice that the goods were not fit for human consumption—only fit for dogs, for instance. A second defence the butcher might raise would be that he had showed all due care and diligence to prevent the offence occurring—but this is rather a shaky defence. A better one would be to prove he had bought the meat under a warranty that it was fit for human consumption, that he had no reason to believe otherwise, and that the meat was in the same condition when he sold it as it had been at the time the warranty was given to him. An attempt was made, in *Walker v Baxter's Butchers* (1977) to argue that food could be described as in the "same state" when thawed as when deep frozen. In this case, after the owner of the food shop had kept frozen pastry in deep freeze for eleven days, he thawed it but it was mouldy. The court held that there was no evidence that the freezing and thawing had affected its state so the defence was successful. Finally, if he can show the offence was actually committed by someone else and that he had used all due diligence to prevent it he can ask that that other person be prosecuted. This particular defence also applies to the person whom *he* points out—eventually, the buck will stop on someone's desk!

In a recent case, *Smedleys Ltd v Breed* (1973) the defence raised was that the caterpillar in the can of peas was an occurrence unavoidable in view of modern methods of production, involving 3,500,000 tins in a single season. Convicted of an offence under the Food and Drugs Act 1955, the defendants appealed relying on section 3(3) of the Act which states "in respect of any food ... containing some extraneous matter, it shall be a defence for the defendant to prove that (its) presence was an unavoidable consequence of the process of collection or preparation".

The appeal failed. The Divisional Court held that although the defendants had shown they had taken all reasonable care in preparation of the food the caterpillar's presence was not, nevertheless, an "unavoidable consequence".

The Lord Chief Justice went on to say:

"There was no doubt that one of the reasons why such a high standard of hygiene in food and drugs was maintained in this country was because manufacturers were required to maintain exceedingly high standards in the preparation of goods."

This statement in fact underlines the whole philosophy behind laws of strict liability such as we see in the Food and Drugs Acts. The idea is that by ruling out the defence of reasonable care (which is a good defence in negligence—a civil suit) businessmen are stimulated to take all possible steps to ensure that welfare regulations are carried out. As we have seen above, liability is not *absolute*; there are defences. But it is strict, and the standards imposed are high.

One word of warning. In order to show that food is unfit for human consumption it is not necessary for the prosecution to prove it would be injurious to health. In *Greig v Goldfinch* (1961) the article in question was a pork pie. It contained a mould under the crust when it was sold. Expert evidence was called to state that such a mould would not cause illness. It was held nevertheless that the pie was still unfit for human consumption.

It is also an offence under the Act to sell to the prejudice of the purchaser any food which is not of the nature, substance or quality demanded. In *Preston v Grant* (1925) a licensee was prosecuted for selling whisky at 42 per cent under proof when the law demanded it be only 35 per cent under proof at maximum. The licensee pointed out there was a notice on the bar telling purchasers that spirits were diluted. Was this a good defence? The court said it was not; the licensee could not prove purchasers had read the notice so could not rely on the defence. On the other hand, the display of an appropriate notice on the wrapper or container will normally be regarded as sufficient notice to a purchaser. As for dilution of whisky, the dilution of spirit with water is permissible provided the strength does not fall below 35 per cent proof. In Scotland, they order things differently—whisky diluted below 35 per cent proof can be sold, but cannot be called whisky!

Under section 7 of the Act regulations can be made concerning the labelling of food and descriptions of their ingredients. In proceedings under the Act for false descriptions concerning the use of labels and advertisements, where the intention is to mislead the purchaser as to the nature, quality or substance of the food the court can find the seller guilty even if the label or advertisement contained an accurate statement of its composition. The retailer has a defence if he can show he did not know and could not reasonably have ascertained the false or misleading nature of the label or advertisement.

The Act provides for a Food Hygiene Advisory Council to advise the Ministers on questions relating to the Act.

Food hygiene regulations

The Food Hygiene (General) Regulations 1970 lay down standards of hygiene for all businesses dealing in food. They state that premises must be sanitary and items of equipment which may come into contact with the food must be kept clean and must be so designed as to prevent contamination. Food containers themselves must be kept free from contamination as must the food itself and if food is kept more than eighteen inches above the ground special precautions must be taken to prevent contamination. All persons handling food must remain clean, cover cuts and abrasions and shall make every attempt to keep their clothing clean. Open food must not be wrapped in printed paper and clean wrappers must be used.

The employer must provide clean sanitary facilities close to hand, and must not allow persons with infectious diseases to work near food. An adequate supply of washing equipment must be provided, lighting, heating and ventilation must be adequate in food rooms which must be kept in a good state of repair. No more refuse should be allowed to accumulate nearby than is reasonably necessary and temperature requirements must be observed. Food unfit for human consumption must be kept separate from food which is so fit and open food must be screened from possible contamination while it is exposed for sale or during actual sale or delivery. Those persons who are engaged in the

108

handling of open food must wear "sufficient clean and washable over-clothing".

Inspection

The food and drugs authorities must appoint public analysts who must be independent of trade or business and sampling officers can take or purchase samples of food for analysis by them. This does not mean that other people cannot also use the services of the public analyst; in fact, any member of the public can submit food for analysis if concerned about it after purchase. A right of entry and inspection is provided for under the Act for any duly authorised officer of the council, acting as a food and drug authority, who produces where required a document duly authenticated. This right of entry extends to any premises, vehicle, stall or other place, but not to private premises—in this last case 24 hours' notice of intended entry must be given to the occupier of the private premises.

But let us assume a retailer has fallen foul of the Act, or Regulations made under the Act. What is likely to happen to him? The answer is he can be fined £100, imprisoned for three months, or both. But that is not the end of the tale—for every day the offence continues after discovery he can be fined a further £5 per day. Moreover, in serious cases where the Hygiene Regulations have been broken the local authority can ask the court to disqualify the premises from further use for such trading. Such a ban could be placed on the premises for a maximum of two years. And disobeying such a disqualification order would be a further offence.

TRADING REPRESENTATIONS (DISABLED PERSONS) ACTS

The Act of 1958 was designed to prevent the practice that had grown up of selling goods from door to door by representing they had been made by blind or otherwise disabled persons. It was not as effective as had been hoped and further legislation was brought in by the Act of 1972. The position now is that the sale or exchange of goods or articles represented as made by, or sold or exchanged for the benefit of the blind, or other disabled persons, is illegal. The only exceptions arise in the case of those organisations or individuals specifically exempted from the Act's provisions.

Nor can the Act be evaded by selling over the telephone. But who are the "exempted bodies"? They are local authorities, certain charities, and companies or associations providing facilities for the employment of disabled persons. Any individual who wishes to trade in this way must show that he is substantially disabled and must actually have produced the goods or articles concerned by his own labour. The Secretary of State may, in addition, exempt a non-profit making body.

The penalties for offences under the Act are a fine of up to £400 on summary conviction. Where the conviction is an indictment there may be a fine or up to two years' imprisonment, or both.

Unsolicited Goods and Services Acts 1971 and 1975

Complaints became common by consumers that goods were being sent to them through the post which they had not in fact asked for. They were in some doubt as to their legal liabilities regarding these goods—if they ignored them, were they liable to pay? Did they need to send them back if they were not required? Did they have to take any special care of the goods while in their possession?

The Act was brought in to provide greater protection for consumers against this practice and in this context "unsolicited" means that the goods are sent to a person without any prior request made by him or on his behalf.

Under the Act, a person who receives unsolicited goods (other than a gift to him) can dispose of them as if they were an unconditional gift in the following circumstances:

(i) the goods must have been sent to him with a view to his hiring them, and

(ii) he has no reasonable cause to believe his hiring or acquisition would be in the course of trade or business, and

(iii) he has neither agreed to take them nor return them.

If the sender does not take the goods back during the next six months after the goods are received (and the person receiving them did not unreasonably refuse the sender permission to take them), they can be disposed of. Alternatively, if the recipient of the goods sends a notice to the sender, not less than 30 days before the six months is up, giving him the opportunity to repossess the goods (and does not unreasonably prevent him from doing so) the goods can be disposed of when the 30 days are up.

But let us assume the goods are sent, unsolicited, and the sender demands payment. In such a case he is liable to a fine not exceeding £200. But he is also liable if he simply *asserts* that payment is due—he does not need to *demand* it. And if he threatens to bring legal action or take other steps to force payment he can be fined up to £400. Moreover, an invoice or similar document stating the amount of pay-

110

ment would in itself classify as an *assertion* under the Act.

The Act also deals with other matters such as payment for unsolicited entries in directories and the receipt of unsolicited books on sexual techniques.

The above rules and regulations are statutory in origin and illustrate the part played by the criminal law in the distributive trades. Similarly, the chapters on sale of goods and hire-purchase show the extent to which Parliament has legislated in contractual matters. But there are other areas of responsibility with which the retailer may be concerned—both in crime, and in civil responsibility: the law of tort. In this next chapter therefore we might concern ourselves with the rights, obligations and liabilities arising in the field of tort and look also at some of the more personal crimes with which the businessman may find himself concerned.

Before doing so, however, we may refer back to the Committee on Consumer Protection Report. Among its numerous recommendations it gave priority to the setting up of a Consumer Council, and this was duly done in 1963, only for it to be discontinued in 1971. A new system of control and a new "watchdog" was set up in 1973.

THE FAIR TRADING ACT 1973

The Act ranged beyond the establishment of a system for the protection of consumers such as arose with the Consumer Council for the opportunity was also taken to overhaul the law relating to Restrictive Trading Agreements, monopolies and mergers, and it replaced with revised provisions the Monopolies and Mergers Acts 1948 and 1965.

The Act created a new office, that of Director General of Fair Trading, and provided for the establishment of a Consumer Protection Advisory Committee. On the recommendation of the Director the Secretary of State is empowered to make orders prohibiting or regulating practices concerning consumer transactions which the Advisory Committee have found to have particularly adverse effects upon the economic interests of consumers. The Director is also given power to bring proceedings before the Restrictive Practices Court against persons who persistently maintain a course of conduct unfair to consumers and detrimental to their interests.

What then are the main duties of the Director? His first duty is one of *review*. He is to keep watch on consumer trade practices in order to ascertain whether they adversely affect the economic interests of consumers, and must also act as watchdog over the carrying on of commercial activities that tend towards monopoly situations or uncompetitive practices. His second duty is of *information*. He is under a duty to inform and assist the Secretary of State about these matters and must make recommendations to him for action. His third function is to act himself by making monopoly references within certain limitations, and taking action, if necessary before the Restrictive Practices Court, to curb conduct unfair to consumers.

But what is meant by "consumer trade practices"? The Act defines them as practices carried on in connection with the supply of goods or services to consumers relating to terms and conditions of supply, the manner in which those terms and conditions are communicated to consumers, the promotion of those supplies and the methods by which payment is demanded or secured. "Consumer" relates to the general public and does not cover a person obtaining goods in the course of a business.

The Consumer Protection Advisory Committee can be asked by Ministers or by the Director to report upon particular consumer trade practices adversely affecting the economic interests of consumers, and the Director must assist the Committee and give it any information he has (except information on particular undertakings regarding monopoly situations).

How does all this work in practice?

Let us assume a large wholesale organisation is carrying out a practice which the Director thinks might affect the economic interests of consumers—concerning the labelling of its goods, for instance. He can draw the attention of the Consumer Advisory Committee to this practice and within a limited period the Committee must report on the labelling practice. The Director will then make proposals to deal with the matter to the Secretary of State. He may then make an order prohibiting the practice, and the enforcement of the order will be the duty of the local weights and measures authorities already charged with enforcing the Trade Descriptions Act 1968.

Let us assume further that the wholesale organisation persists in business activities which are detrimental to consumer interests and unfair to customers. This activity may consist of a breach of criminal law (under the Trade Descriptions Act, or the Food and Drugs Act for instance) or it may be a breach of a civil obligation (such as a breach of contract or commission of a tort such as negligence). In such a case the Director will first of all write to the organisation asking for a written assurance that the practice will end. If such an assurance is given but not observed, or if no such assurance is given at all, the Director may institute proceedings before the Restrictive Practices Court. Moreover, the Director also has the power to bring proceedings against the director, manager, secretary or other officer of

112

a limited company in this situation where he has grounds for proceeding against the company itself—so again, there can be no hiding behind the device of incorporation here.

The Director is also empowered to publish information and advice regarding consumer trade practices wherever he regards this as expedient but he will also have regard to the exclusion of matters which might relate to an individual's private affairs where they might be prejudicially affected or to the affairs of a particular body of persons such as a limited company or a partnership where publication might prejudicially affect their interests.

The Director holds office for five years but can be reappointed. The Consumer Protection Advisory Committee consists of between six and fifteen members, appointed by the Secretary of State, and include among their number persons qualified by experience to advise on supply of goods and services, persons to advise on weights and measures enforcement, and persons to advise by virtue of their experience in consumer protection.

PYRAMID SELLING

In recent years distributor or franchise networks have been established in which those who take part have been able to recover their investment by collecting franchise payments from other people who are subsequently introduced; they may also qualify for special terms or privileges according to the number of sub-agents they introduce.

Such schemes were found to depend for their solvency upon a continuing inflow of franchise payments from agents. When such income no longer came in, the schemes collapsed, and the latest entrants found their investments had been lost.

Under Part XI of the Fair Trading Act it is an offence to take or solicit payments from participators in such pyramid selling schemes if they are induced to make the payments by the prospect of benefiting from the recruitment of further participants.

113

CHAPTER 8

Rights, Obligations and Liabilities

When a plaintiff sues a defendant for breach of contract he is suing for a civil injury, as opposed to an injury occurring through a breach of the criminal law.

The suit that is based on a contract will proceed in the main along duties that have been placed upon the parties by the contract itself. Thus, the retailer who agrees to supply goods to a customer has agreed to be placed under an obligation to that customer, and if he fails to fulfil that obligation he may be sued for breach of contract.

Obligations under the civil law exist other than under contracts, however; these obligations are to be found in the law of tort.

THE NATURE OF TORT

A tort can be defined in the words of Sir John Salmond as: "... a civil wrong for which the remedy is a common law action for un-liquidated damages and which is not exclusively the breach of a con-tract or the breach of a trust or other merely equitable obligation". The latter part of this definition need not concern us, but it would be useful to draw the distinction between tort and contract. As we have seen, the duties under a contract are duties that the parties to the con-tract have fixed for themselves. This is not the case in the law of tort.

The law places duties upon the individual within society. Thus, he may speak his mind but he must not slander his neighbour. He may drive his car along the highway but he must not do it carelessly so as to cause injury to others. He may walk where he will, but he must not trespass on another's land. He may use his property in any way he will, provided that use does not amount to a nuisance to others. These—slander, negligence, trespass, nuisance—are all examples of torts. They are duties placed upon the individual and if he breaks these obligations he may be sued by the person injured by his action.

The first point of distinction between contract and tort is, then, that the duties under contract are fixed by the parties but the duties under the law of tort are fixed by the law itself.

A second point of difference lies in the fact that the obligation fixed in contract is towards the other party to the contract—that is to say, towards a specific person or persons. In tort, however, the duty fixed by the law is towards the public in general, not to any specific person, although any individual injured may then sue for breach of the duty.

This does not mean that it is never possible to have a choice of suing in either contract or tort, for in some cases there is concurrent liability. The passenger in a coach has a contract with the owner of the coach, but if he is injured because of the negligent driving of the coach driver he can sue either in contract or tort. In the same way, there might also be criminal liability: the person who drives a car dangerously might be committing a crime as well as a tort.

In this chapter the question of tortious liability will be dealt with in so far as it is likely to touch the person engaged in the retail trade. The more common torts likely to affect the retailer will therefore be discussed, namely, interference with contracts made by other parties, negligence, nuisance, defamation, passing off, the use of trade names and false imprisonment. The law relating to the liability of the occupier of dangerous premises will also be considered.

INTERFERENCE WITH CONTRACTS

The position here is that where two parties have entered upon a valid and enforceable contract, the third party who interferes so as to cause the contract to be broken by one of the parties will be liable to the innocent party who suffers from the breach. In order to make the third party who interferes liable, it must be shown that he knew, or should have known, not only of the existence of the contract itself but also of the particular term that was broken.

It is necessary here to discuss what is meant by the term "interference". It can, for instance, amount to direct persuasion to bring about the breach of contract. If, for example, a wholesaler agrees to supply goods to a retailer but is persuaded to sell these goods to another retailer who wants to prevent his rival from carrying on his business, the first retailer may sue the wholesaler for breach of contract but he may also sue the second retailer for interfering with the performance of that contract by persuading the wholesaler to break his agreement.

It is obvious that interference will arise where physical violence is used to break the contract—such as the seizing of the goods from the seller before he can take them to the buyer—but basically any dealing which is "inconsistent with the contract" can amount to an "actionable interference". For instance, in *British Motor Trade Assocn v Salvadori* (1949) X agreed not to re-sell BMTA cars except under certain conditions. S bought some cars from X to re-sell at a profit; the sale was in breach of X's agreement with the BMTA. It was held that S had offered a high price to X to induce him to break the contract, so S was liable to BMTA. It will be necessary in these circumstances to show that it was the act of the interfering party which brought about the breach, however; the party suffering from the breach will not succeed if it is shown that the "interferer" was simply taking advantage of a decision by the other contracting party not to carry out the contract. Thus, if Mr Acker decides out of his own head to break his contract with Mr Whacker and sell the goods to Mr Bilk, Mr Whacker cannot sue Mr Bilk for interference with the contract. But if Mr Acker decides to break his contract only *after* he has had a conversation with Mr Bilk, who agrees to take the goods, Mr Whacker may well be able to sue Mr Bilk.

It should be noted that general instructions issued in the course of a trade dispute, such as "Place Mr Egg on the stoplist" or "Refuse to handle Mr Egg's goods" will not amount to interference with Mr Egg's contractual relations where knowledge of the particular contract is not proved. For the Trade Disputes Act 1906 states that "an act done by a person in furtherance of a trade dispute shall not be actionable on the ground only . . . that it is an interference with the trade, business or employment of some other person".

Of recent years the protection given by the Act has been called in question. The situation basically is this. If a union wanted to blacklist one trader they could either persuade his supplier to stop supplying him, or instruct the trader's employees to stop working for him. If they know the supplier is contractually bound to supply the trader their first action would be unlawful; the second would not, unless it could be interpreted as a "stop notice", communicated directly to the supplier, and thus amounting to a *direct* and therefore unlawful inducement.

In this context it is useful to deal with the tort of conspiracy also. Where two or more persons act together in combination in order to damage the plaintiff's trade, business or other interests they commit the tort of conspiracy. This assumes, that the plaintiff can show that he has suffered loss by their action in this way, or by their agreement to so act.

Thus, if several traders together form an organisation to prevent another trader competing within their area, this might well amount to the tort of conspiracy. But it will be a good defence on the part of the combination to show that their main purpose in setting up the organisation was to protect their own legitimate business interests. They will be liable, on the other hand, if they are not acting to protect their business interests, but simply in order to cause the plaintiff loss. The amount of loss he suffers, therefore, is quite irrelevant if the organisation shows that its predominant purpose was to protect its own business interests—even if the plaintiff has been driven out of business he will have no remedy against the combination.

The classic case on this matter is *Crofter Hand Woven Harris Tweed Co v Veitch* (1942). V instructed the dockers not to handle C's yarn or to export the cloth made from it and the dockers acted on these instructions. V was acting in combination with certain mill owners. It was held that C had no remedy since the predominant purpose of the combination was the legitimate interests of the persons combining, V to obtain 100 per cent union membership and the mill owners to eliminate competition.

NEGLIGENCE

The Unfair Contract Terms Act 1977 prevents anyone by contract restricting his liability for death or personal injury arising from his negligence. In respect of other loss or damage he *can* so restrict his liability, but only to the extent that the restriction is reasonable. Nor can a person's agreement to such a term be taken to indicate voluntary acceptance of risk. This statutory interference with contractual "freedom" has no effect on the general principles of liability that arise in tort, however, and in respect to the tort of negligence in particular.

The tort of negligence involves a duty placed upon the individual—the duty of care. The mere fact of carelessness that results in injury to the plaintiff is not enough to cause liability to arise of course; there must have been carelessness in respect of a specific duty to take care. Since 1932 however the scope of the duty of care has been expanded enormously and the basis of its expansion might well be regarded in the words of Lord Atkin: "You must take reasonable care to avoid acts or omissions which you can reasonably foresee would be likely to injure your neighbour. Who then, in law is my neighbour? The answer seems to be—persons who are so closely and directly affected by my act that I ought reasonably to have them in contemplation as being so affected when I am directing my mind to the acts or omissions which are called in question."

The law also draws a distinction between negligent *words* and negligent *acts*. Before 1963 there was no liability for loss arising out of careless misstatements but now if A is "injured" by statements made by B, and B ought reasonably to have had A in contemplation as being one who might suffer harm if the words proved negligent, A can sue B. Even so, A can disclaim responsibility. Suppose a wholesaler desires to begin trade with a new firm and wants to learn of its creditworthiness. The wholesaler asks his banker, who carries out enquiries and tells the wholesaler that the new firm is financially sound. In reliance on this statement the wholesaler supplies goods to the firm only to discover, later, it cannot pay for them. Is the banker who made the careless misstatement liable to the wholesaler? It depends upon whether he disclaimed such liability as in a 1963 case where he wrote on the statement "without responsibility"—he was there held not liable. A pharmacist misdescribing a drug, on the other hand, would be unlikely to resort to such a disclaimer! It should be emphasised also that the loss here was financial and the courts have said they treat such loss differently from damage to person or property. In the case of negligent words, the economic or financial loss can be sued for. But in the case of negligent *acts*, if the only foreseeable loss would have been financial, it cannot be recovered. This does not mean that the law does not recognise a man's financial position can be affected by the deeds of another. It is simply that specific actions by businessmen one against the other can be dealt with under other particular torts. Conspiracy, as we have seen, is one. Passing off, and injurious falsehood are others.

With respect to negligent deeds, the relation of negligence to the retailer can be discussed mainly in the light of liability for dangerous chattels. Before 1932 there was little authority to the effect that the person who supplied goods would be liable for defects in the goods which he should have discovered. In that year the law finally recognised that the consumer needed protection on this point, particularly in view of the fact that mass production and new methods of marketing had meant that it was exceedingly difficult for the consumer to show that anyone possessed knowledge of the defect. Nor could the consumer sue the manufacturer of the goods in contract, because there was no contractual relationship between him and the manufacturer where the consumer had bought the goods from a retailer.

In 1932 the doctrine of the duty to one's neighbour was expounded by Lord Atkin, who then went on to say: "... a manufacturer of products, which he sells in such a form as to show that he intends them to reach the ultimate consumer in the form in which they left him ... owes a duty to the consumer to take ... reasonable care."

This was stated in *Donoghue v Stevenson*. The facts of the case have already been given on page 68.

Since that time therefore there has been liability for defective goods as well as those which are "dangerous in themselves" such as loaded

118

guns, gas, or explosive mixtures; products such as gravestones, drinking water, chisels, food, hair-dye, underwear, motor cars, sweets and buns, are also covered.

In *Clarke v Army and Navy Co-operative Society* (1903) it was disinfectant powder. A sold disinfectant powder which he knew was likely to injure anyone opening the tin. He did not warn the buyer of this. C bought a tin, opened it, and was injured. The court said A was liable in negligence.

The duty probably extends to free samples provided by the manufacturer even though there is no contract of sale between retailer and consumer, but before liability will lie against the manufacturer it must be shown that the consumer used the article exactly as it left the maker and used it for the purposes for which it was intended to be used Thus, if a shopkeeper was in the habit of taking a sweet for himself when serving customers and was injured by a piece of metal in the sweet cutting his tongue he could sue the manufacturer. He bought the sweet for resale, but he was still using it as it was intended to be used. If, on the other hand, an opportunity is given for an intermediate examination by some other person, there will be no liability on the part of the manufacturer.

The practical effect of this is that if the manufacturer sends to the retailer a child's toy which is dangerous because of some defect in its construction, the manufacturer will be liable for any injuries caused when the child to whom the toy is sold uses the toy and is hurt. But if the defect is one which the retailer should have discovered for himself but has not done so, then it is the retailer who will find himself being sued on the ground that he has put into circulation an article which is dangerous. If, on the other hand, inspection of the article so as to discover the defect is impossible—where, for instance, the retailer sells a tin of corned beef which contains half a set of uncleaned false teeth, it is quite obvious that there has been no opportunity for intermediate inspection by the retailer, and the manufacturer will be liable for putting such goods on the market. The defect may not necessarily be in the goods themselves, of course, it may well be a defect in the design of the child's toy, or in the container itself.

Nor is it necessary that the defect should be visible. A shirt that contains invisible chemicals which cause the wearer to contract dermatitis will give rise to an action against the manufacturer by the unfortunate wearer of the shirt—there will have been no opportunity here for "intermediate examination". It might well be that the wearer will not know who is liable for the negligent act. Take the case of a bottle of mineral water which is 50 per cent carbolic acid. Who put the acid in the bottle? Was it the manufacturer, or the bottler? Or was it the carrier of the goods? Or could it have been the retailer?

The point is that the consumer need not lay his finger on the precise person who put the carbolic acid in the mineral water. Nor need he specify what the negligent act was. He is called upon to sue the person who, on the balance of possibility, was responsible for the presence of the carbolic acid. In most cases it will be the manufacturer. But it could conceivably be the retailer.

It should be pointed out, finally, that if the consumer knows of the defect in the goods when he buys them he cannot thereafter complain of the manufacturer's negligence in supplying such goods to the market. In these circumstances the manufacturer owes no duty of care to the consumer.

NUISANCE

To a certain extent the torts of Nuisance and Negligence overlap, but, as we have seen, the emphasis in the tort of Negligence is on the conduct of the person liable. In Nuisance, on the other hand, the emphasis is on the interest which has been "invaded".

Basically, the tort of Nuisance is concerned with the invasion of interests in land. Thus, any person whose enjoyment of the use of his land is interfered with by his neighbour's use of water or fire, smoke or smell, heat, electricity, gas, fumes, disease, noise or even vibrations may find his remedy in an action in nuisance.

In fact there are two kinds of nuisance—public and private. A public nuisance covers such matters as the sale of impure food or the obstruction of the highway: these actions affect the public in general and the individual can sue only if he has received some special injury to himself from the action. Private nuisance is the interference with the enjoyment of land.

To be able to sue, the plaintiff must show that his property has suffered some material injury if he relies on physical injury to found his action. But the injury need not be a physical one suffered by the land, or the house or other property.

Thus, the shopkeeper who sells wet fish will be able to sue if smells emanating from nearby premises produce "sensible personal discomfort" and also damage his business in that customers are driven away and the fish turns green. In the same way, the proprietor of a cafe will be able to sue when the noise from the defendant's premises causes customers to desert the cafe. In *Pwllbach Colliery Co Ltd v Woodman* (1915) the lessor allowed the lessee to carry on the business of coal mining. The lessee, without negligence, caused coal dust to settle on the lessor's slaughter house and the meat and sausages contained

120

there. It was held that the nuisance was not authorised by the lease, and was not a necessary result of the carrying on of the trade, so the lessee was liable to the lessor. But in all these cases the court will consider the locality of the business, for the cafe owner who sets up in business next door to a factory in a region of factories might well be in no position to complain. The court may well state that the plaintiff must take the area, and the premises too for that matter, as he finds them. This, however, can work both ways as is illustrated by *Sturges v Bridgman* (1879). S set up a medical consulting room at the end of his garden. The area was one predominantly occupied by the medical profession. B had carried on a confectionery business next door for the past 20 years. S sued for the nuisance created by the noise from the confectionery. The court said B could not rely on his long use of the property, for the nuisance began only when S complained, nor was S's use of the property unreasonable in that area. B was liable to S.

In all cases a substantial interference will have to be shown, and the plaintiff may well be faced with the defence that his goods are abnormally sensitive. For if the tradesman carries on a delicate trade and the nuisance complained of would not, in any other circumstances, be regarded as an actionable nuisance, he will have no remedy. The delicate goods in *Robinson v Kilvert* (1889) were brown paper. The heat generated by Kilvert on his premises was so great that it damaged the paper used by Robinson in his business, located above Kilvert's premises. *Since the heat would not have interfered with the ordinary business use of the premises*, Robinson could not succeed. The loss had been due to the delicate nature of the goods. If, on the other hand, the nuisance is proved to exist, damages may then be claimed for any delicate goods destroyed. This was the case in *McKinnon Industries Ltd v Walker* (1951) where an orchid grower was able to show that a nuisance had been committed in respect of his property. Once it was shown that a substantial interference had been committed the fact that the orchids were hyper-sensitive was irrelevant. Damage in respect of the sensitive plants as well as other loss could be claimed for.

Assume, for instance, that Mr Petal owns a nursery in which he grows extremely delicate hothouse plants. Next door, Mr Hardcrete's activities causes Petal's expensive hothouse plants to expire from nervous exhaustion. Can Petal sue Hardcrete? The answer will depend upon the circumstances. If the noise and vibrations are not excessive—that is to say, the only damage they could possibly cause would be to expensive hothouse plants of a nervous disposition, Petal cannot sue Hardcrete. But if the noise and vibrations are proved to "sensibly interfere" with Petal's enjoyment of his land then Petal will be able to sue not only on general grounds but also for the damage done to his precious hothouse plants.

Provided the interference is substantial it need not be of any great duration—merely temporary interference can still be sued upon. It may also arise where the defendant has caused a state of affairs to arise, the result of which is that nuisance is caused to the plaintiff. Thus, the shopkeeper who allows his customers or his assistants to throw down wrapping paper on his premises in such a way that a drain is blocked, causing the flooding of the premises next door, will be liable to the party next door in the same way that the shopkeeper's successor who does not trouble to clear the drain will be liable also. The moral of *Sedleigh Denfield v O'Callaghan* (1940) is therefore clear. O allowed a blocked culvert on his property to remain blocked. As a result the adjoining land, owned by S, was flooded. O had created a state of things from which flooding might be expected to result so he was liable in nuisance. If you don't clear up the cause of the nuisance, it's no defence to say it was created by your predecessor. By doing nothing about it you make yourself liable.

While, generally speaking, malice—that is to say the malicious purpose behind the actions of the persons committing the tort—is irrelevant in the law of tort, as far as nuisance is concerned the main purpose of the defendant's activity is taken into account, and malice might well render a normally innocent act an actionable nuisance. In *Hollywood Silver Fox Farm Ltd v Emmett* (1936) the court was told that silver foxes were particularly sensitive animals, and more so during the breeding season. So Emmett, who held a grudge against the farm owners, couldn't claim he had no liability when he fired guns on land adjoining the farm at the particular time when the silver foxes were at their most "sensitive". His malice in so acting made his deeds amount to a nuisance, and the farm owners sued him successfully.

The plaintiff can sue only if he has an interest in the land affected. If the shopkeeper's premises are taken on a lease it is the lessee who will normally sue in respect of the nuisance; the landlord will be able to sue only where the nuisance affects the value of the premises and constitutes an injury to his interest (called his reversion).

DEFAMATION

Defamation takes two forms: libel and slander. A libel is a defamatory statement which is made in a permanent form, such as in a book, newspaper or letter or in a cinema film. A similar statement made in a transient form such as speech is slander. There are other points of difference between the two forms: slander is a tort only, but libel can be criminal as well as tortious. Nor need any special damage be proved in the case of libel (it is said to be actionable "per se") whereas, subject to certain exceptions, a slander can be sued on only if there is proof of actual damage.

The exceptions where slander also is actionable "per se" are slanders imputing that the plaintiff has committed a crime, or is afflicted with a contagious disease of a particular kind, or is an unchaste woman. Of more importance to the retailer is the exception that states that any slander "calculated to disparage the plaintiff in any office, profession, calling, trade or business held or carried on by him at the time of the publication (of the slander)" will be actionable without proof of special damage being necessary. Thus, the shopkeeper who is called corrupt or dishonest can sue under section 2 of the Defamation Act 1952.

But what is a defamatory statement generally? Once again, Lord Atkin might be referred to. "Would the words tend to lower the plaintiff in the estimation of right-thinking members of society generally?" While this test does not cover all possibilities and permutations it does nevertheless serve as a working basis from which to proceed.

The difficulty is that in the case of the tradesman criticism of his products or of his service is often necessary. The retailer who deals in shoddy products should be criticised for the sake of the business as a whole. But the law of defamation gives the trader who deals in shoddy goods an undeserved protection so that it is dangerous to criticise him or his goods by name (although the defences of justification and fair comment are available and may apply). One method of carrying out such criticism without liability has been developed by using the device of club membership for readers; when a magazine criticising products is sold only to members of a club it is privileged from liability and can criticise freely.

In any case, it should be pointed out that criticism of the goods alone is not defamatory; liability arises only when the trader himself is attacked. To say that a bottle of sauce sold by a shopkeeper who makes the sauce himself is bad is not necessarily defamatory, but to say that all the sauce made by that trader is bad may well be defamatory. To say that a trader is incompetent will give rise to liability; to say that he is dishonest is similarly defamatory. But if the words used are merely insulting, or degrading, vulgar abuse, this will not amount to defamation and no liability will follow.

It is not always the case that the statement is obviously defamatory in nature; it may well be that on the face of it the statement is a perfectly innocent one. In such circumstances, it will be the responsibility of the plaintiff to show that the statement amounts to an *in-*

123

nuendo—that is to say, the statement may be interpreted in such a way as to amount to a defamatory remark. An example arose in *Tolley v Fry and Sons Ltd* (1931). F published an advertisement for their chocolate depicting T, an amateur golfer of some fame. T sued in defamation claiming that the advertisement constituted an innuendo that he had been paid for the advertisement, therefore prostituting his amateur status. The court said the advertisement was defamatory, and Tolley was entitled to damages. If the words themselves are defamatory there is no innuendo; it is only where the surrounding circumstances are such that they provide a defamatory meaning for an apparently innocent remark that the innuendo will be pleaded. As an example one might quote the instance of a man erecting a tombstone over the grave of his mistress—"To the memory of my dear wife". His real wife could then sue him on the innuendo that she is defamed as being an immoral woman having lived with him without being married to him.

There may be liability for a defamatory statement even though the defendant did not in fact make it himself. This will be the case where the defendant has disseminated the statement, as will occur in the instance of the bookseller or newsvendor. The defendant will be liable in such circumstances only if he knew or should have known that the statement in the book, etc., was defamatory. If the dissemination was made innocently he will not be liable. This is what happened in *Bottomley v Woolworth & Co* (1932). Woolworth imported publisher's "remainders" of American detective stories. The stories contained defamatory material. It was held the dissemination was innocent and W need not read the stories before disseminating them to discover whether or not they contained defamatory statements. So W was not liable to B. In any case, however, a defendant would be well advised to take advantage of section 4 of the Defamation Act 1952 which states that he may in certain circumstances avoid liability by publishing a suitable correction and a suitable apology to the person aggrieved by the statement.

Other defences available to an action in defamation are to plead consent of the party defamed, truth of the statement made, or to show that the comment is privileged. Finally it may be pleaded that the statement was a fair comment on a matter of public importance.

It may be added that the major problem in defamation cases is deciding exactly what is meant by the defamatory statement, particularly if the defence of truth is used. In 1964 the House of Lords held that a statement in *The Daily Telegraph* to the effect that the Fraud Squad were investigating the affairs of a man called Lewis could not mean Lewis was therefore guilty of fraud. All the newspaper had to prove, when sued, was that the Fraud Squad had in fact carried out the investigation, not that he was guilty of fraud. Even so, many people could have reached in their own minds the inference that there was "no smoke without fire" but Lewis nevertheless failed in his suit.

TORTS AFFECTING BUSINESS INTERESTS

Unlawful means may be used against a trader which are not in themselves actionable as torts but the *use* of such unlawful means in itself will be regarded as tortious. Thus, if a trader suffers severe losses on account of the fraudulent behaviour of the other party an action will lie for damages.

Similarly, wrongful conduct amounting to intimidation of a trader's customers to prevent them dealing with the trader will be an actionable tort. But if the wrongful act consists of the breaking of a duty laid down by statute the trader who is affected by such breach cannot sue. Thus, if heavy import duties are placed on certain goods coming into this country and the trader finds that his rival takes away much of his trade by selling such goods more cheaply—which he is able to do since he has evaded duty on them—the trader cannot sue his rival for breach of statutory duty. A case in point arose in 1941. The Ever Ready Company imported goods into this country even though by statute the company was called upon to make no such import without disclosing the country of origin. The London Armoury Company was in competition as a rival importer; they claimed that Ever Ready had not made the necessary declaration and then sued Ever Ready for breach of this statutory duty. The court denied that Ever Ready were in any way liable to London Armoury for this breach.

Threats made against a trader are not in themselves likely to give rise to a successful action in tort. Only if the threat itself is illegal will liability follow. Thus, a threat to put a trader on a stop list if he does not conform to certain conditions will not be tortious. In the main, it would seem, there must be an element of criminality in the threat to make the person who makes the threat liable in tort. But threats of this nature, even against third parties, will result in a successful action.

It should also be noted that some occupations carry particular obligations. While it is true to say that the principle of freedom of contract exists in the business world as far as a tradesman's decision whether he should deal with a particular person or not is concerned, some occupations demand that the trader have no choice. This is the situation where the trader exercises a common calling such as an innkeeper or carrier. He has a duty to provide his services to the public. If he refuses unreasonably to do so he will be liable to that member of

125

the public. Thus, when Learie Constantine the coloured cricketer and later diplomat was turned away from a hotel (which classified as an inn) he sued on the ground that the hotel had refused to provide services available. The hotel was liable to him in damages. That was in 1944. Nowadays, of course, in similar circumstances the provisions of the Race Relations Act (see p. 47) would be invoked.

INJURIOUS FALSEHOOD

This tort is sometimes known by the title of "slander of goods". It amounts to the disparagement of the quality of goods owned by the plaintiff, or it calls his right to own the goods into question. Indeed, the tort can now be sued upon wherever any damaging lies about a business are published, whether it be in relation to trade name or company shares, patents, copyright or trade marks. Thus, if one trader, to damage his rival, inserts in the local paper a statement that his rival has ceased to carry on business, he can be sued. Even a false statement that the plaintiff's wife, who helped the plaintiff in his drapery business, had been guilty of adultery with the newly appointed parson has been held to be tortious as affecting the business interest of the plaintiff!

The statement must be false, however, it must be published to persons other than the plaintiff and an improper motive or intention to injure on the part of the defendant must also be shown. And, of course, the statement must be a disparaging one. The threat to take proceedings for an infringement of a trade mark or patent can be a disparaging remark where the infringement has not occurred. On the other hand the law takes into account the fact that in the business world advertising is of great importance and if the statement is in the form of an advertisement to the effect that one product is better than another, either generally or in particular respects, no action will lie. The court is not prepared to judge the respective merits of the rival goods and thus provide one of them with a valuable slice of free advertising!

To advertise is one thing, but to make untrue statements, knowing that they are untrue, imputing to the rival sharp practices or inferior methods of workmanship—this would be actionable. Let us take two examples. Suppose a wholesaler buys from a manufacturer some tins of soup made by that manufacturer. He then places labels on those tins which state that his own, rival product was better than any other. If the manufacturer sued he would not succeed because the truth of such a statement is impossible to prove. What is meant by "better"? The statement is really nothing more than advertising "puff": this is

126

not a disparagement and no action for injurious falsehood would stand.

But if, on the other hand, the wholesaler wrote to retail outlets saying that the manufacturer used methods of canning which were inadequate or dangerous and his own methods were better then an action could well lie, if it could be shown that the wholesaler knew the statement was in fact untrue.

It is up to the plaintiff to show that he has suffered some financial loss by reason of the false statement and in some cases this can be done simply by showing a general falling off of custom since the statement was made. The position was in any case affected by the Defamation Act 1952 which stated that special damage need not be proved if the false statement was calculated to cause damage to the plaintiff or to his business, trade or calling.

PASSING OFF

The position has been well stated by Lord Kingsdown: "The fundamental rule is, that one man has no right to put off his goods for sale as the goods of a rival trader . . ." The tort will be committed therefore where one businessman competing within a certain area with a rival businessman represents his goods or services to be those of his rival, in order to deceive the public into thinking that the goods or services are those of his rival.

This will be the case where one trader has built up for his goods a reputation which the rival trader wishes to take advantage of, to the honest trader's detriment. There are several methods by which this tort may be committed.

It may be done in a completely bald-faced manner where one trader sells his goods with a statement that the goods he sells are in fact the plaintiff's goods.

On the other hand it may be that the traders concerned have similar names. If the plaintiff can show that the defendant is engaging in the same line of business and using the similar name in an attempt to pass off his goods as the plaintiff's, he will be able to sue. But he must show evidence of such dishonest purpose where the rival trader is dealing under his own name—or even a name he has recently assumed—for there is generally no right to restrict other people from using names of their choice. Any confusing use of a name for his goods, however, may be evidence of such dishonest purpose, and in some circumstances his good faith will be no defence.

Yet another way in which the passing off might occur is where the rival uses a trade name developed and used by the plaintiff. This does not mean that the person who originally coins a name for a product can later prevent others from describing their product in the same way: if the name simply describes the goods or their nature as is the case with "shredded wheat", "cellular textiles", "nourishing stout", "gripe water" or "vacuum cleaner", other traders cannot be prevented from using such names. But if the name of the product has acquired a special meaning, such as "Yorkshire Relish", the rival trader will commit the tort of passing off if he uses the same name to advertise his product. In *Reddaway v Banham* (1896) B advertised his goods for sale as "camel-hair belting". R claimed that the term had by long and exclusive association with his manufacture come to mean not belting made from camel hair, but belting made by R. The court decided that the term had become a trade name and B could be restrained from using it. But in these cases the burden of showing that the name has acquired a special meaning lies at the door of the plaintiff—though the task will be rendered much easier if the name refers to the place where the original maker manufactured the goods—such as "Chartreuse liqueurs" or "Glenfield Starch". It is always best for the trader who introduces a new product to describe it in a flamboyant, fanciful way, therefore, for he will find it easier to convince the courts that such a name should be applied to his product only!

The tort of passing off will be committed where the plaintiff's trade mark, i.e. a design, picture or other description affixed to his product to identify the goods with him, is used by the defendant. Again, an action for passing off will lie where one trader imitates the appearance of another trader's goods—where, for instance, a baker wraps his loaves in a blue and white waxed paper in an attempt to deceive the public into thinking that they are buying a popular, well advertised loaf made by another bakery firm. This will particularly be the case where the paper carries a name also, which is not dissimilar to the name used by the plaintiff firm.

In the same way if the baker sells loaves which are in fact provided by the rival firm but sells them as the rival's normal produce whereas they are really of a quality inferior to that sold by the rival firm, he will be liable in an action of passing off. It was on this basis that the Gillette Safety Razor Company successfully sued a man called Franks in 1924. He had obtained some used Gillette razor blades and was selling them as "genuine Gillette blades". The company obtained an injunction to prevent him continuing this practice. Thus, a seller who advertises a used product as "the genuine thing" and thereby misleads the public into thinking that he is selling the normal new and current product of the plaintiff can be restrained from doing so by an action for passing off.

One other occasion when the conduct may amount to passing off is worthy of attention. Generally speaking, false advertising alone does not amount to passing off. But if the defendant deliberately creates a market for himself by copying the plaintiff's descriptive matter, such as, for instance, a trade catalogue, in such a way as to induce the public to believe that the goods offered by the defendant are the goods of the plaintiff, the tort of passing off will have been committed. In a case in 1924 E copied the catalogue put out by M in such a way as to induce the general public to believe that the goods offered by E were in fact goods produced by M. E's goods were of inferior quality compared with M's. E's action amounted to passing off.

It should be emphasised that the representation made by the defendant must be calculated to deceive and there must be a business activity in which the plaintiff and defendant are competitors. There was no such common business activity in *McCulloch v May* (1947). Mc was a well-known broadcaster of Children's programmes and was known as Uncle Mac. The defendants made a cereal, "Uncle Mac's Puffed Wheat". Mc sued for an injunction. The court decided his action must fail since the parties were not business rivals and had no common trading activities. Similarly, though Granada Television had made a name for itself in the field of entertainment the court refused in 1972 to prevent the Ford Motor Company from marketing one of its cars as a "Ford Granada". If the tort is proved, however, the plaintiff may ask the court for an injunction to restrain the defendant from such conduct. The other remedy available to him is to sue for damages for the loss of customers, of business reputation and loss of goodwill.

How quickly can a new business, set up without any special advertising campaign, obtain goodwill of a kind that is entitled to protection? In *Stannard v Reay* (1967) S sold fish and chips from a van on the Isle of Wight under the name "Mr Chippy". A few weeks later, R, who had earlier refused to go into partnership with S, went into business using the same name. The judge agreed he should be prevented from using the name "Mr Chippy".

The Crazy Horse Saloon in Paris, on the other hand, was a night club, whose owner objected to an advertising campaign in Britain which stated "Crazy Horse Saloon comes to London" and related to a new place of entertainment near Baker Street Station. Was this a case of passing off? The judge held it was not because a passing off action can be maintained only by a person who uses a name in connection with trade carried on in. this country. The Paris Crazy Horse Saloon had been advertised in Britain but its owner was not in *business* in this country.

Finally, it should be noted that a remedy will be available even though the requirements of the tort of passing off are not completely fulfilled. If the conduct of the defendant is such that he gets the benefit of someone else's goodwill and reputation the court will sometimes allow damages to be claimed against him even though he is not, strictly speaking, a business competitor. In such a case actual damage must be proved by the plaintiff.

The rules laid down by the courts in relation to unfair competition, and the tortious actions we have been discussing here illustrate that in England there is no general rule of law forbidding unfair competition; rather, the law has been built up in a number of directions to prevent unfair competition on a kind of *ad hoc* basis. Closely related to the tort of passing off, however, is the law relating to trade marks for where there is full registration of a trade mark imitative products will often fall foul of the trade mark registration. In fact, most actions lie for passing off rather than infringement of trade marks—sometimes because there are flaws in the registration or because the mark does not really cover the situation. An example arose in the Pullman case of 1919. The defendant called his house by the same name as the plaintiff's factory, then used the similarity to mislead the plaintiff's customers into writing to him. This could not be covered by trade mark registration, but a passing off action could be brought, successfully. It is convenient therefore to follow the discussion of passing off actions with a study of trade marks.

TRADE MARKS

The registration of any person as proprietor of a trade mark in respect of goods gives him the exclusive right to use that mark in relation to those goods. An infringement of a trade mark arises where the mark or some other mark so closely resembling it as to be misleading, is placed on someone else's goods. Thus, "Pem Books" was held to infringe "Pan Books". "Gala" cosmetics, on the other hand, was held not to infringe "Goya". The court in the latter case took account of the fact that both cosmetics had been dealing at the same time whereas "Pem" was a new mark and "Pan" was long established. But the court will also consider the basic idea behind the mark. "Watermatic" toy pistols was held to infringe "Aquamatic" because the idea was the same though the sound of the names was different.

In order to constitute an infringement the mark must be used in the course of trade and must be written or printed. The owner of a trade mark is also able in some circumstances to prevent purchasers of his protected goods from altering the packaging or lettering of the goods, as he may prevent them from using the mark where the condition of the goods has changed.

There are some general exceptions to the rules regarding trade marks, however: accessories and spares can be sold by reference to trade marks used on goods for which they are accessories or spares, where this is reasonably necessary—lenses for particular cameras, for instance. Again, the use by a trader of his own name for business purposes cannot be an infringement of someone else's trade mark. Nor can a trade mark be infringed by an honest description of goods and registration of a trade mark cannot prevent someone who was using the name before registration from continuing to use it, unless the registered owner used it first.

How is a trade mark registered?

First of all the mark must indicate a connection in the course of business between the owner of the mark and the goods. Secondly, the mark must be distinctive—in *Yorkshire Copper Works' Application* (1954) the applicants stated that "Yorkshire" meant their pipe fittings to 100 per cent of the trade but registration was refused, as was "Electrix" for vacuum cleaners because it sounded too much like "Electrics".

The application for registration must be made to the Registrar of Trade Marks at the Patent Office. Goods are divided into thirty-four classes for trade mark purposes and goods are registered sometimes for a selection of goods in one class by the person, firm or company actually using or intending to use the trade mark. Joint applications are sometimes made if the applicants both have a trade connection with the goods but an application by someone not intending to use the mark will be invalid. Anyone can oppose an application, and this is usually done if the new mark is too similar to a mark already used or registered. In 1927 "Nuvol" was successfully opposed by the owners of "Nupol", but "Hovis" were not successful in their opposition to "Ovax" in 1946.

In some cases a mark is registered even though confusion is possible. In *Bass v Nicholson* (1932) an application was made to register a mark including a triangle for bitter beer; Bass opposed it because they already used the Red Triangle mark on their bottled beer. The Registrar allowed the new mark, but only for a white triangle; the House of Lords agreed, but limited the mark further by excluding bottled beer from it. The fact remains, the consumer could well end up somewhat confused!

At any time within seven years of application for registration a trade mark can be removed on the ground it should not have been registered in the first place. Where a mark has been registered in Part A of the register (registration in Part B is easier to get but does not give as good protection as Part A) for seven years the question as to whether it should have been registered at all can be reopened only if registration was obtained by fraud, or if the mark was illegal, immoral, improper or scandalous, or if its registration is likely to confuse or mislead the public.

Once trade marks are registered they need to be kept valid and problems can arise in this respect where there is a change in the way in which the mark is used, or there is a change in ownership, or split ownership occurs. The Registrar will normally give directions in such cases.

Sometimes, a trade mark is licensed—that is, the owner allows a trader to use his mark and gets paid for the privilege. The safest practice in such matters is to apply to the Registrar and show him the arrangement arrived at.

Some registered trade marks become synonymous with the articles themselves—typical examples are "Thermos" and "Yale": vacuum flasks are commonly called thermos flasks and Yale locks may not have been actually made by Yale at all. This raises legal difficulties but if there is a well known and established use, as in these cases mentioned, by the trade as well as the public, registration of the mark would be invalid unless the use of the mark is confined to goods of the owner of the mark. This emphasises the fact that if the owner of a registered trade mark allows a mark like it to be used by the trade as a whole it will probably become descriptive or misleading, and so invalid.

Where a trade mark has been left unused for five years it can be removed from the register unless the owner can show he has been prevented from using it by special circumstances in the trade as a whole. And if a mark has been used over five years for some only of the goods covered by the registration an application can be made to limit the registration by excluding goods on which the mark has not been used. Thus, Columbia pictures applied for such a limiting registration in respect of Columbia records—the latter firm had a mark covering a large variety of goods but used it only for gramophone records.

Although applied for in the same way as trade marks and registered in Part A these are not really trade marks: they simply indicate that the owner has certified the goods as reaching certain standards. An example is "hand-woven" Harris tweed; another is provided by BSI "kite marks".

DECEIT

Deceit appeared as a separate tort in 1789 and has been defined as

132

"a false representation made by the defendant knowingly, or without belief in its truth or recklessly, careless whether it be true or false . . ." There must be an intention that the plaintiff should act upon the statement and the plaintiff must have suffered damage as a result. For instance, assume a customer enters the shop and asks for a Yale lock. Is he really asking for one made by the Yale people themselves, or would he be satisfied with any make of pin-tumbler cylinder lock? If the retailer assumes the latter there may have been nothing more than genuine confusion between them—but there is always the problem that a dishonest trader may use the ambiguity as an excuse to deceive.

If it is shown the trader has acted dishonestly or within the definition of deceit noted above the court will intervene. A defendant trying to get his goods or business mistaken for someone else's will find the courts ready to act. But the elements of this tort have already been dealt with in the rules relating to misrepresentation in Chapter 4 (see page 39). It only remains to point out that a purchaser who has been induced by fraud to buy goods is entitled to recover not only the difference between price paid and market price, but also the profit he would have made had the goods been as they were represented to be.

FALSE IMPRISONMENT

This tort is committed where a person is arrested or imprisoned without lawful justification. This will apply to the preventing of the person from leaving the place where he is. Thus, the customer who is detained in a shop can sue the person detaining him if the detainer has no lawful excuse.

The plaintiff need not prove actual damage; indeed, it is not even necessary that he knows, at the time, that he has been falsely imprisoned. If he goes into a room and is locked in without his knowledge this is false imprisonment, even though the door might be unlocked before he discovers what has happened.

A restraint that is effected by an assertion of authority can amount to false imprisonment, for actual physical touching is not necessary. In *Meering v Grahame-White Aviation Co* (1919) M went to the works office at the request of works policemen to answer questions about thefts. He did not know that he was suspected but he remained in the office for some time while, unknown to him, the works police remained on duty outside. M had been falsely imprisoned. Thus, a person falsely arrested by a policeman need not show that the policeman touched him, to be able to succeed. But what is the case if a person is accused of shoplifting in a store and is asked to go to the manager's office? Will this amount to an assertion of authority on the part of the assistant, where the accused person, to avoid being embarrassed in front of the shoppers, goes unwillingly to the office even though she wants to leave the premises?

The answer is Yes, but if the assistant had reasonable cause to believe that the accused had committed a theft and a theft had in fact occurred, that is a legitimate arrest. However, the law requires that a person who is accused of shoplifting or other "arrestable" offences should be handed over to a police officer or brought before a magistrate within a reasonable time. So it would be in order to take the person before the manager for a decision whether this course should be taken; this would be reasonable. "There are advantages in refusing to give private detectives a free hand and leaving the determination of whether to prosecute or not to a superior official. Whether ... the delay was in fact too great is a matter for the jury." So said Lord Porter in 1952.

Occupier's Liability

The question of liability of the occupier of premises for injuries suffered by persons lawfully on his premises should really be discussed in relation to the tort of negligence, perhaps, but in view of the fact that it is covered by the special legislation of the Occupier's Liability Act 1957 it might conveniently be dealt with here as a separate topic.

It should be pointed out, first of all, that there may be liability towards persons who are not actually on the premises—for instance, where slates from the roof fall on the person next door, or on the highway. In such cases, if the occupier of the premises has been negligent in his maintenance of the roof the injured person can sue. But he will not sue under the Occupier's Liability Act, he will sue in the general tort of negligence.

The purpose of the 1957 Act is to regulate the duty an occupier owes to visitors with regard to the dangerous state of the premises. By "occupier" is meant any person who has physical control or possession of the premises. By "visitors" is meant any persons who have been invited, or have permission (which may be implied) to enter on the premises.

The duty of the occupier relates not only to structural defects in the premises but to any other dangers due to the state of the premises, such as a highly polished floor, for instance, or dangerously stacked goods on the display stand.

What, then, is the duty of care? The Act defines the duty as the "common duty of care"; that is, a duty to take such care as in the circumstances is reasonable, to see that the visitor will be reasonably safe

134

on the premises for the purpose for which he is invited or allowed to be there. If, for instance, he enters a shop to buy a guitar and while there steals a penny-whistle no duty under the Occupier's Liability Act is owed towards him, for he has placed himself in the position of a trespasser.

The amount of care to be exercised by the occupier must take into account the mental and physical state of the visitor, of course; the occupier must be prepared to accept that children are less careful than adults, and also that some dangers may tempt a child to meddle with the dangerous object. But if the person coming on to the premises enters to carry out a task at which he makes his living and is experienced, the occupier can expect that he will appreciate the special risks likely to arise. Thus, the window cleaner who takes no special precautions in cleaning the window which lacks an adequate foothold will not be able to sue the occupier when he is injured in a fall from the window. In *Christmas v General Cleaning Contractors* (1953) C was employed as a window cleaner. He was called upon to work on a high narrow sill where there was no adequate hand or foothold. It was decided that C's employer (not the occupier of the premises) was liable, for he had not laid out a safe system on the premises of the customer whose windows were being cleaned.

Warning the visitor of the dangerous state of the premises does not in itself prevent liability arising, but it may serve to show that the occupier has done all that is reasonable in the circumstances. Assume, for instance, that a shopkeeper is having structural alterations carried out in his shop. If he warns all his customers not to go down to the far end of the shop, he will not then be liable if one of these customers, having been warned, yet goes down to the far end of the shop and falls into the hole left by the workmen. In such circumstances the occupier will have discharged his duty under the Act. Similarly, if the visitor willingly assumes the risk of getting injured, there will be no liability on the part of the shopkeeper if the visitor is injured.

It has been pointed out that if the customer is warned of the existence of the danger but nevertheless goes down to the far end of the shop and is injured the shopkeeper will not be liable. If there is no warning, he will be liable. But what would be the position if the defective state of the premises is unknown to the shopkeeper, having been caused by the negligent act of some workmen who have been working there?

In this situation, the shopkeeper will be liable if the workmen were his employees, for the employer, as we will see in the next chapter, is liable for the acts of his employees carried out in the scope of their employment. But what if the workmen were not his employees, but

135

were contractors called in to do the job? What if they were plasterers employed by a local building firm, ordered by their employer to carry out the work in the shopkeeper's premises? In these circumstances they are known as "independent contractors" and the Act states that the occupier will not be liable for their acts if he had behaved in a reasonable manner in entrusting the work to them.

Thus, if he employs a labourer who is just starting up his own business, without knowing whether the labourer is competent to do the job or not, the shopkeeper will be liable to the customer when the ceiling falls on her. But if the shopkeeper has entrusted the work to a competent local firm he will have acted reasonably and it is the contracting firm only which will be liable, not the shopkeeper. This will be the case particularly where the work involves some special skill not possessed by the occupier; where the work does not involve some special skill responsibility cannot be delegated—such as, for instance, where a person is employed to sweep snow from the front steps. In *Haseldene v Daw and Son Ltd* (1941) D employed an independent contractor to repair the lift on his premises. H was injured when he used the lift. D denied liability for the work of repair carried out by the independent contractor. By employing a reputable firm of lift repairers D had acted reasonably and had discharged his obligations as occupier of the premises.

The occupier may exclude his liability under the Act, of course, by making a special contract with the person who comes on the premises. If he does so, such exclusion will have no effect as far as persons not party to the contract are concerned. Thus, the landlord of premises who continues to use common stairs or passages, etc., can exclude his liability as far as his tenants are concerned, but he will still be liable to the visitors received by the tenants. They are strangers to the contract he has made with his tenants.

So far, the position in relation to visitors who are lawfully on the premises has been discussed. But what if the visitor is a trespasser? The general rule is that no duty of care is owed to a trespasser (with a partial exception in the case of children—the occupier will be liable where he has left an "attractive object" such as an unattended cart on the premises).

Thus, if the trespasser falls into the hole at the far end of the shop he has no remedy; he should not have been there in the first place. But this does not mean that the occupier can place traps to catch the trespasser, such as a spring gun, or a concealed, camouflaged pit. Also, if the occupier knows of the presence of trespassers he will be liable to them for any act of negligence that he commits if it results in injury to the trespassers. In one leading case a contractor, felling a tree, knew that children were playing in the vicinity. If he had looked over his shoulder he would have seen them but he did not do so and failed to warn them when the tree was about to fall. A child was injured by the falling tree. The contractor was liable to the child although it was trespassing. The standard of care was recently discussed in *Herrington v B. R. Board* (1970) where it was said: "... reasonable care is only such as is reasonable in all the circumstances.... The circumstances vary infinitely from case to case."

Finally, it may be pointed out that although it is the occupier of the premises who will normally be liable to the injured person, in some circumstances the landlord of leased premises may be liable even though he himself does not live in part of the leased premises. This will be the case where the tenancy agreement places upon the landlord an obligation to maintain or repair the premises. If a person or his goods are lawfully on the premises any injury sustained through the failure of the landlord to maintain or repair the premises as under the agreement will result in the landlord being sued in respect of that injury. This provision is to be found in the Defective Premises Act 1972, by which the landlord owes a duty to injured persons as though he were in fact the occupier of the premises, and as though the person was on the premises by his invitation or permission. Thus, the law discussed above will then apply to the question of the landlord's liability. Equally, the Act states that if a person takes on work in connection with premises he owes a duty to any person acquiring an interest in that dwelling (a tenant, or a buyer, for instance) to see that the work is done properly. So the retailer who takes on a lease and finds a gas leak has damaged his goods would have the protection of the Act against the firm of builders who were responsible for the leak when carrying out repairs to the premises.

BREACH OF STATUTORY DUTY

The courts have recognised that some statutes give a remedy to an individual who is injured as a result of the failure of the person on whom the statute imposes a duty to carry out that duty. If the injured person has some other remedy available to him the court will be less ready to admit an action for breach of statutory duty. Also, though an employer may be held vicariously liable for a breach of duty by his employee, if the employee is injured as a result of his own breach of statutory duty he can sue the employer under this head only if the employer has been guilty of some fault going beyond that of the employee's.

The remedy is of some importance, however, particularly for the

137

distributive trades, as a result of the passing of the Consumer Safety Act 1978 for rather than bring an action in negligence for the supply of some defective goods it might be simpler for the plaintiff to bring an action for breach of the statutory duty laid down in the 1978 Act. In such an action all he would need to show would be that the breach had occurred and he had been injured—no question of having to prove a duty of care with matters of foreseeability arising.

Such an action would also get away from hurdles provided by the Sale of Goods Act—he need not be the purchaser of the product, recovery of damages will not be concerned with concepts of "merchantability" or "fitness for purpose", and the action could be brought against anyone on whom the Act places the duty.

There is the catch, of course—the goods by which he is injured must not be within that group excluded from the Act—food, fertilisers, animal feeding stuff and certain controlled drugs.

This particular tort does illustrate, however, the manner in which the common law and legislation overlaps in certain areas—and it also emphasises the fact that to the distributor and retailer the criminal, as well as the civil, law has considerable importance.

CRIMINAL LIABILITY

Attention has already been drawn to some of the criminal liability that the retailer or distributor might be faced with: Weights and Measures Acts and the Trade Descriptions Act provide examples. Another example is the Race Relations Act 1976.

Race Relations Act 1976

Successive Acts of 1965, 1968 and 1976 have made it unlawful for an employer to discriminate against employees on grounds of colour, race, ethnic or national origins, and this covers advertisements, recruitment, promotion and dismissal. The Acts also make it unlawful to discriminate on grounds of colour, race, or ethnic or national origins, in respect of:

(a) the provision of goods, facilities and services;
(b) employment;
(c) trade unions, employers and trade organisations; and
(d) the disposal of housing accommodation, business premises or land.

The refusal on the specified grounds to allow access to and use of a place where the public is allowed to go, such as a shop, would be discriminatory. Discrimination in respect of services of a business or trade are made illegal, as is accommodation in a hotel or boarding establishment, or in the provision of facilities for entertainment, recreation, refreshment, transport or travel.

No discrimination may be used by an employer in selection, training, promotion or dismissal of his employees. An exemption arises, however, where the employer can show he is discriminating only to secure or preserve a balance of different racial groups. And if the employee required possesses special attributes held only by persons of certain nationalities discrimination in his favour is possible.

There are a number of particular crimes which are of interest to the retailer and perhaps the most important of these is theft.

Theft

The offence of theft is defined in the Theft Act 1968 as follows: "A person is guilty of theft if he dishonestly appropriates property belonging to another with the intention of permanently depriving the other of it." The offence is punishable with a maximum of ten years' imprisonment and it replaces the old offences of larceny, embezzlement and fraudulent conversion.

The definition itself needs some explanation. By "appropriates" is meant the assumption of the rights of an owner—to behave as though one owns the goods. The obvious example is where the customer walks out of the shop with goods he has not paid for—he has "appropriated" them. But equally, a thing can be appropriated when it has not even been touched. The rogue who points to a car, tells the customer it is his to sell, "sells" it and pockets the proceeds is guilty of theft because he has appropriated the goods by acting as though he owned them.

A difficult case arose in *Davies v Leighton* (1978) where the customer was served in a supermarket with apples, and then went with her apples to the off-licence section of the store. She obtained and paid for wine there, but left the store without paying for the apples. It was argued this was not theft because ownership in the apples passed to her when she received them and it could not be shown, *then*, that she did not intend paying for them. It was held, however, that the property did not pass to her, because she did not pay for them—though had the assistant serving her been in a managerial or other special category, the result might have been different.

Equally, theft can be committed when the goods are lawfully in the thief's possession. The shopkeeper who has been given goods to hold for their owner is a bailee—if he sells those goods he is guilty of theft.

139

But what of the customer who enters the shop, tenders a pound note and asks for change and is given nine tenpenny pieces and one fifty pence piece by mistake? The shopkeeper thought he was giving him ten tenpenny pieces—if the customer retains the money he could be found guilty of theft.

Under the old law there were several ways of committing theft by intimidation or a trick—now they are no longer expressly mentioned but are covered nevertheless by the definition—and where they are not they are covered by other offences such as blackmail. A case in point is *R v McGrath*, a case decided in 1869 but the result would be the same today. A woman at a mock auction was forced to stay in the room until she paid for goods she had not bid for. She paid in order to get out. It was held this was larceny—now it would be theft. She had not really passed the ownership of the coins to him. The result would be the same where the money is obtained by a trick—as in the identity cases discussed on page 37—but it is also covered by the offence of obtaining property by deception.

What about "Finders, keepers"? If a customer finds a wallet in the shop is he entitled to keep it? He is not, because if he does not take reasonable steps to discover the true owner he will be guilty of theft. Nor can he say he did not intend to keep the wallet when he picked it up but decided to do so later, and hoped to get away with it. Formerly, he might have been able to do; now he cannot. It will be theft whenever he formed the intention to keep the wallet. But it will *not* be theft if he reasonably believes the owner will be impossible to trace by taking reasonable steps. This is an unlikely contingency in the example mentioned because the wallet would probably have been dropped by a customer who could well return.

Occasionally, situations arise where the goods supposed to be stolen were in fact obtained with consent of the owner. This would not be theft, but take the case of *R v Turvey* (1946). T approached an employee and suggested he should hand over to T certain goods owned by the employer. The employee reported this and the employer told him to hand the goods to T so he could get caught redhanded. It was held T was not guilty of larceny; under the Theft Act, however, it is likely he would be found guilty.

The offence consists of appropriating "property" dishonestly. "Property" includes money and all personal goods, including, for instance, cheques, shares in a company, or a bank balance. If one retailer draws a cheque on another businessman's bank account in that man's name, it would be a case of theft. Picking growing plants such as flowers or mushrooms or shrubs does not normally amount to theft—but if it is done to sell them, or for some other commercial pur-

140

pose, it would be theft. Wild creatures such as lions cannot be stolen unless they are tamed or kept in captivity; electricity and gas cannot be stolen but to use them dishonestly and without due authority is an offence in itself.

In any case the property must belong to someone, so an article that has been abandoned cannot be stolen. But "belonging" has a special meaning: it denotes possession, rather than ownership. Suppose the retailer has a bicycle stolen from his shop—that is theft. Suppose he lends the bicycle to his son and it is stolen from his son. The thief has committed an offence both against the retailer and against his son. So it follows that an owner can be guilty of stealing his *own* property if he takes it from someone, dishonestly, who has possession of it. A case in point is *Rose v Matt* (1951). The owner left a clock with a shopkeeper as security for a debt he owed. Later, without the knowledge or consent of the shopkeeper, he took the clock back. This would clearly be a case of theft now, as it was larceny then.

It should also be noted that if the act is dishonest it does not matter what the subsequent intentions might be. In *R v Cockburn* (1968) the manager of the shop took some money from the till on the Saturday. His intention was to replace the money on the Monday morning, by putting a cheque from his daughter into the till. It was argued that he had intended putting the money back and really was not aware he was committing a criminal offence—the court still said he was guilty of theft. But what if he had intended putting back the *identical property* he took? In that case it would not have been theft because he would not then have intended permanently to deprive the owner of the goods. If the accused person can show he honestly believed he was *entitled* to take the money he has committed no offence under the Theft Act; again, if he simply believes he has a moral claim to the money (because he considers himself underpaid, for instance) he is guilty of theft.

Some year's ago Goya's portrait of the Duke of Wellington was taken from the National Gallery—there was no intention to permanently deprive the owner so no larceny was committed (except of the frame, which the taker destroyed). The Theft Act now makes such conduct an offence—removal of an article from a public collection is theft. The building must be open to the public, however, and the removal must be without lawful authority.

Robbery

Robbery is an aggravated form of theft. It is committed when force is used before or at the time of the stealing, or when at such time a person is put in fear of being subjected to force. It carries a maximum sentence of life imprisonment. It should be emphasised the force must be used or threatened in order to steal, so using force to escape after the theft is committed would not make the theft robbery.

Fraud

The Theft Act 1968 also created a number of offences involving fraud. One such offence important to the retailer is *obtaining property by deception*.

The offence is committed by one who "by any deception dishonestly obtains property belonging to another with the intention of permanently depriving the other of it". The meaning of "obtains" is the obtaining of ownership, possession or control of the property and it includes the situation where one person takes the goods for someone else to retain. By "deception" is meant "any deception (whether deliberate or reckless) by words or conduct as to fact or as to law, including a deception as to the present intentions of the person using the deception or any other person".

An example of such deception would be the customer who gives a bad cheque for goods—he implies, when he gives the cheque in payment, that he has an account and the cheque is valid. But it does not mean he is representing there will be money in the account when the cheque is presented, so it will be necessary to show he knew the cheque would be dishonoured when he gave it.

Prior to the 1968 Act, a person ordering a meal in a restaurant, knowing he could not pay for it was not guilty of larceny but was guilty of obtaining credit by fraud. Now he would be caught under the Act for obtaining property by deception; the offence we are here dealing with is wider in scope than the old offence, however: *obtaining a pecuniary advantage by deception*.

Further legislation – The Theft Act 1978 – provides instances of obtaining pecuniary advantage by deception. They are:

(i) the obtaining of services from another, by deception, (an example would be obtaining professional advice or dental treatment by false representations, intending not to pay);

(ii) the evasion, by deception, of liability to make a payment (this could be the remission of part or all of an existing liability, or dishonestly inducing a creditor to wait for or forgo payment, or dishonestly obtaining an exemption or abatement of liability to pay);

(iii) making off without having paid for goods supplied, or services rendered, when it is known that payment on the spot is expected (this would cover the meal in the restaurant situation, or "making off" without paying for petrol obtained at a filling station).

The 1968 Act mentions two other circumstances. One arises where the accused "is allowed to borrow by way of overdraft, or to take out any policy of insurance or annuity contract, or obtains an improvement of the terms on which he is allowed to do so". A second case mentioned by the Act of 1968 is where the accused "is given the opportunity to earn remuneration or greater remuneration in an office or employment, or to win money by betting". The man who produces references, or a working career history which is false in order to obtain the post of manager in a large store would be committing an offence under this head.

False accounting

The Theft Act states it is an offence where a person "dishonestly, with a view to gain for himself or another or with intent to cause loss to another (a) destroys, defaces, conceals or falsifies any account or any record or document made or required for accounting purposes; or (b) in furnishing information for any purpose produces or makes use of any account, or any such record or document ... which to his knowledge is or may be misleading, false or deceptive in a material particular".

Blackmail

The Act defines blackmail as the offence committed when a person "with a view to gain for himself or another or with intent to cause loss to another ... makes any unwarranted demand with menaces". In *R v Clear* (1968) the accused, who was to be a witness in a theft case, threatened another person that unless he was paid money he would alter his evidence to the other person's detriment; it was held to be blackmail, even though the other person was unmoved by the threat.

Handling stolen goods

A person can handle stolen goods by receiving them, undertaking their retention, removal, disposal or realisation by or for the benefit of another, or by assisting in this or arranging for it to be done. To commit the offence, however, he must know or believe the goods are stolen goods and act dishonestly in the receiving (etc.) of them.

The definition of stolen goods is wider than may appear at first sight: the person who receives some of the money arising out of the

143

sale of the stolen goods can be convicted of the offence of handling stolen goods.

Goods cease to be stolen goods if their owner (or his agent) discovers them and "exercises acts of dominion" over them. If he merely discovers them, and does not deal with them but merely waits until the criminal returns to collect them, they remain stolen goods, of course.

The common law doctrine of recent possession must also be taken into account in relation to this offence. The customer who is found in possession of a fur coat reported stolen from the furrier's is faced with the presumption that he either stole the fur coat or received it with guilty knowledge. In other words, it is up to him to prove otherwise. How long do goods remain "recently stolen"? A roll of cloth has been held "recently stolen" two months after the theft; but three months was too long in the case of an axe. It all really depends on the kind of goods stolen and the ease with which they can be passed on to others.

Burglary

The Theft Act makes burglary an offence committed where a person (a) enters any building or part of it as a trespasser and with intent to commit certain listed offences (such as theft, or causing unlawful damage) or (b) having entered any building or part of it as a trespasser steals or attempts to steal anything or attempts to commit grievous bodily harm upon someone.

Thus, though a customer may not be *in* the shop as a trespasser, he would become one when he goes behind the counter, thus entering as a trespasser a "part" of the building in which he finds himself, and would be guilty of burglary if he then attempts to steal from the till. On the other hand the customer who enters a shop with the intention of stealing may be guilty of burglary whether he enters while the shop is open to the public or shut.

But what if he entered the department store, intending to buy goods, but then decided to hide and wait until the store closed, so he could steal? His *entry* was not a trespass so he is not a burglar. By staying in the store he is a trespasser but his *entry* was legal. If he then enters some other part of the store, such as another room, or goes behind the counter, he then enters another "part" of the building as a trespasser, and is guilty of burglary.

Forgery

Finally, we come to the offence of forgery. It is a convenient crime with which to end this chapter for it illustrates the interaction of common law and statute law in that although the forgery of a writing with intent to defraud is an offence at common law, in practice forgery is always charged under some statutory provision and usually under the Forgery Act 1913. This Act specifies a number of documents the forgery of which amounts to a criminal offence. Included are: wills, deeds, bank notes, insurance policies, court records and so on, but it also covers *any* document, if the forgery is committed with intent to defraud and any public document if the intent is to defraud or deceive.

Forgery is the making of the false document; it is a separate offence to "utter" or publish the document. In an old case Smith sold baking powder in packets wrapped in printed papers designed to resemble those used by one Borwick, a well-known manufacturer. Was this forgery? The court held it was not for the wrappers were probably not documents and even if they were, they were not *false*—the fraud lay in the improper use of them.

And the retailer should be warned that the mere possession without lawful authority or excuse of a forged banknote, knowing it to be forged, is an offence. So if you don't want fourteen years inside check your till! It is also an offence to utter false coins, knowing them to be false. So is it 2p, or an old penny?

CHAPTER 9

Finance, Insurance and Taxation

The basic problem facing anyone starting a business is capital. The small retailer has to lay out money to make money and the same problem besets a large organisation. Where a company is already in existence to run a distributive business it may be possible to raise further capital to finance expansion by the issue of more shares in the business but this is only one method available for financing the business—and it is hardly available in the case of a small, privately owned business or sole trader. So what other methods are available?

FINANCING A BUSINESS

The funds that are expected to generate profits for the small businessman will often be brought into the business by the owner of the business himself. He may have to raise further cash by way of an overdraft through a bank, or by negotiating a longer term loan by way of mortgage, or through a finance house or other lending institution. A further source of supply can be the suppliers of the goods themselves: trade creditors can be regarded in effect as a source of finance for the business.

In the case of a limited company there are four main ways in which money can be raised without a large-scale issue of shares or debentures (loan certificates). In the first instance there can be an internal financing out of profits. By this method the company retains some of the profits towards the cost of replacing buildings and equipment—in other words it makes provision for depreciation of assets. But equally the company can retain some profits to finance an expansion of its business. It is obvious that this method requires the agreement of shareholders, perhaps at the annual general meeting, because ploughing back profits in this way means that the dividends paid will be smaller.

A second method of financing the business activity is by way of hire purchase. This is the method of financing used by most small organisations who find it cheaper to buy equipment and machinery by hire purchase than by way of bank loans. A variant of this is the credit sale agreement. A further method is simple hiring. All these methods are subject to statutory restrictions, as we have already seen.

A third method of financing a business is by way of private loans. These are made by banks, particularly to finance current trading, but they can be made also by building societies, insurance companies, merchant banks and investment trust societies. A bank advance will usually take the form of an arrangement whereby the borrower is allowed to overdraw the account with the bank up to an agreed limit; interest will then be paid on the amount overdrawn from time to time. Borrowing a fixed sum of money, on the other hand, is more expensive, because interest has to be paid on the whole sum from the date of the loan. Clearing banks tend to be cautious and look at past performance as much as future prospects, before making a loan. They tend to enquire how quickly previous loans have been paid, how long the business has been running, and how the profit record compares with similar firms in the same business.

The fourth method of raising money is by way of the private placing of shares or debentures as the result of negotiations with an investor. In small companies the negotiations are carried out by the directors; in larger companies an intermediary such as a bank or a stockbroker is used.

Property

One of the most important assets the trader will have is the premises from which he carries on his business. He will carry stock, he will own equipment, but it is likely that the shop, or the supermarket, or the warehouse, will amount to a considerable investment in terms of money. However, we have already seen that the ownership of property carries obligations as well as merely amounting to a useful and necessary investment—the law relating to nuisance, for instance, may cause him particular difficulties, as we have seen earlier.

Owning premises can give rise to other problems. The conveyance by which the trader holds legal ownership of the property may well include certain "covenants"—agreements to do or not to do certain things with his property—that will leave him open to a suit if he disregards them.

This is particularly the case where the trader does not *own* the premises, but merely *leases* them from someone else. In such cases the landlord will often insist upon various covenants being included in the lease and he may enforce these covenants if the tenant—the businessman working from the premises—breaks them.

There is one respect in which the tenant of business premises has particular rights over and above those actually appearing in the lease, however. This is in the matter of security of tenure: the Landlord and Tenant Act 1954 stated the principle that tenants of business premises are entitled to a new tenancy at the end of the old one *even if the landlord is unwilling to grant a new one*. This means that if a trader takes the lease of premises to start his business, and at the end of the period of the tenancy wishes to close down or move elsewhere, he can do so. But if he wishes to continue on the same premises he can get a new tenancy even if the landlord is unwilling. By making an application to the county court for the grant of a new tenancy he can successfully hang on in the face of the landlord's opposition.

This protection applies to all business tenancies, whether the tenant is a private individual or a company, and it emphasises the true value of a lease. But there are some specified circumstances where the landlord can resist such a claim. For instance, if the landlord can show that the trader has failed to carry out the terms of the original tenancy or has proved to be an unsatisfactory tenant because of failure to pay rent or maintain and repair the premises as he is liable to do under the lease, the tenant is unlikely to get the court's sympathy in his claim for a renewal. Again, the landlord may be offering the trader suitable alternative premises—if they are really comparable with the premises currently occupied the trader may fail in his request for a new lease. Another ground for the court's refusal of a new lease would be where the landlord wishes to let the whole of the premises and the trader occupies only part of them, or where the landlord requires the premises for demolition or reconstruction, or where he intends to occupy the premises himself and has been the landlord for more than five years.

This last provision is of importance because it prevents the situation where Williams the Grocer finds his tenancy of the premises has come to an end and his new landlord—who bought the premises last year—turns out to be the Grabball Company Ltd, who just *happen* to own in addition the supermarket up the road. It's no good the Grabball Company saying they want to use Williams's premises to expand the supermarket facilities: Williams will be able to get a new lease if he wants one because the Grabball Company will not have been his landlords for the last five years.

All the exceptions mentioned do not in any case denigrate from the basic principle laid down: the court has the power to award a new tenancy of the business premises at the end of the lease for a period not exceeding fourteen years. And even if the landlord succeeds in removing the business tenant under the first three methods noted

148

above he may still be liable to pay compensation to the business tenant, based upon the rateable value of the premises, together with compensation for any alterations or improvements made by the tenant to the premises, which have had the effect of increasing their letting value. Compensation is also payable for goodwill.

It follows from this that in setting up a business the trader who is faced with the choice of buying the premises outright, or becoming a party to a lease, has more than financial matters to bear in mind! And whichever method he uses to establish his business premises he will need to make sure that his investment is safe. This is where insurance comes in.

INSURANCE

The impact of insurance upon commercial life cannot be over-estimated and its importance upon law also is significant since it now means that relatively poor people can still be sued by someone they have injured by their negligence, for it is the insurance company standing behind them who will have to pay the bill.

Any business therefore should be carried on only with the full backing of relevant insurance cover. An insurance policy is a form of contract under which the insured person agrees to pay the insurance company a sum of money, called the premium, in return for the company's assurance that it will pay to the insured person a certain sum of money by way of compensation if a certain event occurs. In a sense it can be regarded as a kind of gamble: the insurance company is making a bet on the future, the insured person also putting down a stake. If the event happens, the insured person collects.

The importance of insurance in business is obvious; some of the risks to which the retailer is exposed are described in this book; many of them can be insured against. Suppose a member of the public is injured by a collapsing ceiling in the department store; suppose a customer falls through a defective floorboard in the small corner shop and breaks a leg. Who will pay the damages? The insurance company—if a policy has been taken out.

There are various kinds of insurance policies that can be taken out.

Liability insurance. This is the kind of policy the cautious retailer would take out to cover contingencies such as those just described. The liability covered might be dangerous premises, or it might be incompetent staff, impure food, damage to customers' property and so on. The retailer may wish to insure himself against any liability arising in his capacity as a retailer, or he may wish merely to specify particular kinds of liability. The premiums payable will often be a brake upon his caution, naturally: the insurance company will take into account the state of the premises, the location of the shop, the type of people being served, the kind of goods being sold, the number of staff—and the general frequency of claims under such a policy. On the answers to these questions will depend the amount payable by way of premium—and some risks will prove to be too expensive to guard against!

It may be added that under the Employers Liability (Compulsory Insurance) Act 1969 every employer must take out an approved insurance policy to cover all possible claims by employees in respect of bodily injuries. In a way this can be likened to compulsory third party insurance in the case of motor cars, for failure to carry out the demands of the Act can lead to a criminal prosecution.

Property insurance. Perhaps the most important policy anyone engaged in the distributive industry should take out with regard to the business premises and the goods stored and sold is a fire insurance policy. Most fire insurance policies are based upon the situation where something is ignited which was not intended to be lit. It makes no difference that the actual ignition took place where ignition is normally expected to take place. Thus, the retailer who lights the fire only to discover that he destroys goods inadvertently left nearby by his assistant can make a claim—the actual cause of the fire is irrelevant, even if caused by the negligence of the retailer or his assistant. The policy will not apply if the fire is caused deliberately, to destroy the goods, of course.

Some perils are not covered by a fire insurance policy: in particular, if damage has been caused by a fire and explosion it will be necessary to show the damage was caused directly by the fire if a claim under the policy is to be made. Damage caused by the concussion of the explosion will not be covered. At least, this is so if the two are separated; if the explosion was caused by the fire itself and the damaged property was situated on the premises a claim could be made. If on the other hand the explosion and the damaged property were off the premises where the fire occurred the policy will not apply. There are some policies which cover loss by concussion even though it is a *fire* policy, but they cover only explosions in domestic boilers or explosions caused by gas appliances used for domestic lighting and heating.

In any claim under a fire insurance policy it must be shown that the damage was the direct and probable result of the fire. This is often difficult to prove. Suppose a fire breaks out in the department store and chemical extinguishers are used to put it out. The chemicals damage some of the stock. Can a claim be made under the policy?

150

Again, in the confusion caused by firemen visiting the premises and putting out the fire someone comes in and helps himself to an expensive fur coat and some jewellery. Is the loss of these items covered by the fire insurance policy? The answer in both cases would be that the loss suffered is sufficiently "proximate" to allow claims to be made. On the other hand, if the premises are severely damaged by the fire and the management decide they will have to rent alternative accommodation elsewhere while the premises are renovated, they could not claim the rental or hire of equipment under the fire insurance policy. The loss suffered would not have been the direct and probable result of the fire—it could be argued the need to rent property really arose because the management could not afford to *buy* alternative accommodation.

While we are on the subject of fire, it would be convenient to draw attention to the provisions of the Fire Precautions Act 1971. The Act states that all premises used for any purpose involving access to the premises by members of the public, paying or otherwise, must be covered by a fire certificate if they are to remain open. This clearly covers businesses in the distributive trade.

Fire certificates are obtainable from the local fire authority who inspect the premises with regard to the means of escape in the event of fire, the type of fire-fighting equipment available on the premises, and the facilities which exist for warning persons on the premises of the outbreak of fire. If the inspector is not satisfied the steps necessary to remedy the situation are stated and a time limit set for them to be carried out.

The matter does not end with the issue of the certificate; regular inspections are thereafter carried out. Alterations or extensions to the premises must be notified to the authority as must the storing of explosive or inflammable substances on the premises.

The certificate itself specifies the use of the premises for which the certificate covers them, and the other matters noted above in the inspection. The certificate may limit the number of persons who may be on the premises at any one time.

Who is responsible for complying with the conditions laid down in the Act? The answer is: the occupier. And he must also make sure the details on which the certificate was drawn up do not alter. He should certainly always be aware of the details since fire certificates must be kept on the premises.

And if the occupier does not get a fire certificate? He will be in trouble—to the extent of a fine up to a maximum of £400, or two years' imprisonment. Or, if the judge is feeling a bit liverish that day and the case is perhaps a bad one—£400 *and* two years'

151

imprisonment!

While fire must remain the single most important hazard facing the distributive trade it is closely run by theft, for the losses suffered by theft in the distributive trades are massive. Previously, a policy to cover all kinds of theft would have been expensive for there were various technical offences falling under the general heading which would have demanded separate cover. Now, since 1968, most of these offences are called, simply, theft and it is not necessary to distinguish so closely between theft, fraud, robbery, embezzlement and so on. It is usual, however, to make specific insurance cover for theft after forcible entry, with separate cover then being required for theft by employees on the premises—the latter is often named as one of the "excepted perils" in a policy.

Any retailer who does take out a theft policy will soon find he may have to mend his ways as far as security is concerned—particularly if he has already suffered loss by theft before taking out his policy. The insurance company will demand strict security and safety precautions and checks to be carried out if the policy is to be taken out and remain valid.

Football supporters are notoriously excitable and tend to get overexcited after their team has won—or lost, for that matter! Shopkeepers in a city centre or near the ground may find themselves in high risk areas as far as their plate glass windows are concerned, for this reason. The problem is that the insurance companies also recognise the high risk involved and will not usually give cover under a general policy, but will pay out compensation only if a special policy is taken out against most of the "accidents" likely to occur to it. Special policies of this kind are needed also for anything else which has a particularly high value or is easily damaged. Thus, dealers in silver, antiques, works of art and so on will need to take out special policies to cover these items.

Some gloomy retailers even take out policies against earthquakes!

Utmost good faith. One further point needs to be made concerning insurance policies. A contract of insurance is said to be *uberrimae fidei*—of the utmost good faith. This means it is a contract of the kind where only one party is in the position of knowing all the material facts and so is under a duty to disclose them to the other. In other words, the businessman who takes out a policy is under a duty to disclose to the insurance company all the material facts that might affect the judgment of the insurers in offering him an insurance policy at a given premium.

One example of a non-disclosure of a material fact would be the situation where the insurance company asks the retailer if any other company has declined to offer him cover. In *Glicksman v Lancashire and General Insurance Co.* (1927) G and H were partners and made a proposal to L for burglary insurance. G had been refused before; the firm had not. G did not tell the company of the refusal. Did this amount to non-disclosure of a material fact? The court held it did—even though H had not been concerned, G's failure, as a *partner* in the business, to disclose the refusal was held to affect the matter. Again, there was non-disclosure of a relevant fact in a 1957 case where after an insurance policy was taken out to cover loss of or damage to skins and furs it was discovered that the chairman of the insured company had been convicted in 1933 for receiving stolen furs. The insurance company should have been told. A more recent example arose in 1966 in *Roselodge Ltd v Castle*. Diamond merchants insured their diamonds against all risks but failed to state their sales manager had been convicted of diamond smuggling. They thought the fact immaterial. The court thought otherwise when the director of the company was robbed of diamonds with violence. Their claim under the policy was dismissed, for failure to disclose such material facts under a contract of utmost good faith makes the policy voidable—the insurers can deny liability on it.

One further example arose in 1969. The plaintiffs effected an all risks policy in respect of "new clothes in bales for export . . . including transit from the assured's premises". Over 200 bales of leather jerkins were lost but the claim was lost too, because of the non-disclosure of a material fact—the fact that the goods were Army surplus and at least 20 years old. While not affecting the fact of loss at all, it was a material fact which would have affected the underwriter's judgment. This is an example of a situation where mere silence can amount to misrepresentation (see page 39).

CHEQUES

The Bills of Exchange Act 1882 defines a cheque as a bill of exchange drawn on a banker and payable on demand. It is an order in writing addressed to the bank and signed by the person making it, demanding that the bank pay on demand the sum mentioned, either to the order of the person mentioned on the cheque or to him personally, or if no specific person is named, to the bearer of the cheque.

A bank is not bound to honour an undated cheque and a post dated cheque presented by the retailer may be answered by the bank's bland statement that the account holder had withdrawn everything from the account two days previously. In any case, a cheque must be presented within a reasonable time. If the bank dishonours the cheque wrongly it

153

will be liable to the drawer of the cheque, to the extent of the loss if the drawer is a trader. And if the bank pays out on a cheque that has been stopped, it will be liable to the drawer of the cheque.

Crossed cheques

The important thing to remember about cheques is that they are classified in law as "negotiable instruments". The characteristics of negotiable instruments are that the title to them passes by mere delivery, no notice of assignment needs to be given to the person liable on the instrument, the holder can sue in his own name on the instrument, and the holder who has taken in good faith and for value is not affected by the fact that a previous holder may have had only a defective title to the instrument—where, for instance, the cheque was stolen.

It follows that if the distributor pays the wholesaler for the goods by cheque, the wholesaler can *endorse* the cheque by adding his signature and then pass the cheque on to the exporter in payment of the wholesaler's debt to him. But certain rules apply to cheques which are crossed in one of the ways mentioned below. A crossed cheque will not be paid over the counter of the bank—payment will be made only through another bank. This is one of the basic reasons for crossing cheques—it prevents fraudulent practices, for the thief stealing the cheque cannot get cash for it since it must be paid into the collecting bank. In the time that elapses between presentation of the cheque and payment the theft is likely to be discovered.

There are four kinds of crossings that might be used.

General crossing: two lines are drawn parallel across the cheque with or without the addition of the words "and company".

Special crossing: two parallel lines are drawn across the cheque and the name of the banker is written between the lines. The cheque will be paid only to that bank.

Not negotiable: the addition of these words across the cheque, with or without the name of the banker, make the cheque a crossed cheque. The person who takes such a cheque obtains and can give no better title than the person from whom he took the cheque—in the case of a thief, none.

A/c payee: this type of crossing is not in fact legally recognised but it does give the true owner of the cheque a better protection than the usual crossings mentioned above. Its effect in banking practice is to place a duty on the collecting bank to make sure that it collects for the payee named on the cheque, or otherwise to ensure that the customer has the authority of the payee. The cheque remains negotiable, but failure of the bank to make the necessary enquiries would make it liable to the true owner of the cheque. This brings us to the whole question of the liability of bankers on cheques.

Bankers' liability

In general, bankers accept money from and collect cheques for customers and place them to their credit. They also honour cheques drawn on them by their customers when they are presented for payment and debit the customers' accounts, and they keep current accounts in their books in which the credits and debits are entered.

All this is familiar enough but what happens when a bank pays out on a cheque which has been forged? If it is the signature of the drawer which has been forged the bank will be liable on that cheque—that is, it cannot debit the drawer's account but must bear the loss itself. But if it is an *endorsement* that is forged, the banker is protected if he pays out in good faith and in the ordinary course of business. The same applies if the *endorsement* is irregular or missing.

But what if the cheque had been crossed? The law states that in such circumstances, if he pays the cheque drawn on him in good faith and without negligence to a banker (if crossed generally) or to the banker to whom it is crossed (if crossed specially), he is in the same position as if he had paid the true owner of the bill.

Again, if the banker receives payment of a crossed or uncrossed cheque for a customer with no, or defective, title, but receives it in good faith and without negligence he will not incur liability merely because he has received payment.

These provisions protecting bankers are to be found in the Bills of Exchange Act 1882 and the Cheques Act 1957.

The words "in good faith and without negligence" have been mentioned in these provisions, but what does negligence by a banker mean? In 1968 a judge stated that four principles should guide a court in deciding whether a bank has been negligent.

First, the standard of care required by a banker is that which would be the normal practice of careful bankers.

Second, this standard of care does not demand that bankers subject accounts to microscopic examination.

Third, in considering whether a bank has been negligent in receiving a cheque and collecting money for it a court must scrutinise the circumstances in which a bank accepts a new customer and opens an account.

Fourth, the burden lies upon the defendant to show that he acted without negligence.

There are a number of examples which have already been decided to be negligence by a banker—opening an account without enquiring into the identity or circumstances of the customer, receiving payment of a cheque for a customer when the cheque is drawn in favour of the customer's employer without making inquiries as to the customer's title to the cheque, not noticing the account from time to time and considering whether it is a proper or a suspicious one.

But if an open cheque payable to bearer is presented the bank need not make inquiries unless the circumstances themselves are suspicious, and the bank can make payment over the counter quite safely. But what if the retailer finds that an employee of his has taken his cheque book, forged the retailer's signature and drawn money from the account for his own purposes? In such a case the banker cannot debit the retailer's account—he must not pay out on a forged signature. Similarly, the bank will be liable to the retailer if the signature is genuine but the amount on the cheque has been fraudulently altered.

A word of warning, however. The businessman is under a duty to warn the bank of any forgeries he has discovered and he is also under a duty to take reasonable and ordinary precautions against forgery. If he fails to take such precautions and the natural result of his neglect is to allow a forger to draw money from his account it is the businessman who must bear the loss, not the bank. So the retailer who signs a blank cheque and leaves his assistant to fill in the amount and the payee is asking for trouble—and if the assistant makes off with a lot of money the retailer cannot blame the bank.

One particular problem for bankers has arisen because of computerisation. The computer sorts out cheques by branch and account number printed on the cheque in magnetic ink. In a recent case the customer altered the branch name in *ordinary* ink—which the computer cannot "read". He then countermanded payment, but the computer ignored the inked change, sent the cheque to the original branch and payment was made. In such circumstances the bank could be liable to the customer unless notice had been given to him that he should not use the cheques for payment through another branch.

Promissory notes

Like a cheque, a promissory note is a negotiable instrument. It is defined as an unconditional promise in writing made by one person to another, signed by the maker, engaging to pay on a fixed or determinable future time, or on demand, a sum certain in money to or to the order of a specified person or bearer.

It can be made by more than one person and the makers may be

156

liable jointly or as individuals. If the note is payable on demand it must be presented within a reasonable time to make the *endorser* liable, though this does not apply as far as the *maker* of the note is concerned. Presentment for payment is necessary to make the *endorser* liable, but again this is not necessary as far as the maker is concerned unless the note is payable at a certain place (it must then be presented at that place to make the maker liable).

CREDIT CARDS

Consumer credit generally was the subject of the Crowther Report in 1971; it argued for an overhaul of the law relating to consumer credit and this was implemented in the Consumer Credit Act 1974.

One of the forms of credit to be covered was the credit card. Of recent years, of the various forms of credit available to prospective borrowers, the credit card has become increasingly popular and increasingly available. Most credit cards, which are now caught by the provisions of the Consumer Credit Act 1974, operate on the basis of a three party system which works in the way described below.

The three parties are the card holder, the issuer of the card and the retailer. The card holder enters into a legal contractual relationship with the firm issuing the card. The terms of the agreement are contained in a printed form delivered to the holder with the card. The contract is completed when the holder signs his name on the back of the card. Under the agreement the holder will usually agree to reimburse the issuer of the card (usually monthly, with interests payable in the event of late payment) for goods or services supplied to the holder by a retailer. Copies of all sales or service vouchers will then be sent to the holder by the issuer with a statement and a request for payment to be made.

The retailer will also have entered a contract with the issuer. Armed with the card the holder goes to the retailer and enters a contract with him— he obtains goods from the retailer, the retailer transmits to the issuer the invoices or vouchers and is paid by the issuer in relation to those vouchers or invoices. The payment is at a discount of course—this being the profit margin for the issuer. The issuer then sends the statement and request for payment along with copies of the vouchers or invoices to the cardholder.

The effect is that the cardholder need not pay for the goods or services when he gets them from the retailer; he is given credit as a cardholder and pays on his monthly account, either the total cost or a percentage of it.

The usual terms of a credit card agreement demand the signature of

157

the cardholder, this being the basis of the contract. Other terms will normally be that:

(1) use of the card is restricted to the person named up to the amount stated and until the date of expiry noted;

(2) all sales and cash advance vouchers issued under the card will be charged to the account held by the issuer and a statement will be sent to the cardholder each month;

(3) the cardholder will pay to the issuer within a specified number of days (sometimes 25) the minimum sum stated or any greater sum the cardholder chooses (the minimum sum is often about 5 per cent of the outstanding balance);

(4) interest will be charged on the amounts of all vouchers debited to the cardholder's account (sometimes no interest is charged on amounts paid by the cardholder in respect of sales vouchers within 25 days of their appearing on a statement—in other words, pay early and avoid interest);

(5) sums paid are applied first to pay off interest accrued and then to pay off the cardholder's liability for cash advances and sales vouchers;

(6) the card remains the property of the issuer and can be cancelled without notice.

If the cardholder dies or becomes bankrupt the sums owing on the account are still payable, of course. Usually, there is also a term demanding that the issuer should be informed immediately the card is lost or stolen, for the opportunities for fraud on credit cards are obvious; indeed, of recent years with the proliferation of such cards the frauds perpetrated on them have moved into the realm of big business themselves!

COMMERCIAL SECURITIES AND GUARANTEES

This conveniently brings us to the matter of commercial securities and guarantees. It may be that when a retailer is owed money he is offered goods to hold until such time as the money is paid. Or, on the other hand, the debtor says he cannot pay but another person will stand as his guarantor. Let us take the question of guarantees first, since they have already been discussed earlier (see page 48).

Guarantees must not be confused with the "guarantees" or "warranties" put out by manufacturers concerning their goods whereby they "guarantee" that if the goods are defective they will be repaired or replaced free of charge or for a nominal charge. A contract of guarantee is a contract by one person to be answerable for the debt default or miscarriage of another. The characteristics of such contracts are that there must be three parties: the principal debtor, the principal creditor, and the guarantor; and the liability of the guarantor must be secondary only—that is to say, it is the principal debtor who is liable first, the guarantor becoming liable only if the debtor defaults.

Guarantees must also be distinguished from indemnities. A contract of indemnity arises where one party promises to be liable for the debt of the other *in any event*. That is, there is no secondary liability in the case of the indemnity—the person offering the indemnity is primarily liable on the promise. The distinction between the two is important because contracts of guarantee, to be enforceable, must be made in writing and signed by the guarantor. A contract of indemnity need not be in writing.

The retailer who is faced with the promise by the young man to pay for the goods supplied to his girl friend had therefore better make sure where the primary liability lies, and distinguish between guarantees and indemnities! If the young man is to act as guarantor—get it in writing!

It follows from this that the retailer could not demand payment from a guarantor until the debtor is in default. And if any conditions have been laid down to be fulfilled before the guarantor becomes liable they must be so fulfilled—for instance, if A agrees to be guarantor if C, D and E will also agree, he cannot be made liable if any one of the others refuses.

A guarantee may be intended to cover one transaction or it may be intended to cover a series of transactions. In the latter case it is called a continuing guarantee. An example would be a guarantee to stand surety for payment for goods delivered at monthly intervals over a year.

If the original contract between debtor and creditor is void, the guarantor cannot be held to his promise, so where an overdraft for a minor was guaranteed the guarantor was not liable to the bank because the original agreement was void under the Infants' Relief Act 1874.

It may be the retailer who acts as guarantor for another colleague in the trade. What are his rights against that colleague if the date for payment of the debt has come? In the first instance, he has the right to require the creditor to attempt to get payment from the debtor, by a court action if necessary. If this fails, and he finds himself sued by the creditor on the guarantee the retailer can set off against the creditor any claim the debtor might have. And where he has paid the debt to the creditor he has the right to take over any rights the creditor might have in respect of the debt to which the guarantee relates. Thus, if the creditor would have ranked as a preferential creditor, the guarantor can take over that position having paid off the creditor.

Contracts of guarantee relating to hire-purchase, credit sale or conditional sale agreements and any securities given by a guarantor are enforceable only if copies of the main and the guarantee agreements are supplied to the guarantor in the prescribed manner. It is useful here to refer once more to recourse agreements (see page 87) between a finance company and a car dealer: the car dealer there agrees to *indemnify* the finance company if the hire-purchaser defaults, so this is not a contract of guarantee. A noteworthy result is that the finance company can recover from the dealer under a recourse agreement the whole amount of the damages suffered—not just the amount by which the hire-purchaser of the car was in arrears when he defaulted. This is because the dealer takes upon himself the mantle of principal debtor.

As for the debtor, the guarantor has certain rights against him too. He can demand that the debtor relieve him from liability for paying the debt—by paying it off himself. And after payment is made he can demand to be indemnified by the principal debtor against all payments properly made. Finally, if the guarantor is sued by the principal creditor he can bring the principal debtor into the action and claim indemnity from him.

Where there are several guarantors acting together and one pays more than his share he can claim contributions from the others.

A guarantor will be discharged if the contract between the debtor and creditor is varied in some way without his consent. Similarly, if the creditor agrees to give the debtor more time to pay the guarantor will be discharged. He will also be discharged if the creditor omits to do something he is bound to do to protect the guarantor, or if he gives up any security held by him in respect of the guaranteed debt. The guarantor's liability will be at an end where he is expressly or by implication discharged from his debt or where the guarantee is revoked.

Securities

The legal term for a person who holds goods for their safe custody, or on loan or pawn, or for their hire or hire-purchase is a *bailee*. The person who hands him the goods is called a *bailor*.

The bailee is under a duty to take reasonable care of the goods while they are in his care, and the standard of his conduct is determined by the circumstances of each particular case. But the burden lies on the bailee to show he has acted without negligence. If he *can* show he acted with reasonable care he is not liable for any loss or damage the goods might sustain.

The bailee must of course return the goods in accordance with the terms of the contract. But if they are delivered to him for repair, for instance, and when the goods are ready the bailor refuses to pay for the repairs and refuses to take delivery of the goods the bailee, after giving due notice, can sell the goods. He can then retain his charges out of the proceeds of sale, but must pay the balance to the bailor (and see page 162).

Sometimes special contracts are made which exempt the bailee from liability for negligence. Where Mr Rutter deposited his car with one Palmer for sale on commission, he failed to get damages from Palmer when the car was damaged as it was shown to a prospective buyer. The reason? There was a clause in the contract stating: "Customers' cars are driven by our staff at customers' own risk".

In the case of goods loaned for use by the bailee he is not liable for fair wear and tear as long as he does not deviate from the conditions of the loan.

Pawn is the delivery of goods to a person (the pawnee) by the owner (the pawnor) as security for a loan. Ownership stays with the pawnor; possession goes to the pawnee, who must take reasonable care of the goods, cannot use them, and must give them up when the pawnor wishes to redeem them within the stipulated time or, if no time has been stipulated, within a reasonable time after demand for repayment has been made. If the pawnor does not redeem the goods the pawnee can sell them, keep his charges and expenses and hand the balance to the pawnor.

Additionally, we come to the form of security known as *lien*. A lien can arise where the retailer has goods in his possession owned by a customer who owes the retailer money. The retailer can retain those goods until such time as the debt is paid. But the possession must be rightful, and once possession is lost the lien is lost. Possessory liens may be general or particular. A general lien is a right to retain possession of someone's goods until all claims against that person have been satisfied. A particular lien is a right to retain goods until all charges incurred *in respect of those goods* have been paid. In 1917 Mr Green had let his car on hire purchase to Mr X who agreed to keep it in good repair and working condition. Mr X sent it to All Motors Ltd for repair but then fell behind in his hire-purchase payments so Green terminated the agreement. All Motors Ltd refused to return the car until the costs of repair were paid. The court said they were entitled to this lien for X had had Green's authority to act as he did. It should be noted that if the agreement had ended *before* the car went for repair there would have been no lien available. In any case a particular lien does not arise until the work done on the goods is completed (unless the owner prevented this) and the goods in question have been im-

161

proved by the work done on them. An agreement to *maintain* a car gives rise to no lien, because maintenance does not *improve* a car, it merely keeps it in its present condition.

Possessory liens are enforced by keeping the goods; there is no right of resale. Exceptions have been noted on pages 76 and 160.

It is relevant to add here that the question of the disposal of goods left by a customer for repair or other treatment and then not collected is governed by the Torts (Interference with Goods) Act 1977, which repealed the Disposal of Uncollected Goods Act 1952. By sections 12 and 13 of the 1977 Act, where the "bailee", relying on the provisions of the Act, sells goods to a third party he passes to that third party only such title as the bailor possesses. It may be, of course, that the title to the goods vested in the bailor is defective.

If there is a genuine dispute between the parties concerning the price charged or the quality of repair or treatment, the bailee's right to sell is suspended.

Once the articles are sold the bailee can retain the money due to him and the charges arising and paid out of the public auction. He may also charge a reasonable sum for storage of the goods and the cost if any of insuring the goods. The rest of the money must be paid to the bailor.

Within seven days of the sale the bailee must prepare a record of the sale and keep it for six years, together with a copy of his notice of intention to sell, and the certificate of posting of the letter containing the notice. He must produce these at any reasonable time to the bailor for inspection.

In the Act the expression "bailee" means the person to whom the goods are delivered—a shoe repairer for instance will be the bailee to whom the customer, the owner of the shoes (the bailor) delivers the shoes for repair.

VALUE ADDED TAX

One of the most significant results of Britain's entry into the Common Market was the introduction of a new tax called Value Added Tax. It was introduced by the Finance Act 1972, took effect as from 1st April 1973 and replaced both purchase tax and selective employment tax. In addition to VAT a tax of ten per cent was charged on new or imported cars to offset the loss of purchase tax on those items.

VAT is chargeable on the supply by way of business of all goods and services other than the exempted goods. The tax is borne by the ultimate consumer but its collection is made in instalments at each successive stage in the process of production or the chain of distribution. Thus, manufacturers, processors, wholesalers, retailers, or others concerned will each pay VAT. Each instalment payable is calculated upon the increase in value of the chargeable item resulting in the completion of the stage in question, whether it be manufacture or distribution.

The system works like this: the organisation which places the luncheon meat in tins will fix a selling price of, say, 50p per tin. The wholesaler who buys from him will pay 55p per tin—50p going to the canner, 5p being collected as VAT. Similarly, when the wholesaler fixes a price on the tin of, say, 60p, the retailer will pay him 66p, and when the retailer fixes a price of 70p the housewife will pay him 77p—in each case VAT is added at 15 per cent.

In each case, the persons selling the tins of meat collect VAT, but equally, each is then entitled, when he accounts to the Exchequer for the VAT collected, to deduct from the VAT collected, the VAT he has paid. Thus, the retailer will pay, in the above example, 7p on each tin to the Exchequer but will reclaim 6p paid to the wholesaler.

All persons engaged in the supply of goods or services chargeable to tax are liable to pay VAT (unlike for instance the individual selling his house) and should therefore register with HM Customs and Excise. Failure to register has serious repercussions, for the liability to *pay* VAT still remains, but the unregistered person cannot recover VAT paid. Only if the person is registered can he recover VAT paid on goods or services supplied to him.

Where the total annual value of the goods and services chargeable to tax (including those "zero rated", that is, charged to tax at a nil rate) supplied by a business do not exceed £10,000 the proprietor will not be treated as a taxable person and may choose whether or not to apply to be registered. So what happens if a trader decides to remain unregistered because his turnover is less than £10,000? He will still have to charge VAT on his "outputs" (the goods sold by him) but he cannot recover tax paid on his "inputs" (goods bought by him).

A single rate of tax applies to all goods that are not zero rated or exempted. The rate is 15 per cent but it can be changed by the Treasury. Zero rating applies to all items of food and drink other than those commodities formerly subject to purchase tax and food supplied in the course of catering. It also applies to house construction, fares, domestic fuel, lighting, newspapers, periodicals and books. Zero rating also applies to exports.

The problems that arose over the calculations small retailers might have to make in respect of VAT were early recognised and schemes were published by Customs and Excise to simplify the calculations that retailers might have to make under the system. The schemes in fact provided a choice of methods for calculating tax from gross takings instead of having to record each separate transaction for tax purposes. Scheme 2, always regarded as the scheme most likely to be used by small retailers was quickly modified in response to representations and after consultation with interested trade bodies. Scheme 2 does not require the different lines of goods sold by retailers to be the subject of separate calculations but allows for different retail margins to be set on different lines of goods. The original scheme provided for a standard addition of one-eighth to the amount arrived at by the basic calculation. That original version remains only for retailers who have a turnover in excess of £50,000. Small retailers whose annual turnover is below that figure could use the modified version where the one-eighth addition is not made.

A further revision occurred in relation to "gross takings"—the basis of the retailer's output tax calculation. Defined essentially on the basis of cash receipts, gross takings can also be defined, by those retailers who so wish, as cash receipts and sales to account customers, when the customer is debited instead of when the customer actually pays the account.

If this system is used, however, the retailer adopting it must use it in uniform fashion for all his sales to account customers.

But what items are exempted from VAT?

Health, education, most postal services, property transactions, rents (but not hotel accommodation), and insurance are exempt from VAT. A number of VAT Regulations have been issued: by No. 2 Order 1973 the following transaction is to be treated as a supply of services—"the exchange of a reconditioned article for an unserviceable article of a similar kind by a person who regularly offers in the course of his business to provide a reconditioning facility by that means". The transactions intended to be covered are those commonly existing in the vehicle and machinery spare parts trade. Similarly, an order has been issued providing for the tax chargeable on the supply of a used caravan by a taxable person to be charged only on any excess of the price he obtains for the caravan over what he paid for it.

Are there any legitimate ways in which businessmen can reduce the burden of VAT on the business? One way (and there are very few of them) would be to make purchases from non-registered suppliers, but these should really be avoided. The supplier cannot charge VAT on his invoice although he will have borne it on his purchases so his price will presumably be geared to take this into account. The supplier, in such circumstances, is likely to be in business only in a small way—he could not otherwise afford to remain unregistered. Any savings made are thus likely to be small. And if the nonregistered supplier's price is less than a registered supplier's price before charging VAT there will be no saving at all. One other way concerns pension funds. Nearly all the output of a pension fund is exempt from VAT. Some of the inputs will bear VAT and the pension fund cannot recover this tax. In those large companies which bear the marginal cost of their pension funds it would be in their interest to pay expenses such as audit fees on behalf of the pension fund so they can recover the VAT.

Credit notes are not covered by the 1972 Act but in practice credit notes are accepted by Customs to adjust invoices received from the taxable person. But what about credit given to a customer to compensate him for some loss—such as goods damaged in transit through the negligence of the supplier? The credit does not attract VAT but the supplier should still add it to the credit cancelling the original charge for the goods. Returnable containers provide another headache. The retailer is well advised to charge VAT on deposits for containers dispatched, and to credit VAT on "containers returned" deposits. In this way the net charge for containers made to the customer will have borne VAT. Otherwise, the customer could argue he need not pay VAT on the deposit until he has had the container for a year (under section 7(2)(c) of the Act), if he does not pay the deposit.

Finally, we come to bad debts. These cannot be treated as a deduction from the supplier's liability for VAT. The argument is that it is probable that the tax charged by the supplier to the bad debtor was repaid by Customs to the bad debtor, so to refund the VAT to the supplier would be a case of making two refunds. As against that, bad debts are a normal business expense and prices are really designed to cover them and in other countries VAT operation allows for deduction of bad debts. Moreover, since they were allowed as a deduction for purchase tax why not under VAT? But perhaps strongest of the arguments is that cash retailers can exclude dishonoured cheques as part of their sales, so why should not credit traders be allowed to do so? But such is the situation, so the retailer is duly warned. If he cannot recover the money due from the customer and decides to write it off he'll have to write off the VAT in addition.

One further point—if you give a staff party or provide business entertainment you don't pay VAT, but you do if you supply gifts of services, such as free holidays to your staff. VAT is also payable on gifts of goods (including Christmas gifts) to staff or customers, long service awards to staff and the proportion of petrol supplied to staff and used by them for private purposes.

165

CHAPTER 10

Employers and Employees

The contract of employment whereby one person agrees to provide personal services for another is in no way different from the types of contracts already discussed in Chapter 4. The principles there mentioned apply equally to the contract of employment and it is not proposed here to reiterate what was stated in Chapter 4. Nevertheless, certain points already mentioned may be emphasised here in view of their importance in the contract of employment.

Firstly, though this text will speak of employer and employee, it should be noted that the time-honoured legal terminology for the relationship is "master" and "servant". This terminology is useful in that it serves to distinguish between the "servant" and the independent contractor. This distinction, already mentioned, is based upon the test: can the employer control not only what the employee does but the way in which he does it? If he can, the employee is a servant, but if the employer can control only *what* is done, the employee is an independent contractor. Reference to the chauffeur (servant) and the taxi-driver (independent contractor) may make the distinction clear.

While it would be more in accordance to speak of master and servant, in accordance with legal practice, that is, the use of the words employer and employee will nevertheless be used here in view of the fact that the master/servant terminology tends to be regarded as a little outdated these days—and even resented. This can be illustrated by the remark of the crane driver who was asked in court whether his actions were controlled by his employer, or by the person for whom he was doing some contracting work: "No one tells *me* what to do!" Admirably independent perhaps, but hardly useful to the court trying to decide which employer is to be liable for his actions!

When reference is made to the employer/employee relationship in these pages, therefore, it is the master/servant relationship which is being discussed, not the position of the independent contractor. This will be left until later in this chapter when the vicarious liability (liability for the torts committed by another) of employers will be discussed in more detail.

As far as the contract of service is concerned, then, it differs but little from ordinary contracts. It might be worthwhile, however, to mention the position of the minor again in this context. Generally speaking, a minor will not be bound by any contract of service which he enters unless it is substantially for his benefit. This does not mean that if there is one clause in the contract which is not to his benefit he can avoid liability on the contract. The court will look at the contract as a whole and decide if, as a whole, it is to the minor's benefit. If it is, it will be enforced against him, even if there are clauses which penalise him in some way. If the contract as a whole is not to his benefit, he can avoid it.

Thus, if the minor enters a contract of employment whereby he is called upon to take part in a works sick benefit scheme, the scheme will be looked at as a whole by the court if he tries to avoid the contract on the ground that the scheme penalises him since he is not paid for certain types of illness. The fact of non-payment in itself will not mean that it is therefore "not to his benefit". Similarly, if the contract of service places severe obligations upon the minor, while the employer is called upon to do very little under the contract, the court will look at the contract as a whole to decide if it is beneficial to the minor.

The position of the corporation is also noteworthy. If it has been formed by statute, or under the Companies Acts 1948–67, its powers will be restricted by the statute and the Articles of Association respectively. Thus, the person who is employed by the corporation may find that the corporation is not in fact empowered (by the statute, or by the Articles) to make such an appointment. He will thus find himself out of a job, although he can, of course, demand payment for the work he has done and which has been accepted by the corporation. The position is affected by the European Communities Act 1972 to some extent however. Section 9(1) states that if the person dealing with the company has acted in good faith the action taken by the company directors shall be regarded as one within the power of the company to do. It would *not* protect the would-be employee who *knows* the company does not have power to make the contract because he would not be "in good faith".

In the case of the unincorporated association, the body itself cannot make a valid contract of employment, for it does not possess legal personality, as we have seen in Chapter 3. In that circumstance, the person who has been employed will, in the event of unjust dismissal, or refusal to pay wages, etc., have a remedy against the committee of the association, or the individual who actually appointed him, acting as an agent for the association.

What form must the contract of employment take? As is the case with the ordinary contract, it may be made expressly, by word of mouth, or in writing, or it may arise by implication from the conduct of the parties. Usually, of course, it will be made expressly, and it should, in most circumstances, note both the duration of the contract and the wages or salary payable.

What if the duration of the contract is not actually stated? If this is the case, then the attitude of the courts has been that the duration should be determined from external appearances: in other words regard must be paid to the conduct of the parties, the periods at which wages are paid by the employer, the custom as to length of employment that applies in the particular trade. If there is clear evidence that the length of time is other than that suggested by the circumstances mentioned above, of course, then the circumstances will not disturb such evidence. Thus, the fact that trade custom is that the contract should last for one month only will not affect a contract where the parties have expressly agreed that the employment should be for two months.

It is quite possible that no specific period is mentioned; in these circumstances the contract should state what amount of notice is necessary. The position as to notice is now governed by statute but before Parliament took a hand, in the event of no trade custom existing to act as a guide, the court would have to decide what amounted to reasonable notice.

Thus, it was decided that a newspaper editor was entitled to twelve months' notice, a foreign correspondent six months, a film editor one month, a shop manager one month, a milk carrier one week, a foreman one week, and while a clerk was entitled to three months' notice a chorus girl was entitled to two weeks.

The position under the Contracts of Employment Act 1972 will now be examined in some detail.

Contracts of Employment Act 1972

The 1972 Act is the main Act but has been amended by the Employment Protection Act 1975.

The rules laid down by the legislation apply only to cases where the employee has been in employment continuously for at least thirteen weeks and it should be emphasised that the periods of notice stipulated are *minimum* periods so a contract of employment may directly or by implication still demand longer periods.

The situation regarding notice is as follows.

For employees who have been continuously employed:

(a) from 13 to 104 weeks, one week's notice is required;
(b) from 104 to 260 weeks, two weeks' notice;
(c) from 260 to 520 weeks, four weeks' notice;
(d) from 520 to 780 weeks, six weeks' notice;
(e) for 780 weeks or more, eight weeks' notice is necessary.

So, the employer is obliged under the Act to give these minimum periods of notice. But what of the employee? The situation here is different. The Act states that no matter how long he might have served beyond the minimum 13 weeks he is required to give the employer only one week's notice. Once again, let it be emphasised that his contract may nevertheless demand a longer period.

The parties to the contract cannot demand *shorter* periods though they can demand longer ones. It is always open to either party to waive his right as to notice, of course, and an employee can always accept payment in lieu of notice. Moreover the Act does not prevent one party from terminating the contract without notice where the other has committed a serious breach of contract justifying the action.

Reference has already been made to "continuous employment". What does this mean?

The Act is quite specific about it. Any week in which the employee's contract requires him to work for at least 16 hours counts as a week of employment. Once he is qualified for any right under the Act he remains so qualified unless and until his contract ceases to require at least 8 hours per week, and in such a week, he actually works for fewer than 16 hours. Further, any worker who is continuously employed for five years under a contract which normally requires at least 8 hours per week is deemed to be continously employed.

If the employee is incapable of work through sickness or injury for not more than 26 weeks his continuity of employment is not broken; nor is it broken if he is absent from work because of a temporary cessation of work, or is absent in such circumstances that by arrangement or custom he is regarded as continuing in employment of the employer.

But what if the employee changes employers where the business is sold to someone else? In such cases continuity of employment is not broken, any more than it is where there has been a change of partners in the firm, or a transfer of employment under some Act of Parliament, or employment by personal representatives when the employer has died.

The receipt of redundancy payment under the Redundancy Payments Act 1965 will break continuity of employment, however, even if the employee is immediately employed thereafter by the same employer.

What happens if there is a strike or a lockout? The period of all lockouts count towards continuous employment (a lockout is the closing of the place of employment, the suspension of work or the refusal by the employer to employ persons because of a dispute). In the case of a strike, the striking employee will find the period he is on strike will not count towards the calculation of his period of employment (his 13 weeks or his 260 weeks and so on) but equally it will not break his continuity of employment (if it did he would have to start his period of qualification all over again).

How much should the employee be paid during the period of notice? The general object of the Contracts of Employment Act in this respect is to ensure that the employee gets a guaranteed wage while under notice and to prevent either party excluding or limiting this right. The first thing to discover is whether the contract of employment is governed by normal working hours. If it is the employee will get a guaranteed minimum wage during notice if he is prevented from earning that wage because the employer provides no work, or he cannot work through sickness or injury, or is absent from work on holiday due to him under his terms of employment. The amount he gets will depend on the circumstances—if his remuneration normally varies with the amount of work done, for instance, he will be entitled to the average hourly rate paid in the four weeks fully completed before notice (overtime bonuses being excluded). Also, sick or holiday pay given to the employee during the period of notice will go towards making up the employer's statutory liability.

If the contract is not governed by normal working hours the employer must pay the employee not less than the average weekly rate of remuneration during the twelve weeks ending with the last complete week before notice was given. Once again, all this depends upon the employee being ready and willing to work (although the exceptions noted above regarding illness and injury or holidays also apply). And if the employee asks for and is granted leave there is no liability to pay the guaranteed wage then.

So much for the question of notice. The Act also has something to say about terms and conditions of employment. Prior to the 1963 Act it had become apparent that legislation on the matter was necessary because of the casual nature of many contracts of employment, particularly in smaller firms, where the employees in particular were often not at all clear as to what the terms and conditions attached to the job might be.

Accordingly the Act now compels employers to give employees

170

written information as to the terms of the contract. The information must be given not later than 13 weeks after employment starts. This does not mean that in a small family business the father must give such notice to his family, for the Act excludes close relatives from the scope of the Act where they are the employees in question.

What must the written statement contain?

The Act stipulates it must identify the parties and state the date when the contract began and then give the following particulars:

    (a) the scale or rate of payment or the method by which payment is calculated;

    (b) the intervals at which payment is to be made;

    (c) any terms and conditions relating to hours of work;

    (d) any terms and conditions relating to holidays, public holidays and holiday pay, sickness, injury and sick pay, pension rights and pension schemes, the length of notice to be given and received to end the contract;

    (e) a note indicating the nature of the employee's rights relating to membership of a trade union or to refuse such membership and the effect of any agency shop agreement (if any) on those rights;

    (f) a note specifying to whom he can apply to invoke grievance procedures, the manner in which the application must be made and the subsequent steps to be taken (reference to a document where these matters can be found will be sufficient);

    (g) in the case of a fixed term contract the date when it expires.

Changes in the terms and conditions of employment affecting these matters must be communicated in writing to the employee within one month of the change.

Additionally, by the Employment Protection Act 1975 all employees have the right to receive an itemised pay statement, in writing, on or before each payment of wages or salary.

The Act has significantly improved the position that formerly stood. It may be pointed out that the provisions of the Act can be avoided by the employer merely giving the employee a written contract of employment but similar particulars must be given. There are also some flaws in the statute: the written particulars need not be given before thirteen weeks have elasped and during that thirteen weeks disputes as to the terms and conditions may well arise. Moreover, the distributive trade, like some others, does have a fairly large turnover of staff—young people often drift in and out of jobs, or change employment from one shop to another with some regularity, and such personnel, changing jobs before the thirteen weeks elapse, could well never see the particulars of their employment.

One final point may be made. The written particulars that are sent to the employee under the terms of the Act do not constitute the contract and need not be signed. The contract of employment can be enforced even though the employer has failed to comply with the Act.

This section began with a discussion of termination of the contract with notice; we may now examine the termination of contracts of employment without notice.

Termination Without Notice

The 1972 Act as amended by the Employment Protection Act 1975 covers the situation with respect to the giving of notice to end the employment. In some circumstances the giving of notice is not necessary: the employer may exercise his right of summary dismissal. The right is not affected in any way by the Contracts of Employment Act.

There are several grounds on which the employer may dismiss his employee summarily, and thus terminate the contract of employment without notice. He will be quite justified in taking this action, for instance, where the employee has been disobedient. If the employee insists on going home early, or refuses to do a particular job which is within the scope of her contract, or insists on continually doing something forbidden by his employer—smoking on the shop premises, for instance—the employer will be justified in dismissing the employee without notice.

Similarly, no notice will be necessary where the employee has been guilty of neglect of his duties. The neglect might amount to damage to stock or machinery, or to loss of trade; in these circumstances the employer may dismiss the employee summarily.

A third ground on which an employer may terminate the contract of employment without notice arises where the employee has been guilty of misconduct. Insolence alone can be regarded as misconduct but it is hardly likely that a single, isolated example of insolent behaviour on the part of the employee would justify his instant dismissal by the employer. It would depend very largely on what the insolent act amounted to, and what acts might be sufficiently serious to warrant summary dismissal might be left to the imagination. Certainly, where the insolence comprises several acts over a period this would be a ground of dismissal on the ground of misconduct. Similarly, if the chief clerk in the store uses funds belonging to his employers to play the Stock Exchange, or the horses, this would justify instant dismissal, as would any act that would be inconsistent with the employee's performance of his duties under his contract.

172

There is even evidence to show that the misconduct need not be connected with the employment: it might be something which has been done outside the work. Thus, the employee who is convicted of a criminal offence outside work could be dismissed, on the ground that it affected the reputation built up by the employer. A single act of dishonesty connected with the business is, of course, a perfectly sound reason for instant dismissal without notice by the employer. But not doing too well on a day release course at the local Technical College is not!

The incompetence of the employee is also a good ground for summary dismissal. If the employer has advertised for a trained man he is entitled to expect that the man who answers the advertisement and obtains the position will display those qualities expected from the advertisement. Thus, if he is employed as a scene painter he should be able to paint scenery; if he is employed as a salesman, he should be a trained salesman; if she is employed as a cashier she should be able to undertake a cashier's duty with competence. Under this heading of incompetency falls the question of the lazy employee also. Persistent laziness on the part of the employee will classify as incompetency and the employer will be justified in dismissing summarily.

It should be noted that the question of competence may well be a subjective one—that is to say, who is to decide whether a person is incompetent or not? It can depend so much on the views of the individual employer or employee. But if the employer states in the contract that he will be justified in dismissing the employee summarily "if he is dissatisfied with his work" the employee will have no remedy when he is dismissed nor can he demand to be told what the grounds for his dismissal are: all the employer need say is—"I am dissatisfied with your work". The questions of his reasons for dismissal simply will not arise.

It is possible that illness of the employee might be a reason for instant dismissal without notice, but much will depend on the nature of the illness and the length of the employment. The duration of the illness will also be relevant, of course: the shop manager who is told by his doctor that he must take a complete rest, when his contract is to end in six months' time, may well find himself being dismissed.

In the above circumstances, then, the employee may be dismissed without notice. Wherever there is summary dismissal for a good cause no reason need be given to the employee, though courtesy would demand that this should be done. If it is not done, the employee will have no remedy nevertheless. But if there is a good cause for dismissal and the employer does not know of it, he cannot later sue the employee for a "golden handshake" he might have given him when he wanted to end his contract before it expired. He cannot say that he need not have given the employee the money because he could have dismissed him summarily at the time: the point is, he did not dismiss him summarily at the time, so he cannot claim the return of the payment.

This was decided in *Bell v Lever Bros Ltd* (1932) which also decided the employee is under no duty to his employer to tell him of reasons which would justify his instant dismissal. The facts were that Bell was under a contract to serve as managing director for five years but before the period ended Bell agreed to accept a "golden handshake" of £30,000. After the money was paid the company discovered Bell had committed various acts for which he could have been dismissed without compensation. The court said the company could not get its £30,000 back.

If the employer does nothing about the employee's insolence, or disobedience or misconduct or other ground for instant dismissal, this can amount to condonation of the employee's conduct. In that circumstance, he cannot later dismiss the employee summarily. Thus, if the manager takes no steps against the employee when he is disobedient, he cannot use this disobedience as a ground for dismissal when, at a later date, he wants to dismiss him for some other reason, such as a disagreement over something unconnected with employment.

Where the employee has been properly dismissed he cannot recover any payment for work he does after the date of dismissal. For instance, the employee might refuse to regard the dismissal as justified and might turn up to work the following morning, continuing as though nothing has happened. He will be unable to claim any payment for his morning's work. He has been properly dismissed and the dismissal takes effect immediately.

If, on the other hand, he has been dismissed summarily without good reason he can claim that he has been dismissed for no good cause. In these circumstances he can recover not only the wages that he would have received had he been given proper notice but he might be able to claim even more, on the grounds of breach of contract through the unjust dismissal. This does not mean that the assistant who is entitled to two weeks' notice but who is unjustly dismissed summarily can then sit back at home during those two weeks and take life easily, on the supposition that he is entitled to damages and this will more than cover the wages he would have earned. He is under an obligation to minimise his loss, as we have already seen when discussing the measure of damages in contract. Thus, he should go out and attempt to obtain a similar position; only if he fails to do so will he be able to claim the full amount of his loss. As to what his loss actually is, it should be noted that any financial losses he makes, such as train fares in looking for another job, or loss of luncheon facilities, etc., can be claimed for, but no damages will be payable as compensation for injured feelings.

In *Brace v Calder* (1895) a partnership was dissolved and this meant Brace, effectively, was dismissed. But two of the partners offered him a similar job. He refused so the court said he was entitled to nominal damages only. But the duty to mitigate has to be judged from the facts of each case. In a 1967 case a managing director earning £7,500 a year was replaced after two years by another man. He had three years of his contract to run, and was offered the *assistant* managing director's position at the same salary. He refused it. He looked elsewhere for a job—at first in the £8–10,000 salary range but eventually lowered his sights to £4,000 a year. The court said he had not acted unreasonably in the circumstances, refusing a post as assistant and he was awarded one years' loss of salary at £7,500 and two years at £4,500, the assumption being made he would soon get a job at about £3,000 per annum.

So far we have discussed the situation where the employer dismisses the employee, but what is the situation where the employee walks out of his employment, in breach of his contract?

Where the employee walks out without giving the relevant notice it is open to the employer to sue him for damages. In practice, of course, this never happens other than at the very top level, where a managing director or some other highly paid executive breaks his contract. It simply is not worth the employer's while to sue his shop assistant. But he does have the legal right to do so. Furthermore, it should be noted that if the employee walks out like this, he is entitled to no wages payable since the last payment.

Thus, if the employee's wage is paid weekly, on a Friday, he will be able to claim nothing, where he walks out on a Thursday, for the work he has done on the Saturday, Monday, Tuesday, Wednesday and Thursday. The employer is justified in refusing payment. This assumes, of course, that the employee is paid on a weekly basis. If the wage is paid on a daily basis, however, such wages could be claimed.

Suspension of the employee or placing him on short time will be allowed only where such arrangements are in accordance with trade custom or under the terms of the contract. If this is not the case, notice of termination of the contract must be given.

It is possible that the contract may be terminated in other ways than the ones mentioned above. In a partnership, the death of one or other of the partners may terminate the contract. If the employee is in the employ of a firm composed of several partners he is employed by

175

the partners: a change in the partnership will therefore amount to termination of his contract. If the employer becomes bankrupt, this can bring about the end of the contract. The bankruptcy of the employee, of course, would not. The sale or other disposal of a business does not mean the owner need no longer employ the assistant. If the employee's wages are not paid he can sue his employer. If there is an obligation to provide *work* the sale of the business can amount to a breach of contract. But what if a wholesaler does not dispose of his business but merely moves it—say from Newcastle to Gateshead? Much will then depend upon the interpretation of the contract as to whether an order to work at the new location will or will not be a lawful order. If it is *not* lawful the employee can refuse to go and can treat the contract as discharged. Thus, when Mr O'Brien, who had worked and lived in the Liverpool area, refused to work in Cumberland it was held he was perfectly entitled to refuse. Finally, it is possible that the contract will be terminated automatically where the employing company is wound up, and it goes without saying perhaps that the contract can at any time be terminated by the mutual consent of the parties.

It is important to realise in this context that one need not wait until the contract is actually broken before one sues. Assume Mr Egg employs Mr Nogg as store manager. After a dispute Mr Nogg states flatly that he is not going to work out his notice. As soon as he declares such an intention Mr Egg can take proceedings to sue for breach of contract. This is called an "anticipatory breach" for obvious reasons. In fact, Mr Egg would be well advised to pursue his remedies immediately, on the grounds of the "anticipatory breach". The reason why, is that contracts are sometimes discharged on the grounds of frustration or impossibility as we have seen in Chapter 4. What would happen if Mr Egg laughed, and said, "I don't believe you—you'll be back!" and then Mr Nogg storms out of the store only to be knocked down by a car in the road? In fact, the liabilities of Mr Nogg under the contract would then be discharged, because he cannot turn up to work anyway, on account of his injuries.

Thus, if Mr Egg had started proceedings at once he could have sued. If he waits for performance of the contract, he might lose his remedy. The example given is, of course, not a good one since Mr Egg would not have time to start proceedings before Mr Nogg was run over! Nevertheless, it may serve as an example that shows the position clearly. Other examples may be found in contracts for the sale of goods, as in *Avery v Bowden* (1856). B agreed to load a cargo of wheat on A's ship at Odessa within a certain time. B subsequently refused to load the cargo. A would not accept this refusal and as time went on continued to demand performance of the agreement. Before

176

the last day of the time period the Crimean War broke out, rendering the performance of the contract illegal. The court decided the contract had been discharged before A had begun to treat it as broken. A had therefore lost his opportunity to sue for breach.

In these ways then, the contract of employment may be terminated. It would be useful at this point to discuss the remedies available to the parties where the contract has been broken.

Before looking at the remedies available for breach of contract, however, some reference should be made to the law relating to redundancy.

Redundancy

If an employee lost his job before 1965 he was unable to obtain compensation except by way of damages for breach of contract (see page 53) but the Redundancy Payments Act 1965 changed matters considerably. The main purpose of the Act is to give the employee compensation for loss of his job, whether or not unemployment results. The Act cannot be avoided, parties cannot contract out of it (except where agreements are exempted, or in the special cases relating to fixed term contracts—see page 179).

A lump sum redundancy payment applies only to employees who have been continuously employed for at least 104 weeks by an employer and who have been dismissed by reason of redundancy or have been laid off or kept on short time. Service up to and including the week which began before the employee became eighteen does not count. It should be added that the Act does not apply to employees who are husbands or wives of the employer or to domestic servants whose employer is a close relative. Nor does it apply to employees under certain fixed term contracts, persons who work less than 21 hours a week, persons under 18 or over 65 (60 for women), and employees who have been dismissed for misconduct or who have unreasonably refused re-engagement or alternative employment.

What is meant by redundancy? The effect of the Act is that a person will be redundant if, for instance, his shopkeeper employer closes down the business, or closes it down in the place where the employee works, or no longer has need for the kind of work the employee has been employed to carry out. An example would arise where checkout points were installed in a shop, making counter staff unnecessary—they would be redundant. The introduction of *new* checkout systems with which an employee could not cope would not lead to redundancy, for the dismissal then could be one for incompetency. In *O'Brien v Associated Fire Alarms Ltd* (1968) the electrician employed in Liverpool who was asked to work in Cumberland was really asked to do so because of the shortage of work in Liverpool, so he was entitled to a redundancy payment; when Mr Hindle asked for redundancy payment from Percival Boats Ltd in 1969, however, they pointed out he was a skilled woodworker, they were changing over to fibreglass and his work was uneconomic—he was "too good and too slow". He got no redundancy payment.

There has to be a *dismissal* before a claim can be made. Let us assume the supermarket management announce to their staff that the supermarket will be closing down under reorganisation in the near future. The assistant who "jumps the gun" and takes another job elsewhere will not be able to claim redundancy payment—she would not have been dismissed.

On the other hand, if due warning is given by the employer that the employment will end, say, in March, and the employee then gives notice that she wishes it to end in February and no objection is raised by the employer in writing, a redundancy payment will be due. A written notice from the employer objecting to the premature termination and asking the employee to withdraw her notice, may then lead to the industrial tribunal having to decide whether a payment is due and how much should be paid if anything.

Dismissal also has a somewhat extended meaning, as can be seen in Marriott's case in 1970. He was employed by the Oxford and District Co-operative Society Ltd, and was told that his status was to be reduced and his wage reduced by £1 a week because of a running down of his department. He protested, but accepted two weeks of this while he sought a new job; he then gave one week's notice to the Society and claimed redundancy payment. The Court of Appeal said he must be successful: the reduction in wage had been a breach of contract, he had not accepted this without protest, so he had been "dismissed" within the terms of the Act.

If the supermarket gives the manager notice of termination and then renews the contract of the manager, or re-engages him under a new contract of employment, he cannot use the notice of termination to claim a redundancy payment provided the contractual terms and conditions are much the same and take effect immediately, or in other cases the renewal or re-engagement follows an offer in writing from the supermarket before the ending of the employment.

What happens if an employee carries on working for the employer even after notice of dismissal? He may then find he has lost his right to redundancy pay because he has not been dismissed. And if he refuses to accept an offer to continue after being dismissed? Much will depend upon whether the offer is "suitable". Let us assume a supermarket manager is employed in the one store for several years and is then dismissed, and offered employment in the same capacity but on a "mobile" basis, working for periods of time in each of the stores in the chain, as a relief. His refusal would probably not be unreasonable and he could claim a redundancy payment. In *Morganite Crucible Ltd v Street* (1972) an audio typist who did a little clerical work was dismissed and then was offered alternative employment with an associated company where she would have more clerical work to do. She refused it, arguing it represented clerical rather than typing work, and in any case it would not last for more than twelve months. The Court agreed with her second ground but not her first, but the National Industrial Relations Court agreed with neither—the offer was for regular employment and it would be reasonable only to refuse temporary employment.

Whether an offer has been unreasonably refused will often depend upon personal factors: the poor state of health of an employee's wife has been held to justify refusal of a different job.

Reference was earlier made to fixed term contracts. An employee serving under a fixed term contract can get redundancy pay if he is dismissed prematurely because of redundancy but if he was engaged for two years or more there are two special rules that apply:

(i) if there is a written agreement that no such payment can arise if the contract is not renewed, he cannot claim redundancy when it is not renewed (he still can for *premature* dismissal, of course);
(ii) if he entered the contract before December 6, 1965, he cannot claim a redundancy payment under any circumstances.

How much is the employee entitled to by way of redundancy payment?

This depends upon the length of his continuous service with the employer. He must show at least 104 weeks of continuous service after the age of eighteen. Then, he can claim:

(i) half a week's pay for each year of employment between ages 18–21;
(ii) one week's pay for each year of employment between ages 22–40;
(iii) one and a half week's pay for each year of employment between ages 41–65.

The maximum service which can be counted is twenty years counting back from the end of the service. A year is 52 weeks, not a calendar year. The redundancy payment is reduced by one-twelfth for every completed month served beyond the male employee's 64th birthday so he is entitled to nothing if he reaches 65 before dismissal. For a woman the reduction is for every month served beyond 59 years.

The employer is responsible for the repayment but he can recover a rebate from the Central Redundancy Fund to which he will have been paying contributions.

Continuous employment is largely defined as it is under the Contracts of Employment Act 1972.

Unfair dismissal

The discussion earlier was concerned with wrongful dismissal, but what of "unfair" dismissal? At common law no action for unfair dismissal could be brought but as we have seen a man dismissed for redundancy can now claim a redundancy payment and, furthermore, by Schedule 1 of the Trade Union and Labour Relations Act, as amended, with certain exceptions, anyone unfairly dismissed can point to his dismissal as an unfair industrial practice.

The Act states that dismissal would be unfair if:

(a) the reason for dismissal was that the employee was exercising or wished to exercise his rights with regard to trade union membership;

(b) if the reason given was redundancy but others in similar situations had not been dismissed and he had been singled out because of his trade union activities and rights, or was selected for dismissal in contravention of agreed procedures and there was no special reason for the contravention.

Dismissal of a woman because she is pregnant is automatically unfair unless her pregnancy means she cannot do her work properly or it would be illegal for her to do the work while pregnant and the employer has offered suitable alternative work, if any is available.

All other reasons are *presumed* unfair but the employer can prove otherwise by showing the principal reason for dismissal was related to the capability, conduct, redundancy or some other substantial reason concerning the employee himself. He must also show he acted reasonably in dismissing the employee.

The remedy for unfair dismissal? An industrial tribunal can award compensation to the complaining employee. This is calculated in three stages: a basic award, worked out by reference to length of service (as with redundancy payments), a compensatory award, assessed in a way similar to damages for breach of contract, and an additional award where a re-instatement or re-engagement order has been dis-

180

obeyed by the employer.

Employees over retiring age are not covered by the provisions for unfair dismissal, nor are spouses who are employees, one of the other. Nor do the provisions apply when a fixed-term contract for two years or more ends, if before that date the employee agreed in writing to exclude any such claim. For this purpose, it was held in *BBC v Ioannou* (1975) a fixed term contract which gives either party a right to terminate by notice before the contract expires is not sufficient, and an exclusion in such a contract is void.

It should be noted that the remedies of the employee for wrongful dismissal have not been replaced by the statutory concept of unfair dismissal. Thus, if there is dismissal without proper notice there can be a remedy at common law—and such dismissal can be wrongful, it seems, without being unfair. An example arose in *Treganowan v Robert Knee Ltd* (1975) where the employee was dismissed without notice for boasting about her sex life, thus making the atmosphere at work unpleasant. She was held to have been *fairly* dismissed, but since notice should have been given the dismissal had been wrongful and she could claim damages.

Before we proceed to the common law remedies for breach of the contract of employment, however, we may discuss briefly certain other statutory rights that the employer must be aware of.

SPECIAL STATUTORY RIGHTS

Apart from the requirements of the Contracts of Employment Act, as amended, and the Redundancy Payments Act 1965, there are certain other statutory obligations and duties placed upon employers, apart from the obligations which will be noted later, arising out of the common law.

Sex Discrimination Act 1975

This Act makes it unlawful for the retailer or distributor to discriminate on grounds of sex when advertising a post, engaging employees or stating details of the terms offered. Thus, to advertise for a "salesgirl" could be an offence under the Act. It is similarly unlawful to discriminate in the promotion, training, transfer or other benefits, facilities or services. Equally, discrimination in selection for dismissal, short time or other detriments is illegal.

Though the provisions are designed to protect women in employment they apply equally to men and so discrimination is permissible only when the man (or woman) advertised for has, by reason of the

181

particular sex, a genuine occupational qualification for the job. It would also be permissible where it could be shown that decency or privacy might demand selection. In *Peake v Automotive Products* (1977) the complaint was made that men were being discriminated against because women employees were allowed to leave five minutes early to avoid the rush at the factory gates, but this was held to be a minor act of chivalry in the interests of safety, and not discrimination.

Equal Pay Act 1970

This Act, which covers pay, hours, holidays and sick pay provides that a woman's terms of employment shall be no less favourable than those of a man doing broadly similar work.

Complaints are heard by industrial tribunals which can order compensation, including compensation for hurt feelings, as was the case in *Gubala v Crompton Parkinson Ltd* (1977) where Mrs G was selected for redundancy ahead of a male colleague with the same length of service. She obtained compensation for unfair dismissal and £400 for hurt feelings.

It may be added that women are given further rights, under the Employment Protection Act 1975 in respect of maternity leave —under section 34 it is unfair to dismiss a woman employee merely because she is pregnant. Subject to certain conditions, including two years' continuous employment, a pregnant woman may claim up to 29 weeks' maternity leave and up to 6 weeks' maternity pay. The employer can claim a rebate of the money paid from the Government.

Disabled Persons (Employment) Act 1958

By this Act an employer who employs more than 20 workers is required to employ a three per cent quota of disabled persons provided suitable work is available. Non-compliance with these provisions can be a criminal offence.

These provisions are, of course, statutory. It has already been noted that they do not affect the common law remedies for breach of the contract of employment. But what are these remedies?

REMEDIES FOR BREACH OF CONTRACT

It would be convenient to deal first of all with the remedies that may be claimed by the employer, and then the remedies available to the employee.

182

Employer

As we have already seen above, in certain circumstances it is open to the employer to dismiss the employee summarily. Since these circumstances have already been discussed at some length the remedy of summary dismissal needs no further discussion here.

It might well be that there are no grounds for summary dismissal. Where this is the case the employee can still be dismissed immediately by the employer but the employer will then be called upon to pay the employee's wages in lieu of notice.

Thus, if he is bound to give his employee two weeks' notice, he can dismiss the employee immediately but will have to pay him the wages that he would have earned during those two weeks.

At one time it would have been possible to say that the employer also had the remedy of chastisement available to him where the employee was guilty of misconduct, but this remedy would hardly be exercised these days outside the father/son relationship!

It is always open to the employer to sue for any damage that he has suffered as a result of the employee's conduct. He can sue for damages, which will be related to the actual loss that he has suffered by the breach of contract. This does not mean that all losses can be sued for, as has already been pointed out: it is only those losses that arise naturally out of the breach of contract that will be used as the basis for assessing the compensation payable to the employer.

The remedy of the Injunction can also be used by the employer against the employee. Since this is a remedy that originated in the Court of Chancery it is discretionary in nature (the court decides whether it should be awarded—it cannot be demanded by the plaintiff) and the employer will have to show that he deserves the remedy: that is, he has behaved in a proper manner and the employee is taking unfair advantage of him. We have already seen that the remedy of Specific Performance does not lie in a contract of employment, but that the Injunction can be used to bring about much the same result where the employee is forbidden to work for any other employer (see page 56).

Employee

In the same way that in certain circumstances the employer may bring about the summary termination of the contract, so the employee may summarily end his contract with the employer. The employee who is called upon by his employer to take risks that were not within the terms of the original contract may regard that contract as terminated and his obligations under it discharged. Similarly, changes in

183

the conditions of his employment may allow him to terminate his contract as in the O'Brian case, for in such a case the terms of the contract have been changed without his consent. Thus, since contracts are based on agreements, the employer cannot change the terms without obtaining the consent of the employee to the changes.

If the employee has been dismissed without notice but for no good cause he can sue for the wages payable to him where proper notice should have been given. It is possible that in the case of wrongful dismissal he may be able to obtain more than simply the wages payable: if, for instance, he is a waiter who is wrongfully dismissed he may claim not only the amount of his wages but also the average amount of tips that he would have received from customers had he still been at work.

On the other hand it may well be that he will be faced with the defence of misconduct on his part, or the employer may claim that the employee had wrongfully walked out of his employment or that the employee has already been paid sick pay.

Where he does not sue for wages that are due he might bring an action for damages for wrongful dismissal. The same principles as to mitigation of loss and measure of damages apply in this circumstance as we have seen in other circumstances.

Yet another remedy that he might ask for is that of *Quantum Meruit*, which has already been discussed in Chapter 4. In the contract of employment the question of apportionment of wages arises, however: he will be able to sue on a *Quantum Meruit* where the frustration of the contract was not self-induced, but if the wages cannot be regarded as apportionable he might have difficulty in succeeding.

Finally, he might ask the court for an Injunction to be enforced against the employer, but it should be noted that the Injunction is a remedy which is negative in effect, so that if its result will be positive in nature it will not be given. Thus, an Injunction to prevent the employer from dismissing the employee might well be regarded as too positive in nature to be allowed by the court.

OBLIGATIONS OF THE PARTIES

Now that the remedies of both employer and employee have been discussed it would be convenient to turn to the question of the obligation of the parties to the contract of employment. In this context, once again, the obligations of the employer will first be dealt with, before proceeding to the question of the employee's obligations. Since obligations connote rights also, it is quite obvious that where there is a positive obligation placed upon one party, the result is in most instances that a corresponding right is the entitlement of the other. There will, therefore, be no need to discuss the respective rights of the parties: they are implied in the discussion of the obligations of the contracting parties.

Employer

The first, and perhaps obvious obligation placed upon the employer is to pay the wages agreed upon under the contract. If there are no wages agreed upon, then the payment of wages will be presumed by the court if it is shown that the work done by the employee has been accepted by the employer.

The employer's obligation to pay wages is affected by the Truck Acts by which payment must be in coin, and not in goods, no stipulations must be made as to the manner in which the wages can be spent, and no excessive deductions are to be made. These Acts were somewhat relaxed by the Payment of Wages Act 1960 which allows for payment in ways not authorised under the Truck Acts. These are by payment into a bank account in the name of the employee by postal order, cheque, or money order. But the employee must receive at or before the time of payment a written statement of the gross wages before deduction, the amount of each deduction, and the net amount due. And any employee who does not want to be paid this way can get his desire by giving written notice to the employer.

The list of deductions allowed under the Truck Acts is exhaustive but other statutes deal with matters such as income tax and National Insurance, while attachment of earnings is covered by the Attachment of Earnings Act 1971.

The payment of wages may also be affected by the Wages Councils Act 1959 under which Wages Councils may be established in particular industries if the Minister thinks that there is no adequate machinery to regulate the remuneration of employees within that industry. In this matter, he is the sole judge. The function of a Wages Council is to submit wages regulation proposals to the Minister, to fix the remuneration and holidays either generally or for particular work. The Minister may then act on these and make a Wages Council order, or he may refer the matter back for further consideration.

Thus, where there is a proper contract with agreed wages to be paid, the employee may be able to claim extra wages if he can show that he has done extra work which has been accepted by his employer. The agreement to pay extra wages for the extra work will be implied.

If the contract contains provisions as to free board and medical

185

attention these will be enforced; if they do not appear in the contract they will not, obviously, be implied. If, on the other hand, the employee is injured and the employer orders special attention for him—a private room in a nursing home for instance—then it is the employer who will have to pay for the attention.

In certain circumstances there will be an obligation placed upon the employer to provide work for the employee. This will be the case where a representative is employed on a basic salary plus commission basis. If the employee is not given work he cannot earn commission: it is the obligation of the employer to provide work in these circumstances, provided the contract states nothing to the contrary.

A general duty can also be said to have arisen between employer and employee whereby employers should behave reasonably and responsibly towards their employees. It could be said that both parties should show mutual respect towards each other—which is not always possible at sales time in a large store! Certainly, arbitrary and inconsiderate action taken by an employer can amount to a breach of contract and if it is serious enough it can be regarded as an implied dismissal of the employee—with all the consequences that arise from such an action.

One example would be where an employee is asked to carry out deliveries in a van which he knows to be in an unsafe condition—with faulty brakes, perhaps. If this led to his refusal, and a consequent deterioration of relationships with the management, his decision to leave as a result *could* be taken as a dismissal and he might be able to claim damages, successfully.

In *Cox v Philips Industries Ltd* (1976) C wrote a reasonable letter of protest to his employers about his salary. Shortly afterwards, he was demoted, and his duties were henceforth vague: he did not know what to do and nobody told him. He became depressed and ill. The court held the employer had broken the contract by treating him in this manner and he obtained £500 damages. In *Wares v Caithness Leather Products Ltd* (1974) an employer who used foul language to a woman employee was held to have broken his contract—but this situation will always depend upon the circumstances. Such language might not be a breach of contract on, for instance, a sea-going vessel!

Apart from these duties, there is also a duty placed upon the employer to indemnify the employee for any loss or injuries he might receive during the course of his employment. If he is acting outside that employment, or if he is in breach of his own duty under the contract, it may well be that he will be unable to claim an indemnity from the employer, but much will depend on the circumstances.

There is no general duty placed on the employer to insure his employee against injury (except for such obligations as those imposed by the National Insurance Act 1946, the National Insurance (Industrial Injuries) Act 1946, and the National Health Service Contributions Act 1957), but where the employee drives a car for the employer of course he must take out such insurance as is prescribed. Apart from this, however, it is a wise employer who insures the safety of his employees.

One particular situation often causes a certain amount of difficulty in the employer/employee relationship. This is the question of the "character reference". Very often the employee thinks that he is entitled to such a reference, and the employer himself often regards it as a duty incumbent upon him to give one.

In fact, of course, no such duty exists. The giving of a character reference is entirely discretionary, and the employer is under no obligation to the employee to do what he asks. Nevertheless, in practice, the employer does give such references during the term of employment, or at its termination. In so doing he should be extremely careful.

The danger is that if he does not state in the reference what he honestly believes to be true concerning the employee he may find himself being sued by the employee's new employer in fraud or deceit. Thus, the employer who is so glad to see the back of the employee that he gives him a glowing, entirely unjustified reference, stating that the man is as honest as the day is long, may find himself liable to the new employer who takes on the employee on the strength of the recommendation and is robbed of all his takings.

Generally speaking, however, there is no liability for merely careless statements. This has long been the rule, with the exception of certain special relationships such as solicitor and client. Even so, negligence in the writing of a reference can lead to liability if the employer knows or ought to know that the prospective employer seeking his advice will rely on that advice. If he does not act carefully he might find himself liable for financial loss arising.

The employer should therefore write out his reference with care. He need not disclose all the information available to him: he may say, without liability to anyone, that he is releasing an employee because of a "decrease in business" even though the decrease is due to the employee's dishonesty, of which he is aware. But any positive statement that he makes must be made in good faith. Even then he might find himself being sued—not by the new employer, but by the employee, who regards the statement as libellous. In such a case, the employer giving the reference may plead that the document is subject to qualified privilege, but as can be seen from the foregoing, the very giving of character references is an action fraught with peril!

They have even been dealt with by the criminal law. Section 16 of the Theft Act 1968 states that any person who by deception dishonestly gets for himself or another any financial advantage can end up with five years in prison. So if the supermarket director gives a reference containing false statements about a manager he wants to get rid of (or is friendly with) so that the manager gets a plum job he could well be guilty of an offence under the 1968 Act.

A most important obligation placed upon the employer is that as to the safety of his servant. To this end he is called upon by several Acts of Parliament to provide competent staff, to provide safe working conditions, proper tools and machinery, effective fencing of dangerous machinery, etc. As far as the retailer is concerned the position is largely governed by the Offices, Shops and Railways Premises Act 1963 which came into effect in 1964. This Act took the place of the Offices Act 1960 which was largely unused, and covered also certain sections of the Shops Act 1950. Some details of the last-mentioned Act are given on page 190. It extends the scope of the operation of provisions relating to the safety of employees as well as to their health and welfare.

The Act itself is really further recognition of the principle that the employer should provide basic minimum standards of working conditions, and particularly so in the case of the office or shop worker who, with the high cost of floor space in the towns, finds himself working in even more cramped conditions than he imagined possible.

Under the Act, an office is a place used mainly for administrative or clerical work, and a shop is a place where wholesale and retail trade is carried on, so this will include cafes, restaurants, hotel bars and public houses. One noteworthy point is that the small shopkeeper who employs close relatives or only part-time help is not covered by the Act, so the provisions will not apply to him (unless the part-time help works for more than twenty-one hours a week). The reason for such exclusion is said to be the fear that small shopkeepers might be driven out of business if they were called upon to meet the financial obligations incurred under the Act.

With regard to safety provisions for the employee, these in the main follow the model laid down in the Factories Act: bacon slicers and other dangerous machines must be properly guarded or fenced, floors and stairs, passages and handrails must be firm and secure, and Factories Act provisions are closely followed in relation to fire precaution and first-aid requirements. The Act lays down general provisions relating to health, safety and welfare which will in due course be replaced by provisions made under the Health and Safety at Work

188

Act 1974.

The Act requires that suitable and sufficient sanitary conveniences must be provided at conveniently accessible places and must be kept clean, maintained, effectively lighted and ventilated. There must also be suitable facilities for washing. Detailed provisions are to be found in the Sanitary Conveniences Regulations 1964 and the Washing Facilities Regulations 1964.

An adequate supply of drinking water must be provided, as must accommodation for clothing not worn during working hours and for all employees who have the chance to sit down—without detriment to their work, of course—suitable seating must be provided. And if employees eat their meals on the premises adequate facilities for eating meals must be made available.

A first aid box or cupboard must be provided and maintained—and more than one if there are more than 150 employees. The box must be in the charge of a responsible person and if there are more than 150 employees there must also be a properly trained first aid officer employed and named.

The Act is also concerned with temperature, lighting and ventilation of premises on which people may be working. Adequate provision must be made for securing and maintaining, by the circulation of sufficient supplies of fresh or artificially purified air, the ventilation of every room in which persons are employed to work. Guidance on lighting standards is given by the Department of Employment.

Similarly a reasonable temperature must be maintained in every workroom and where the work done does not involve severe physical effort the temperature must be at least 16 degrees Centigrade after the first hour. A thermometer must also be provided. But the retailer who seeks to raise the temperature with smelly oil stoves might find himself in trouble: the heating method must not induce injurious or offensive fumes! On the other hand these temperature provisions do not apply to workrooms—such as a store for instance—where persons work for short periods only. Nor do they apply to the shop itself as a whole, necessarily: if the public are to come in it might not be reasonably practicable to maintain the temperature mentioned—this would certainly be the case where the goods need to be kept in cold storage, for instance. But in such cases there must be some convenient and accessible place where the employees working there can go to warm themselves.

The Act is concerned also with space for employees. The general requirement is that, taking into account furniture, machinery, equipment and so on, the room must not be so overcrowded as to cause risk of injury to the health of the persons working there. As a guideline, the

189

Act states there must be at least 40 square feet of floor space and 400 cubic feet of capacity for each employee—but this is without prejudice to the general requirement.

Floors, steps, stairs, passages and gangways must be sound, properly maintained and kept clean and free from obstruction. There are provisions also for the guarding of floor openings and stairs with handrails.

The administration of the Act is left partly to local authorities and partly to the Department. The inspection of offices and shops to see that they conform to the regulations issued lies with the local authorities, but the Secretary of State for Employment is called upon to set up a small central inspectorate to deal with difficulties of co-ordinating local groups. Offices and shops on railway premises fall under the control of Factory Inspectors, however.

The employer is made specifically liable in addition under the Employers Liability (Defective Equipment) Act 1969. This states that if an employee suffers personal injury because of defective equipment provided by the employer for business purposes it will be useless for the employer to argue that the defect is due wholly or in part to some other person—such as the manufacturer of the equipment or some other employee who had used it, damaged it and made it dangerous. The injury arising is, under the Act, regarded also as the responsibility of the employer.

This means in a sense that the employer is strictly liable and the injured employee does not have to prove the employer was *negligent*. But his own *contributory* negligence can be used as a defence by the employer, who can also claim against others, such as the manufacturer or other, negligent, person responsible. The whole idea behind the Act, of course, is to make it easier for injured persons to sue. But it should be emphasised the Act applies only to equipment supplied *for business purposes*.

The Shops Acts

A series of Acts have been passed relating to hours of work and conditions in shops; the 1950 Act was the most comprehensive and was amended by the Shops (Early Closing Days) Act 1965. The provisions in these Acts which dealt with health and comfort have now been repealed and replaced by those in the Offices, Shops and Railway Premises Act 1963.

The Shops Acts are therefore concerned now with hours of opening.

A shop is defined by the Act as including any premises where any

190

retail trade or business is carried on and a shop assistant as one concerned wholly or mainly in a shop, in connection with the serving of customers or the receipt of orders or the despatch of goods. It would seem that the business must be concerned with selling goods to purchasers who do not intend to resell. The shop itself can, on the other hand, include a coin-operated launderette. And a person can be a shop assistant even though he has no connection with the customers direct.

The main provisions of the 1950 Act are as follows.

(1) Every shop must be closed not later than 1 p.m. in the afternoon on one weekday each week. The 1965 Act makes the shop occupier responsible for fixing the day and displaying a notice stating the day in the shop. The early closing provision does not apply to some shops, such as those selling intoxicating liquor, refreshments, meat, fish, milk, and similar articles.

(2) Every shop must close by 8 p.m. except on the late day, which may be 9 p.m. (a Saturday unless fixed for some other day by the local authority). A Closing Order may also be made fixing the hours at which in certain areas all shops (or those of a certain class) are to be closed for serving of customers.

(3) On at least one weekday in each week shop assistants must be allowed a holiday after 1.30 p.m. (except in the week before a bank holiday if the assistant is not employed on the bank holiday, and if the employment of the shop assistant ceases not later than 1.30 p.m. on another day in the same week as the bank holiday). Every young person wholly or mainly employed about the business of a shop is regarded as being a shop assistant and so the half-holiday provisions apply (unless he was employed for less than 25 hours in the week).

(4) No shop assistant may be employed for more than six hours without an interval of twenty minutes being allowed during that period—in the case of young persons, the period is five hours. On half days the period is five and a half hours. Forty-five minutes must be allowed for dinner if the assistant is employed between 11.30 and 2.30 p.m., but it must be one hour if dinner is not taken in the shop. If the assistant is employed between 4 p.m. and 7 p.m. thirty minutes must be allowed for tea.

(5) As far as Sunday employment is concerned the 1950 Act states that four hours' or more working on a Sunday entitles the shop assistant to a whole day's holiday in lieu—other than the half holiday he might be entitled to. For less than four hours' work, a half holiday can be claimed. There are certain exceptions to this rule, e.g. in shops selling refreshments. As for Sunday opening, the general rule is it is forbidden but many shops such as newsagents are exempted from this.

191

(6) Young persons (that is, persons below 18 years of age) are subject to special rules. Between ages 16–18 they cannot be employed for more than 48 working hours in a week; under 16 years of age they cannot be employed for more than 44 hours in a week (with the raising of the school leaving age this provision is probably no longer necessary, except in the case of school holidays). Overtime beyond these hours can be worked but not for more than six weeks in a year, or for more than 50 hours in a year, or for more than twelve hours in one week. Special rules apply to shops serving meals, liquor or refreshments, and where the business is concerned with accessories for aircraft, motor vehicles and cycles.

What will happen if the shopkeeper shows that he did not know, or could not reasonably have discovered that a young person had been employed over the maximum (where he has also been employed by another retailer, for instance)? In such a case it would be a good defence to a charge under the Act.

Night work by young persons in shops is prevented though some relaxations are allowed, for instance in the delivery of milk or the serving of meals, which might occur before 6 a.m. or after 10 p.m.

Responsibility for enforcing the Acts lies with the local authorities. The person primarily liable under the Act is the occupier of the shop, though he can shift the blame onto the actual offender.

The Young Persons (Employment) Acts 1938 and 1964 deal with certain other employments such as the collection of goods or the carrying, unloading or loading of goods incidental to their collection or delivery. A 48 hours' maximum is laid down for young persons (44 for under 16s) and a limited amount of overtime allowed. Prescribed intervals are laid down for rest periods and meals, half holidays and Sunday working. The Shops Act 1950 provides that in some employments, such as a residential hotel, an employer may choose to apply either the provisions of the Shops Act or the Young Persons (Employment) Act 1938.

An employer who has persons under eighteen working for him must keep a complete record of their hours of work, mealbreaks, rest intervals and overtime. Alternatively he can keep and display a notice stating what these shall be and then simply record any deviations that actually occur. Failure to follow these requirements would be an offence under the Act.

Employee

The contract of employment is one whereby the employee agrees to provide service to his employer: the first and primary obligation of the employee is, therefore, that of personal service. The employer is entitled to expect that the employee will do the work he is employed to do. If the assistant is employed to serve in the shop the employer would be justifiably annoyed if she took off one afternoon a week to do a part-time job, having one of her friends to come in and take her place at the counter!

It has already been pointed out that one of the grounds for summary dismissal of an employee is disobedience. Thus, this leads to the corollary that the employee is under an obligation to obey his employer in so far as the orders given are reasonable and within the scope of the employment. Nowadays, the whole question of whether an employee needs to do any particular job is governed largely by trade union attitudes, but in general the principle of obedience remains.

What is the situation where the employee is aware of the fact that certain of the other employees are behaving in a dishonest manner? Should he report their conduct to the employer? The courts have in fact been quite clear on this point: the employee is not breaking the law if he fails to disclose any information he possesses about conduct detrimental to his employer. If he knows that his colleagues are indulging in sharp practices he would be wise to inform his employer of the fact, nevertheless.

It is quite true that this ignores the reality of the situation, where the employee feels bound not to betray his friends, but in the contract of employment his loyalty lies towards his employer. His loyalty is bought by the employer. If he does not disclose his colleagues' misdemeanours to his employer the result may well be that he will find himself being dismissed and in such a case he will have no remedy.

The strange situation is that although he is under a duty to disclose dishonest acts carried out by other employees he is under no obligation to disclose his own acts of the same nature! The principle here is that the employee cannot be expected to indict himself. Thus, if two employees together systematically swindle their employer each is under a duty to disclose the other's activities to the employer, but not his own.

What is the practical result of such a situation? It can mean that a salesman will be dismissed for not informing his employer of the manager's dishonesty—or indeed of any act constituting disloyalty towards the employer. But if, on the other hand, the salesman has himself been dishonest but has his contract terminated for other reasons and is paid a pension or is given a gratuity, the employer cannot later demand the return of the gratuity on the grounds that if he had known of the employee's dishonesty earlier he would have given no such gratuity. The employee is not bound to tell his employer of his own peccadilloes: he need not indict himself.

Almost as part of the foregoing, there is a duty placed upon the employee to give faithful, honest service to his employer. This means that not only must he refrain from acts of dishonesty but he must also refrain from acts which will damage his employer's business.

If the employee is an electrician, he should not work in his spare time doing jobs that could have been done by his employer. The shop assistant who sees that a particular item in the shop is in great demand must not buy stocks of such items and sell them himself. It is the duty of the employee to look after his employer's interests and this he will not do if he sets up in competition himself, or works for a rival firm during his off-duty hours.

In the same way that the employer is called upon to indemnify the employee for any loss or injury the employee has suffered during the course of his employment, so the employee must indemnify his employer for any loss caused by the action of the employee. This was the situation in *Romford Ice and Cold Storage Co Ltd v Lister* (1957). L was employed as a lorry driver and his father was mate. The son's negligence caused injury to the father, who sued the employer. The employer was held vicariously liable for the son's negligence. The employer sued the son for his negligence and for breach of contract. It was held that the son was liable to the employer.

Thus, if the employee negligently drops a heavy crate of tinned goods on to a customer's foot it is extremely unlikely that the customer will go to the trouble of suing the employee. It will not be worth his while, since he is far more likely to obtain compensation for his injury from the employer, and as we will see shortly the employer is liable for the acts of his employee to a certain extent.

The customer will, therefore, sue the employer. If he succeeds, the employer will have suffered financial loss through the negligence of his employee. It may well be that he will then demand an indemnity from the negligent employee, and this he is entitled to do. The practical result may well be that the employee will have to pay to the employer the damages that the customer will have received from the employer. This assumes that the employee is in a financial position to do this.

There is also a duty incumbent upon the employee to account for all profits that he makes in his employment. The courts have construed this situation very strictly: any profit made by the employee will be payable to the employer if the profit can be regarded as having been made by virtue of the fact of employment. This prevents the employee making money secretly, "on the side", to the detriment of his employer's receipts.

194

Indeed, if the contract is one for exclusive employment, as it will in most cases be, all money earned by the employee must be paid to the employer and if the work is extra to the employment, that is, done outside the normal contract of employment, there may be liability in other directions, as we have already seen, where the employee works, in competition with his employer, for a rival firm. In *Hivac v Park Royal Scientific Instruments* (1946) H made midget valves for hearing aids. P set up in competition and some of H's employees spent their Sundays working for P. The court decided an implied term must be read into their agreements that the workmen should not break faith to H by doing any act which would injure H's business, and an injunction restraining the inducement of this breach of contract would be granted.

The question of secrecy can also arise. Since the employee is under a duty to provide faithful, honest service he should not tell trade competitors of his employer's trade secrets. Obviously the situation here will depend very largely upon the circumstances of the employment and of the trade itself. Nevertheless, if it is possible to generalise and state that if the information is such that it might be of use to a competitor, or of detriment to the employer's trade if disclosed, the employee is under a duty not to disclose such information.

Thus, he should not disclose the existence of special markets, or the source of special supplies, to his employer's trade competitors or others who might use such information to the employer's detriment. He should not disclose the new system of accounts used by his employer, he should not disclose exactly how much the amount of his employer's sales are each week, or how they are made up.

It has already been pointed out that where fraudulent behaviour on the part of employees is concerned there is no *duty* as such to disclose, but the employee may be dismissable if the circumstances are not disclosed.

In a discussion of the question of trade secrets and the prohibition placed upon the employee from disclosing such secrets, it would be convenient to mention the question of patents and copyright.

The ownership of a patent depends on whether the patented article was developed by the employee on his own account or was developed by him, working as his employer's tool, so to speak. It is quite obvious that the employer who directs the employee to develop a particular process or system or article, etc., is merely using the employee as a tool and the patent will belong to the employer. The situation is slightly more difficult to decide where the employer does not direct the employee to apply his energies to this particular task, but during the course of his employment the employee discovers certain information which enables him to develop the system, in his own time perhaps.

There again, basically, the patent belongs to the employer. But if the employee has brought up the idea himself he can be regarded at least as a joint owner of the patent rights, or even the sole owner. In circumstances such as these, where the patent is developed in the "firm's time" even if the employee is entitled to the patent rights it might well be that it is only the employer who is entitled to the benefits of the patented system or article.

In practice, most employers cover these contingencies by making special reference to the problem, either by claiming all rights themselves, or by agreeing to joint ownership of patent rights, or by in effect buying such rights from the employee with a bonus payable to him.

Much the same sort of situation arises in the case of copyright. The important question to be answered is—"Was the writing done in the course of the author's employment?" If it was, it is the employer who will obtain copyright in the written work, unless there are other arrangements made by the parties. If it is extraneous to the matter of the writer's employment then it is he who will be entitled to the copyright in the work.

It goes without saying, finally, that on the termination of the employment the employee should not make use of any secret information that he has acquired during the course of his employment. Thus, a list of customers who like particular products at a particular time, or a method used by the old firm which is unique and not written down, should not be used by the employee who leaves to set up in competition.

The question of restraint of trade arises in relation to the contract of employment, but since this has already been discussed in Chapter 4 it will suffice to mention it but briefly here.

The terms restricting the employee must be imposed only to protect trade secrets or business connections and must not restrict the employee unduly in the exercise of the particular skills that he has acquired. Nor must the restriction be too wide in nature.

In deciding whether the restriction is reasonable the courts will inquire, therefore, into the nature of the business, to discover whether the possibility of trade secrets, etc., arises; the position held by the employee, for obviously the junior employee who cannot damage the employer should not be restrained; the extent of the promise of non-competition, for if the employer's business extends over a three-mile radius it would be unreasonable to make the covenant extend over a ten-mile radius; and the usage of the trade, to discover whether such restrictions are customary within that particular type of employment.

196

It may be added that though the restrictive covenant may bind the employee when he leaves the firm, this will not be the case where the employer has wrongfully dismissed the employee. By wrongfully dismissing him he has by implication waived any rights that he might have had to enforce the covenant. The employer has broken his contract, so he cannot thereafter attempt to enforce one of the clauses in that contract.

Liabilities to Third Parties

The scope of the contract of employment is such that it can affect not only the two parties to the contract but also parties who stand outside the contract.

Such liability can arise in contract, tort, or under criminal law. Some discussion has already been undertaken with respect to the question of interference with contractual relations: this may here be dispensed with.

Contract

The employee who acts without his employer's authority will make himself liable to third parties who suffer loss as a result of his conduct. The employer will not be liable himself, for he has not authorised the employee to act in this way.

This situation differs where the relationship of Principal and Agent arises. If the employee does not have authority and signs a document in his own name, or is an agent but does not disclose the fact of the agency, he will make himself personally liable for his actions. But where the relationship of Principal and Agent arises generally, the effect of the employee's action is to bind the employer in relation to the third party.

This can be explained by pointing out that the agent is nothing more than a tool; he is employed by the Principal to make a contract *for the Principal* with a third party. Once the contract is completed, the agent drops out of sight, and the two parties to the contract are the employer (principal) and the other contracting party (third party).

The situations in which an employee can make his employer liable in contract are:

(1) where he has been expressly authorised by the employer to make the contract;
(2) where he has *implied* authority to make the contract;
(3) where the employer has held out the employee as a person who

has power to make such contracts and
(4) where he later agrees to be bound by (ratifies) an unauthorised contract.

Thus, where the employee is employed to buy goods on credit for the employer, the employer must pay for the goods. The agent thus employed can bind the employer to such contracts even where the authority to do so is lacking, provided that to all intents and purposes such authority is his. This was the case in *Watteau v Fenwick* (1893). H sold his public house to F but remained on as manager. W, who knew nothing about the transaction, sold cigars to H for the use of the public house. F had expressly forbidden H to buy cigars. W sued F for the price. F could not use his instruction to H as a defence since W knew nothing about it and it was ordinarily within the powers of a manager or owner to buy cigars for the public house. It was decided F was liable for the price. Thus, if the shop manager has always given orders to the salesman when he calls, the shop owner will be liable on such contracts made even though he has expressly forbidden the employee to make such orders in future. For this amounts to a private arrangement between him and the employee, one which the salesman cannot be expected to know about. As far as he is concerned, the manager has authority to make the orders. When they are made, therefore, the owner will be bound.

The practical effect of such a situation can be clearly seen where, after a stormy interview, the owner of the shop dismisses the manager, with effect from the day's end. If, then, the salesman walks in and the manager maliciously places orders for goods not wanted by the owner, and those goods are within the usual powers of the manager to order, the orders he makes—even though he has been dismissed—will be enforceable against the employer. In *Summers v Solomon* (1857) A customarily accepted orders from B who was acting as C's agent. When B was dismissed from his employment B continued to fraudulently pledge C's credit with A. The court decided C was liable to A for the price of the goods supplied.

Quite obviously, to be safe from such situations the employer should make it known to persons customarily dealing with his employee that the employee is no longer in his service, otherwise he might find himself faced with some very large bills! It is always open to him to sue the employee, of course, but that does not detract from his liability on the orders that the employee has given.

If, on the other hand, the orders given were not within the scope of the employee's authority the employer might well be able to escape liability on the ground that there was no reason to suppose on the

198

salesman's part that such authority had been given to the employee.

An employee who has made a contract on behalf of his employer will sometimes *himself* be liable to the other contracting party. This will be so, for instance, where he has stated he has authority to make the contract but in fact he has no such authority. If the employer later refuses to ratify the agreement the employee will be liable to the other party. He may also be liable under the particular usage of the trade; where he signs a bill of exchange without adding he is signing for his employer; or where he enters a contract on behalf of his employer without disclosing the existence of the employer.

Tort

Tortious liability under the contract of employment is largely concerned with the doctrine of vicarious liability. This has already been touched upon in Chapter 6, but it may be discussed further here. It was pointed out earlier that the employer will be liable for the acts of his employee provided that they are carried out in the course and within the scope of his employment.

To what extent are actions regarded as falling within the scope of employment? What will happen, for instance, if the employee is given the task of parcelling up goods downstairs, and he takes time off to smoke a cigarette which causes a fire that demolishes the premises next door? Will the employer be liable for the damage done to the neighbour's premises?

"Well," he might say, "I employed the lad to parcel goods, not smoke cigarettes. It was the smoking that started the fire, not the parcelling of goods. I'm not liable."

In fact, he would be wrong. He would be liable, for the courts have said that actions such as lighting a cigarette can be regarded as normally incidental to the performance of the employment and as such will incur liability.

Similarly, where the office staff wash their hands before leaving the premises and negligently leave a tap running which floods the premises below, it will be useless for the employer to cry—"But he washed his hands after hours!"

He will be liable on the same principle as that stated above. It is to be regarded as part of the employment.

Nor would it avail the employer to say that he is not liable because:

"I expressly told the employee not to do the act complained of!"

Express prohibition will not excuse the employer from liability provided that the action was done within the scope of employment. Thus, if the employer expressly warns his vanman not to drive over thirty miles an hour this will be no defence for him when the van driver negligently knocks down an old lady. The employer might point out that he employs the van driver to drive, not to knock down old ladies, but the point is that he is liable for the van driver's negligence nevertheless, for he employs him to drive, and he was driving when he caused the accident.

On the other hand, there will be no liability where the act is clearly outside the scope of employment. The employer is liable for the knocking down of the old lady, but if the van driver has taken the van during his lunch hour to take his girl friend for a drive it is hardly the employer who can be regarded as liable for any consequences arising—whether it be the knocking down of old ladies, or any other negligent act committed by the employee. In *Poland v Parr and Sons* (1927) H was employed as a lorry driver by P. Reasonably believing that a boy was stealing sugar from his employer's lorry he struck the boy, who fell into the road, was injured, and had a leg amputated. The court decided the employee was acting in defence of his employer's property and P was liable to the plaintiff.

It is possible that the act of the employee was done for his own personal benefit. Thus, the employee might have stolen some money from a customer's handbag. The mere fact of personal benefit does not automatically exclude the liability of the employer for his employee's actions. If he employs the assistant to carry Mr Meek's goods, and the employee steals some of these goods, Mr Meek is perfectly able to sue the employer even though the act was for the employee's personal benefit.

Nor will it matter that the action taken by the employee was motivated by pure malice or ill will. The general rule is still good: if the act was committed within the scope of employment the employer will be liable for that act. In a case reported in 1948 an intoxicated customer was refused a drink. He picked up a glass and threw it at the barman, then turned to leave. The barman picked up a piece of the broken glass and threw it at the retreating drunk. A splinter of the glass struck him in the eye. Although the act was done out of resentment it was a wrongful mode of keeping order—which the barman was employed to do—and the employer was liable. Thus, the assistant who is employed to keep order at the door during sales time by allowing only six people through at a time will be personally liable if she punches the lady in the red hat on the nose when she pushes her way through. The employer will not be liable, for he employs the assistant to keep order, not to cause disorder by assaulting a customer. But if the assistant closes the door in the woman's face and the red-hatted lady's finger is caught and pinched, the employer *will* be liable, for the assistant has done only what she is employed to do. The fact that she has done it negligently means that the employer is liable.

It has already been noted that no liability falls to the employer where the employee is not a "servant" but "an independent contractor". This is certainly true as a generality, but in particular circumstances liability on the part of the employer will arise.

The employer is under a duty to make his premises safe for the public and for his employees also. If his lift is not working, or his flooring needs repair, he is under a duty to make them safe. Thus, he should get the repairs carried out, and if he does this by employing an independent contractor he may yet be liable if the work is faulty. If his choice of workman was reasonable—that is, he employed a reputable firm to do the work—it is the firm which is liable, not the employer. But if he employed a friend who knew little about lifts or floors, the employer has not discharged his duty by delegating the work to the independent contractor.

Similarly, the employer is under a duty to provide proper tools and machinery for his employees. If he gives them a new bacon slicer of his own invention and make, or a new type of cake tongs which will not pick up or hold cakes, then it is the employer who will be liable for the sliced finger in the bacon and the cake-stained woollen suit.

Formerly, he would not be liable if it could be shown that the bacon slicer was provided by a reputable firm and was of a standard make and pattern, and that the cake tongs were similarly supplied and made. The remedy would lie only against the manufacturer, the independent contractor, in this case and not against the employer, for he had behaved properly in such circumstances and had effectively delegated his duty to take care.

The situation has now been changed as a result of the Employers Liability (Defective Equipment) Act 1969 (see page 190) which has meant that his duty of care cannot be delegated.

Crime

Generally, the employer is not liable for crimes committed by his employee: his guilty intent cannot be imputed to his employer. It is different where the employer *ordered* the employee to commit the crime, or if knowing he was doing it he failed to stop him.

There are particular cases in addition where the employer can be liable vicariously. One arises where the employee commits a public nuisance—such as where the supermarket manager allows rubbish to be piled at the back of the store and blocks the drains. The employer can be indicted even though the nuisance was committed against his orders. A second case arises where an employee publishes a criminal libel—with or without the employer's authority. The employer can in this situation plead the two defences of "no authority consent or knowledge" and "due care and caution" however.

Some statutes expressly make an employer liable—the Food and Drugs Act 1955 is an example. They are of the kind regulating the conduct of trade and business, and no guilty intent needs to be proved. The Licensing Acts provide further examples of employer liability: only the licensee can commit the offence.

Moreover, a retailer can "sell" goods even when he is nowhere near the shop and has given express orders. In *Cooper v Moore* (1898) D sold American hams in his shops. He told his assistants they were to be described only as "breakfast hams". While he was away an assistant sold a ham as a "Scotch ham". D was convicted under the Merchandise Marks Act 1887, now replaced by the Trade Descriptions Act.

Even more serious is the example provided by *Allen v Whitehead* (1930). The proprietor of a cafe delegated control of the premises to a manager. He had a warning from the police that prostitutes were using the cafe. He told the manager this was not to be allowed, and he had a notice to this effect fixed to the cafe wall. He visited the premises twice a week and saw no prostitutes. Later, the prostitutes began to congregate again in the cafe, to the manager's knowledge. W's ignorance of the fact was held to be no defence and he was convicted.

In fact, in 1965, the House of Lords did emphasise that where a statute uses the word "knowingly" this would generally exclude vicarious liability—thus meeting some of the criticisms voiced against Allen's case above. Two of the judges stated, however, that an exception exists in licensing cases, where management has been delegated to an employee. And in 1969, in *R v Winsor* the holder of an on-licence was convicted where his manager sold liquor to a person who ought not to have been served. There had been a delegation of management so knowledge of the manager could be imputed to the licensee. This was not the case, on the other hand, in the *Tesco Supermarket* case (see page 99) where the employer was held not liable.

THE CONTRACT OF APPRENTICESHIP

The contract of apprenticeship differs from the contract of service, which is what has been discussed up to this point. In the contract of apprenticeship the apprentice is legally bound to another person in order to learn a trade or calling. The master teaches, the apprentice learns by serving the master. The master binds himself to instruct and teach the apprentice in his trade, profession or business.

Formerly, the contract of apprenticeship had to be made under seal to be effective, but now it is enough if it is made in writing. But the minor who enters a contract of apprenticeship must personally agree to it, otherwise it will not be binding upon him. Thus, it cannot be made for him by his father, for instance.

The contract of apprenticeship will normally impose certain obligations upon the employer. Thus, in most instances, the employer will be called upon to provide board and lodging or wages in lieu, together with any medical attention necessary. If the contract makes no special provisions to the contrary, the employer cannot send the apprentice outside the United Kingdom.

The apprentice also will have obligations, however. He must continue to serve the employer while he is willing to teach. If the employer abandons the business, there is nothing for the apprentice to learn and in those circumstances the apprentice is released from his obligation. But he must not absent himself from his work without good cause, and generally he is under an obligation to do as the employer directs. This applies even if he is called upon to work for another employer.

Where the two parties to the contract have a dispute which they cannot resolve it may be settled for them in a magistrate's court.

The contract of apprenticeship will be terminated if the employer changes his business, for then he will be unable to teach the apprentice other than theoretically. The contract may also be terminated by subsequent agreement of the parties, and if the apprentice is guilty of some misconduct this may entitle the employer to end the contract, if the situation is provided for in the contract. Otherwise, the contract may be terminated by order of the court or, since the contract is a personal one between the parties, by the death of either the employer or the apprentice.

APPENDIX 1

Extracts from the Sale of Goods Act 1893 as amended by the Supply of Goods (Implied Terms) Act 1973 and the Unfair Contract Terms Act 1977

Section 11(1) (b): Whether a stipulation in a contract of sale is a condition, the breach of which may give rise to a right to treat the contract as repudiated, or a warranty, the breach of which may give rise to a claim for damages but not to a right to reject the goods and treat the contract as repudiated, depends in each case upon the construction of the contract. A stipulation may be a condition, though called a warranty in the contract.

Section 12(1): In every contract of sale, other than one to which subsection (2) of this section applies, there is:

(a) an implied condition on the part of the seller that in the case of a sale, he has a right to sell the goods, and in the case of an agreement to sell, he will have a right to sell the goods at the time when the property is to pass; and

(b) an implied warranty that the goods are free, and will remain free until the time when the property is to pass, from any charge or encumbrance not disclosed or known to the buyer before the contract is made and that the buyer will enjoy quiet possession of the goods except so far as it may be disturbed by the owner or other person entitled to the benefit of any charge or encumbrance so disclosed or known.

(2) In a contract of sale, in the case of which there appears from the contract or is to be inferred from the circumstances of the contract an intention that the seller should transfer only such title as he or a third person may have there is:

(a) an implied warranty that all charges or encumbrances known to the seller and not known to the buyer have been disclosed to the buyer before the contract is made; and

(b) an implied warranty that neither—
   (i) the seller; nor
   (ii) in a case where the parties to the contract intend that the seller should transfer only such title as a third person may have, that person; nor

(iii) anyone claiming through or under the seller or that third person otherwise than under a charge or encumbrance disclosed or known to the buyer before the contract is made;

will disturb the buyer's quiet possession of the goods.

Section 13: (1) Where there is a contract for the sale of goods by description, there is an implied condition that the goods shall correspond with the description, and if the sale be by sample, as well as by description, it is not sufficient that the bulk of the goods corresponds with the sample if the goods do not also correspond with the description.

(2) A sale of goods shall not be prevented from being a sale by description by reason only that, being exposed for sale or hire, they are selected by the buyer.

Section 14: (1) Except as provided by this section, and section 15 of this Act and subject to the provisions of any other enactment, there is no implied condition or warranty as to the quality or fitness for any particular purpose of goods supplied under a contract of sale.

(2) Where the seller sells goods in the course of a business, there is an implied condition that the goods supplied under the contract are of merchantable quality, except that there is no such condition:

(a) as regards defects specifically drawn to the buyer's attention before the contract is made; or

(b) if the buyer examines the goods before the contract is made, as regards defects which that examination ought to reveal.

(3) Where the seller sells goods in the course of a business and the buyer, expressly or by implication, makes known to the seller any particular purpose for which the goods are being bought, there is an implied condition that the goods supplied under the contract are reasonably fit for that purpose, whether or not that is the purpose for which such goods are commonly supplied, except where the circumstances show that the buyer does not rely, or that it is unreasonable for him to rely, on the seller's skill or judgment.

(4) An implied condition or warranty as to quality or fitness for a particular purpose may be annexed to a contract of sale by usage.

(5) The foregoing provisions of this section apply to a sale by a person who in the course of a business is acting as agent for another as they apply to a sale by a principal in the course of a business, except where that other is not selling in the course of a business and either the buyer knows that fact or reasonable steps are taken to bring it to the notice of the buyer before the contract is made.

Section 15: (1) A contract of sale is a contract for sale by sample where there is a term in the contract, express or implied, to that effect.

(2) In the case of a contract for sale by sample:

(a) there is an implied condition that the bulk shall correspond with the sample in quality;

(b) there is an implied condition that the buyer shall have a reasonable opportunity of comparing the bulk with the sample;

(c) there is an implied condition that the goods shall be free from any defect rendering them unmerchantable which would not be apparent on reasonable examination of the sample.

Section 55: (1) Where any right, duty, or liability would arise under a contract of sale of goods by implication of law, it may be negatived or varied by express agreement, or by the course of dealing between the parties, or by usage if the usage is such as to bind both parties to the contract, but the foregoing provision shall have effect subject to the following provisions of this section.

(2) An express condition or warranty does not negative a condition or warranty implied by this Act unless inconsistent therewith.

Section 62: (1) Goods of any kind are of merchantable quality within the meaning of this Act if they are as fit for the purpose or purposes for which goods of that kind are commonly bought as it is reasonable to expect having regard to any description applied to them, the price (if relevant) and all the other relevant circumstances; and any reference in this Act to unmerchantable goods shall be construed accordingly.

Unfair Contract Terms Act 1977

6.—(1) Liability for breach of the obligations arising from—

(a) section 12 of the Sale of Goods Act 1893 (seller's implied undertakings as to title, etc.);

(b) section 8 of the Supply of Goods (Implied Terms) Act 1973 (the corresponding thing in relation to hire-purchase),

cannot be excluded or restricted by reference to any contract term.

(2) As against a person dealing as consumer, liability for breach of the obligations arising from—

(a) sections 13, 14 or 15 of the 1893 Act (seller's implied undertakings as to conformity of goods with description or sample, or as to their quality or fitness for a particular purpose);

(b) sections 9, 10 or 11 of the 1973 Act (the corresponding things in relation to hire-purchase), cannot be excluded or restricted by reference to any contract term.

(3) As against a person dealing otherwise than as consumer, the liability specified in subsection (2) above can be excluded or restricted by reference to a contract term, but only in so far as the term satisfies the requirement of reasonableness.

206

(4) The liabilities referred to in this section are not only the business liabilities defined by section 1(3), but include those arising under any contract of sale of goods or hire-purchase agreement.

7.—(1) Where the possession or ownership of goods passes under or in pursuance of a contract not governed by the law of sale of goods or hire-purchase, subsections (2) to (4) below apply as regards the effect (if any) to be given to contract terms excluding or restricting liability for breach of obligation arising by implication of law from the nature of the contract.

(2) As against a person dealing as consumer, liability in respect of the goods' correspondence with description or sample, or their quality or fitness for any particular purpose, cannot be excluded or restricted by reference to any such term.

(3) As against a person dealing otherwise than as consumer, that liability can be excluded or restricted by reference to such a term, but only in so far as the term satisfies the requirement of reasonableness.

(4) Liability in respect of—

(a) the right to transfer ownership of the goods, or give possession; or

(b) the assurance of quiet possession to a person taking goods in pursuance of the contract, cannot be excluded or restricted by reference to any such term except in so far as the term satisfies the requirement of reasonableness.

(5) This section does not apply in the case of goods passing on a redemption of trading stamps within the Trading Stamps Act 1964 or the Trading Stamps Act (Northern Ireland) 1965.

11.—(1) In relation to a contract term, the requirement of reasonableness for the purposes of this Part of this Act, section 3 of the Misrepresentation Act 1967 and section 3 of the Misrepresentation Act (Northern Ireland) 1967 is that the term shall have been a fair and reasonable one to be included having regard to the circumstances which were, or ought reasonably to have been, known to or in the contemplation of the parties when the contract was made.

(2) In determining for the purposes of sections 6 or 7 above whether a contract term satisfies the requirement of reasonableness, regard shall be had in particular to the matters specified in Schedule 2 to this Act; but this subsection does not prevent the court or arbitrator from holding, in accordance with any rule of law, that a term which purports to exclude or restrict any relevant liability is not a term of the contract.

(3) In relation to a notice (not being a notice having contractual effect), the requirement of reasonableness under this Act is that it should be fair and reasonable to allow reliance on it, having regard to

all the circumstances obtaining when the liability arose or (but for the notice) would have arisen.

(4) Where by reference to a contract term or notice a person seeks to restrict liability to a specified sum of money, and the question arises (under this or any other Act) whether the term or notice satisfies the requirement of reasonableness, regard shall be had in particular (but without prejudice to subsection (2) above in the case of contract terms) to—

    (a) the resources which he could expect to be available to him for the purpose of meeting the liability should it arise; and

    (b) how far it was open to him to cover himself by insurance.

(5) It is for those claiming that a contract term or notice satisfies the requirement of reasonableness to show that it does.

12.—(1) A party to a contract "deals as consumer" in relation to another party if—

    (a) he neither makes the contract in the course of a business nor holds himself out as doing so; and

    (b) the other party does make the contract in the course of a business; and

    (c) in the case of a contract governed by the law of sale of goods or hire-purchase, or by section 7 of this Act, the goods passing under or in pursuance of the contract are of a type ordinarily supplied for private use or consumption.

(2) But on a sale by auction or by competitive tender the buyer is not in any circumstances to be regarded as dealing as consumer.

(3) Subject to this, it is for those claiming that a party does not deal as consumer to show that he does not.

APPENDIX 2

Extract from the Treaty establishing the European Economic Community, Rome 1957.
Part Three, Title 1, Chapter 1, Section 1

Article 85

(1) The following shall be prohibited as incompatible with the common market: all agreements between undertakings, decisions by associations of undertakings and concerted practices which may affect trade between Member States and which have as their object or effect the prevention, restriction or distortion of competition within the common market, and in particular those which:

(a) directly or indirectly fix purchase or selling prices or any other trading conditions;

(b) limit or control production, markets, technical development, or investment;

(c) share markets or sources of supply;

(d) apply dissimilar conditions to equivalent transactions with other trading parties, thereby placing them at a competitive disadvantage;

(e) make the conclusion of contracts subject to acceptance by the other parties of supplementary obligations which, by their nature or according to commercial usage, have no connection with the subject of such contracts.

(2) Any agreements or decisions prohibited pursuant to this Article shall be automatically void.

(3) The provisions of paragraph 1 may, however, be declared inapplicable in the case of:

—any agreement or category of agreements between undertakings;

—any decision or category of decisions by associations of undertakings;

—any concerted practice or category of concerted practices;

which contributes to improving the production or distribution of goods or to promoting technical or economic progress, while allowing consumers a fair share of the resulting benefit, and which does not:

(a) impose on the undertakings concerned restrictions which are

not indispensable to the attainment of these objectives;
(b) afford such undertakings the possiblity of eliminating competition in respect of a substantial part of the products in question.

Article 86

Any abuse by one or more undertakings of a dominant position within the common market or in a substantial part of it shall be prohibited as incompatible with the common market in so far as it may affect trade between Member States. Such abuse may, in particular, consist in:

(a) directly or indirectly imposing unfair purchase or selling prices or other unfair trading conditions;
(b) limiting production, markets or technical development to the prejudice of consumers;
(c) applying dissimilar conditions to equivalent transactions with other trading parties, thereby placing them at a competitive disadvantage;
(d) making the conclusion of contracts subject to acceptance by the other parties of supplementary obligations which, by their nature or according to commercial usage, have no connection with the subject of such contracts.

APPENDIX 3

The Unfair Contract Terms Act 1977

This Act became operative on February 1, 1978. The object of the Act is to restrict the extent to which liability can be avoided for breach of contract and negligence. It has an impact, therefore, both upon the law of contract and the law of tort.

The Act regulates only "business liability"—things done in the course of business or arising from the occupation of business premises. It introduces, *inter alia*, the following provisions.

(1) Liability for death or personal injury resulting from negligence cannot be excluded or restricted either by a term of the contract or by notice (section 2)

(2) Liability for other loss or damage arising from negligence is subject to the test of "reasonableness" (section 2)

(3) Agreement to or awareness of such a term or notice is not of itself to be taken as indicating voluntary acceptance of risk (*volenti non fit injuria*) (section 2(3)).

(4) In all sales to a person dealing as a consumer restriction of liability or exclusion of liability for breach of contract are subject to the requirement of "reasonableness" (section 3).

(5) Notwithstanding that a contract has been terminated by breach or by a party electing to treat it as repudiated a term of that contract which is required to meet the requirement of reasonableness may, nevertheless, be found to do so and be given effect to (section 9).

(6) The test of reasonableness is also imposed on terms in a contract which require a party dealing as a consumer to indemnify another for any liability by reason of the other's negligence or breach of contract (section 4).

(7) Anything in writing is said to be a guarantee "if it contains or purports to contain some promise or assurance (however worded or presented) that defects will be made good by complete or partial replacement, or by repair, monetary compensation or otherwise." In such contracts no term can exclude or restrict liability arising from the goods proving defective (section 5).

211

(8) Where the goods are in private use ("consumer use" in the Act) there can be no exclusion or restriction of manufacturer's liability or distributor's liability for defective goods.

(9) Attempts to avoid negligence liability or to exclude or restrict obligations or duties under the Act are controlled by section 13(1).

(10) The test of reasonableness applies when the contract was made in the case of a contractual term (section 11(1), but also when the liability arose in the case of a non-contractual notice (section 11(3)).

(11) The onus of proving reasonableness lies upon the person so claiming (section 11(5)).

Certain contracts are excluded from all or some of the Act's provisions. Contracts of insurance are totally excluded. Other contracts are excluded so far as they relate to the creation, transfer, or termination of an interest in land, or of a right or interest in a patent or trademark. Equally excluded are contracts relating to creation or dissolution of companies or partnerships, and the creation or transfer of securities.

Index

214

216